An Introduction to the New Testament

Witnesses to God's New Work

Charles B. Cousar

Westminster John Knox Press
LOUISVILLE • LONDON

Book design by Sharon Adams
Cover design by Night & Day Design

First edition
Published by Westminster John Knox Press
Louisville, Kentucky

This book is printed on acid-free paper that meets the American National Standards Institute Z39.48 standard. ♾

PRINTED IN THE UNITED STATES OF AMERICA

06 07 08 09 10 11 12 13 14 15—10 9 8 7 6 5 4 3 2 1

Library of Congress Cataloging-in-Publication Data is on file at the Library of Congress, Washington, D.C.

ISBN-13: 978-0-664-22413-4
ISBN-10: 0-664-22413-X

For
Walter Brueggemann,
Beverly Roberts Gaventa,
Shirley C. Guthrie,
George W. Stroup

Contents

Preface

One always has a number of persons to thank when writing a book. Footnotes are but one way of expressing indebtedness. Many students, colleagues, and friends, whose names are not found in the bibliography, have contributed ideas, and the book is richer for their contributions. Carey Newman, then academic book editor of Westminster John Knox Press, gave me the "assignment" to write this book. I am grateful for his prodding (though he soon left to go to Baylor University). The staff of the John Bulow Campbell Library has been gracious in getting materials for me when I needed them. Davis Hankins has improved the text immensely by proofreading the manuscript and preparing the final copy. Christopher Henry has ably compiled the indexes. Betty, my devoted wife, has given patient and faithful support throughout the entire project. It is nice to have a spouse who is a copy editor by trade and can answer those pesky questions that inevitably arise, like where the comma goes.

Richard S. Dietrich, a former faculty colleague and now a pastor in Virginia, has graciously allowed me to borrow his poetic rendition of Jude, a book alive with strong metaphors. His treatment of the brief letter not only highlights the fierce language of the text, but also calls attention to the numerous Old Testament references found on its pages.

No one has had as rich and supportive group of colleagues as I have had in my four decades at Columbia Theological Seminary. The words of encouragement, the conversations over lunch, and their own work have been a tremendous stimulation. This book is dedicated to four special friends, who have regularly read my material, have offered invaluable feedback, and have taught me more than they will ever know. They are Walter Brueggemann,

Beverly Roberts Gaventa (now at Princeton Theological Seminary), Shirley Guthrie (who came to an untimely death in 2004), and George Stroup. To all four I owe a profound debt of gratitude.

CHARLES B. COUSAR
Lent 2006

Introduction

The assignment to write a "postcritical introduction" to the New Testament for the life of the church is a daunting one. From the age of the Enlightenment to almost the present time, the whole genre of "introduction" (*Einleitung*) has been identified with critical scholarship. As Feine-Behm-Kümmel put it, "The science of introduction is, accordingly, a strict historical discipline."[1]

An "introduction" would be expected to treat the historical matters of the origin of the New Testament writings, their collection, authorship, dating, governance, and the textual tradition of the collection. As it relates to the Christian theologian, the "introduction" was meant to determine a historical foundation on which Christian reflection could take place. An example of this historical-critical approach is the over-eight-hundred-page "Introduction" of Adolf Hilgenfeld, written in 1875.[2] As William Baird has noted, "Virtually every question of historical criticism is addressed, and the analysis is supported by massive well-documented research."[3]

By the time of the First World War, however, there was a shift to an interest in a history of literature, and with it a preoccupation with the prehistory of the form of the New Testament writings. This literary perspective developed out of the history-of-religions school and sought to place the New Testament texts in the historical contexts out of which they arose. Influenced by the Old Testament scholar Hermann Gunkel, attention was focused on the earliest traditions of the Gospels. The form-critical works of Karl Ludwig Schmidt and Martin Dibelius on the Gospel of Mark appeared in 1919 and Rudolf Bultmann's monumental *History of the Synoptic Tradition* in 1921. While none of these books were introductions in the strict sense of the term, their influence on the production of introductions in the early half of the twentieth century was immense.

The latter half of the twentieth century, however, has witnessed a considerable change in the genre of introduction. Often written for classroom use in colleges and seminaries, writers have tended to reduce the critical material and have surveyed the canonical character of the New Testament writings. One thinks of Brevard Childs, *The New Testament as Canon: An Introduction* (1984) or Bart D. Ehrman, *The New Testament: A Historical Introduction to the Early Christian Writings* (2004, 3rd edition) or Carl R. Holladay, *A Critical Introduction to the New Testament*, 2 vols. (2005). It is surprising, however, to discover how much time and space is given to the rehashing of historical-critical questions, even those about which there is considerable agreement as to the solution. The reason for this volume of writing is primarily that the readers of these volumes apparently need to be introduced to the critical issues as well as to the content of the canonical books.

So what is a postcritical introduction to the New Testament? My understanding of the term "postcritical" derives primarily from Paul Ricoeur, who contends that our relation to the biblical text must be a hermeneutical one.

> The kerygma is not first of all the interpretation of a text; it is the announcement of a person. In this sense, the word of God is, not the Bible, but Jesus Christ. But a problem arises continually from the fact that this kerygma is itself expressed in a witness, in the stories, and soon after in the texts that contain the very first confession of faith of the community. These texts conceal a first level of interpretation. We ourselves are no longer those witnesses who have seen. We are the hearers who listen to the witnesses: *fides ex auditu*. Hence we can only believe by listening and by interpreting a text which is itself already an interpretation. In short, our relation, not only to the Old Testament, but also to the New Testament itself, is a hermeneutic relation.[4]

In developing his hermeneutical arc, Ricoeur posits that the initial reading of the text is no more than a hunch. The reader is aware that there can be no appeal to the intentions of the author or to the historical circumstances in which the text appears. Thus the reader is left to estimate, even to guess at the meaning of the passage (called the "first naiveté").

A second stage in the circle is the critical stage, which Ricoeur labels "distantiation." The work is "distantiated" from the writer; the interpreter is not hunting for the intention of the author, nor for the historical situation common to the author and his original readers—"not the expectations or feelings of those original readers; not even the understanding of themselves as historical and cultural phenomena. What has to be appropriated is the text itself, conceived in a dynamic way as the direction of thought opened up by the text."[5] This approach does not imply an authorless text. As Ricoeur notes, "The tie between the speaker and the discourse is not abolished, but distended and complicated."[6]

Put another way, the meaning is not to be discovered in the world behind the text or even in the world of the text itself, but in the world in front of the text. Hermeneutics is not the science of uncovering the meaning that a text's author may have intended, but a consideration of the application or appropriation of the text.

Though Ricoeur speaks of "the desert of criticism" from which we wish to be called,[7] he sees no way to bypass the critical stage and return to a reactionary or even sophisticated precritical stage. The "second naiveté" is not simply the first naiveté writ large, but is truly a postcritical stage, in which the work of the historical and literary criticism is engaged and yet not in isolation from a theological use of Scripture. "A fusion of horizons" (to borrow Gadamer's phrase)[8] occurs between the text and the world appropriated in front of the text.

Another of Ricoeur's concepts becomes significant at this point: "the surplus of meaning."[9] Ricoeur is concerned that a text should mean all that it can mean. To limit a text to what the author intended it to mean and to arrive at a single interpretation is to constrict the text. Rather, each text has multiple meanings. Furthermore, this "surplus of meaning" pushes one back to the text time and again and invites fresh imaginative encounters. Texts are fertile and always have still more fruit to yield.

Most of the critical positions taken in this book are mainline and are assumed and not debated—for example, the priority of Mark, the seven undisputed letters of Paul, and the book of Acts as a second volume of the Gospel of Luke. They are noted in their appropriate places in order that the reader may be aware of what is taking place. One will not find here a thorough discussion of collating the Acts account of Paul with the Paul of the letters, nor will one find here information about the social setting of the first-century churches. The critical positions I have taken are not, however, without impact on the interpretations offered. I have simply tried to maintain faithfully the assignment, namely to write a postcritical introduction, which I take to mean a theological introduction.

I have begun the book with Paul and his letters, but have treated the letters in the canonical rather than historical order, in part because scholars do not agree on the historical sequencing of the letters. Does Galatians or 1 Thessalonians come first? Is Romans or Philippians the last of Paul's letters? I have a hunch that 1 Thessalonians comes first and Romans last; however, in the face of indecision, it seems wise to stick with the canonical sequence.

One chapter in the book clearly represents more of a critical than a postcritical perspective: the one on "The Historical Jesus," which is the issue in current New Testament studies where, in reading much of the debate, one feels thrown back into the nineteenth century, rehashing old questions. In fact, as early as the time of Augustine, who made an elaborate case for rationally harmonizing alleged contradictions between the Gospels and Origen, who argued that the contradictions were intentional to force readers to face the true spiritual and mystical sense of the text, the matter was before the church.[10] Each generation since has had to wrestle not so much with details that differ from Gospel to Gospel as with the complementary dimensions of Christology that diverse narrative accounts have provided. Thus, in this chapter I have surveyed the recent history of the problem, have sought to clarify what I think is at stake in the current research, and have stated why I am content with a literary approach to the Gospels. Others who have more invested in the historical-critical stance toward the understanding of Jesus will no doubt find this chapter lacking. The book is written, however, primarily for use in the church, for seminary and church college classes, and for pastors who assume the regular responsibility of teaching and preaching in congregations.

The subtitle "Witnesses to God's New Work" is a way of recognizing that the New Testament is not a monolithic proclamation of God's good news, but rather represents a varied collection of statements, all bearing testimony to the single figure of Jesus crucified and risen, God's gift of newness. The variety of the witnesses at times is baffling to the reader, who finds them full of tensions, paradoxes, and apparent contradictions. We shall face these tensions as they arise, and yet it is helpful to be reminded that the canon cannot serve as the ultimate basis for unity, but only "one God and Father of all, who is above all and through all and in all" (Eph 4:6) and who has acted in Christ to bring "one new humanity" (Eph 2:15).[11]

"Newness" refers to God's invasion of human history in Jesus. While the adjective "new" can be used to describe someone who is young and thus is "new" with respect to time,[12] it is remarkable how many of the witnesses use the adjective "new" to characterize what is distinctive, what is different from the ordinary, what is eschatological.[13]

Paul speaks of the new creation in Christ (Gal 6:15; 2 Cor 5:17) and of "the new life of the Spirit" (Rom 7:6). In Ephesians we read of "the one new humanity" that replaces both Jew and Gentile (Eph 2:15). Mark's crowds were puzzled after Jesus exorcized a demonic spirit from a man, and they kept on asking one another, "What is this? A new teaching—with authority!" (Mark 1:27). Jesus then warns of the danger of putting new wine into old wineskins (Mark 2:22). Hebrews invites readers to a new and living way (Heb 10:20) and cites Jeremiah's promise of a new covenant (Jer 31:31–34) to critique the old covenant (Heb 8:8–13). The Johannine tradition speaks of a new commandment that we love one another (John 13:34; 1 John 2:7–8; 2 John 5–6), promises "a new heaven and a new earth" (Rev 21:1), and declares that the one seated on the throne is making "all things new" (Rev 21:5).

Since the "new" is repeatedly anticipated by writers in the Old Testament (Isa 42:9; 43:19; 48:6; Jer 31:31–34), it must not be taken as a supersessionist category (i.e., as the new superseding the old and rendering it obsolete). As Brueggemann puts it, "The 'Old-New' linkage does not suggest the disposal of the Old Testament in Christian reading, but, rather, insists that the Old Testament is indispensably important in a Christian reading of the New Testament."[14] One can hardly make sense of the New Testament, apart from the categories and images of the Old Testament. An instructive image is Matthew's scribe, who, like the head of the household, brings out of his storehouse things both new and old. Such a person is in training for "the kingdom of heaven" (13:52).

This introduction will not serve as a substitute for reading the biblical text itself. It rather has been written with the assumption that users of the book will need a Bible open before them at all times. A concluding chapter is an encouragement to readers to study the New Testament on their own.

The select bibliography at the close of the book includes commentaries that for the most part seek to illumine the text theologically. Many are brief treatments, not even strictly commentaries, but are engaged in reflection on the text in the general vein of Ricoeur's "second naiveté."

PART ONE

The Pauline Letters

1

Introduction to the Pauline Letters

The first theologian of the Christian church, at least whose writings we have in the New Testament, was the apostle Paul. Paul was dead before any of the Gospels were written. But since the order of the canonical documents places Matthew, Mark, Luke, and John before the letters of Paul, it may seem strange to take up the letters before the stories of Jesus. Paul's letters, however, were in circulation at an early date, even likely within Paul's lifetime (Galatians: "To the churches of Galatia" [1:2]). After his death, the pseudonymous Colossians anticipates circulation to other communities (4:16), and Ephesians, written to a historical situation but not a purely local one, indicates that it "was intended for broad dissemination from the outset and like Colossians offers indirect early evidence that other (authentic) letters of Paul were circulating outside the communities to which they were first addressed."[1] The evidence seems to indicate that Paul's missionary enterprise had "a corporate structure and a school dimension and that Paul and his associates thought it important to formulate the apostle's teaching in writing and to employ those writings in the furtherance of Paul's missionary aims."[2] Thus we begin with Paul, the earliest Christian theologian.

To speak of Paul as the earliest Christian theologian does not, however, mean that he was the founder of Christianity. From his own letters we learn that there was Christianity before Paul. He was baptized and received into a Christian community like anyone else. In his letters he cites liturgical material that the church had already been using in its worship. One can cite 1 Corinthians 11:23–26; 15:3–8; and Philippians 2:6–11 as explicit examples of pre-Pauline Christian material, which the apostle takes over and interprets in the contexts of the earliest churches. A. M. Hunter, one of the earliest scholars to identify pre-Pauline elements in the letters, states his purpose as to take Paul out of his apostolic insularity and to set him in the midst of early Christianity—to see him not as a lone pioneer blazing, single-handed, the trail of early Christianity, but as one of a gallant company of pioneers; or (to change the figure) to see him not as a sort of spiritual Columbus 'voyaging through strange seas of thought alone,' but as one sailing (as the historical Paul did sail) in company with others in the apostolic ship.[3]

And yet Paul remains the figure who wrote the earliest books that were later canonized, and for two or three decades at least he was the figure to be reckoned with in the early churches.[4] Interestingly, Paul's letters in the early part of the second century are rarely mentioned (e.g., by Clement of Rome, Ignatius of Antioch, and Polycarp), nor is his theology engaged in any way until Marcion appears on the scene in the middle of the second century, perhaps because as they were written to particular communities, the letters needed time to be universalized and accepted by other communities.[5]

Setting aside the book of Acts, what we learn of Paul from his letters is that he was a Jew of Pharisaic persuasion, of the tribe of Benjamin; that he probably spoke Aramaic (in addition to Greek); that he was zealous for the tradition of his ancestors to the point of harassing the church; and that, regarding the righteousness of the law, he was beyond reproach. At some point in his life he experienced the risen Christ and on the basis of that encounter was moved to become an itinerant missionary carrying the gospel to non-Jews. Together with a cadre of fellow workers, he traveled through Syria, Cilicia, Galatia, Asia Minor, and Greece, preaching the good news and starting house churches. He planned to travel to Rome and carry on a mission from there to Spain. According to Acts, he reached Rome as a prisoner and preached the gospel for two years "with all boldness and without hindrance" (Acts 28:31). Acts supplies additional information about Paul and his ministries, but since that information comes secondhanded and often does not mesh with what Paul wrote in his letters, it is not taken as accurately.

Before considering the specific letters themselves, we should note six important observations about the study of Paul as a theologian. First, *Paul wrote letters*. His letters communicate with the Christian groups he started, often to address problems that arose within the communities and, in one case (Romans), to introduce himself to a church he had not yet visited. In many cases the letters served in place of a personal visit. Collections of Paul's letters appeared at a fairly early date. Though Luke, in writing Acts, makes no mention of Paul's having written letters, Clement of Rome (95–96 CE) cites them in a way that suggests copies were available, and possibly a collection of them existed.[6] No one knows how and exactly when Paul's letters were collected into a corpus, whether gradually as churches shared documents with other churches or as the result of a single figure (e.g., Timothy, Onesimus, or Luke), except that Marcion in the mid-second century clearly exhibits familiarity with ten letters of Paul.[7]

Paul undoubtedly wrote his letters with an eye toward their being read aloud in the receiving congregations (1 Thess 5:27). The best estimate of the literacy rate in the first century is 10 to 15 percent. People were used to recitations of various sorts, such as public declarations and official decrees, being read in assemblies. It was truly an oral culture.

Two features about Paul's letters are noteworthy:

1. They reflect a sophisticated and varied use of argumentation. These letters are not the works of a busy pastor hastily dictating on the run. Even Galatians, with its highly charged rhetoric, reflects a disciplined and carefully crafted argument. Whether Paul received formal training in rhetoric is anybody's guess. It would have been difficult for any educated person to avoid the basic forms of argumentation, since they were practiced in nearly every mode of communication.

2. This sophistication indicates significant scholastic activity within the communities to which they were written. Both Jewish and Christian groups placed a high value on texts, and particularly on the Septuagint (the Old Testament translated into Greek). Frequent and often lengthy readings, followed by exposition, made the writings more accessible to the entire community. The letters themselves display careful attention to the Jewish Scriptures and anticipate readers who know and value the stories they contain.

A second observation to keep in mind is that *Paul was a Jew*. He tells us this repeatedly—both before and after his transforming experience with Jesus Christ. In facing opponents in Corinth, he claims both his ethnic heritage and his religious roots. "Are they Hebrews? So am I. Are they Israelites? So am I. Are they descendants of Abraham? So am I" (2 Cor 11:22). In puzzling over the Jews' rejection of Jesus, he speaks of his "kindred according to the flesh. They are Israelites, and to them belong the adoption, the glory, the covenants, the giving of the law, the worship, and the promises: to them belong the patriarchs, and from them, according to the flesh, comes the Messiah" (Rom 9:3–5).

His transforming experience—when Christ was revealed to him—did not make him any less a Jew in his own eyes than before the experience ("I myself am an Israelite, a descendant of Abraham, a member of the tribe of Benjamin" [Rom 11:1]). The modern concept of "converting" from Judaism to Christianity would have been foreign to Paul. To be sure, Paul's world was reconfigured by the Christ experience. At the same time, he clung to the traditional Jewish understanding of God, to Israel's election as the special people of God, its calling to be a light to the nations, and to the future consummation of God's reign. He distinguished between Jews who accepted Christ as Messiah and those who did not (Rom 9:6b–8), but the distinction did not make Christian Jews any less Jewish than non-Christian Jews.

Why is it important for us to remain mindful of Paul's identity as a Jew? Because students in a postmodern era who encounter Paul's letters such as Galatians for the first time often judge Paul rigid and insensitive. He had sharp conflicts with other Jewish groups who also had an ecumenical attitude toward the reception of non-Jews into the people of God. Students too quickly assume that Paul is attacking Judaism and ignore that he writes as a Jewish Christian to counter another Jewish Christian group. It is one thing for a Jew to have written the letter to the Galatians with its harsh rhetoric and aggressive style to the Jewish Christian missionaries who had infiltrated the congregations there and demanded that Gentile converts be circumcised, and another thing for modern gentiles to read the letter wrenched out of this initial context.

Third, still claiming his Jewish heritage, Paul nevertheless saw and identified himself as *"an apostle to the Gentiles"* (Rom 11:13). Though Acts portrays Paul's mission as beginning in various towns and cities by first preaching in the synagogues and—only after having been rejected there—then turning to non-Jews, his letters tell a quite different story. Paul's ministry was primarily among Gentiles. At a meeting in Jerusalem the leaders recognized his apostleship to the Gentiles just as they did Peter's apostleship to the Jews (Gal 2:7–8).

Why? What was the catalyst that led Paul to his passionate mission to non-Jews? There have been several suggestions. Francis Watson contends that Paul did in fact begin his ministry among the Jews, but out of frustration over their lack of response to the gospel, he turned to the Gentiles. He abandoned parts of the Mosaic law in order to make it easier for Gentiles to become Christians. The setting aside of legal restrictions was more a matter of expediency than of theology.[8]

Daniel Boyarin, on the other hand, argues that Paul became restless with a Jewish God that demanded circumcision and set table taboos creating divisions among people of various ethnic backgrounds. Influenced by a syncretistic blend of biblical universalism (that Israel had a mission to save all of humanity and to bring them to the worship of the one true God) and of a Hellenistic idea of universalism (that all the gods were really different names for the one God), Paul walked the Damascus road "with a very troubled mind." It was this unrest with the rigorous restrictions of Judaism that led him to discover in Jesus' resurrection a spiritual and universal model. It enabled him to transcend the particular confines of the Torah and find a message for all.[9]

Both of these two positions contain serious problems. Watson has an impossible task of dredging up verses from the letters that might hint that Paul first went to the synagogues and only turned to the Gentiles out of frustration. On occasion Paul mentioned being among Jews (1 Cor 9:20–21) and either being persecuted by them (2 Cor 11:24) or being acknowledged by them (Gal 1:18–24), but these scattered references hardly warrant an early mission to the Jews.

Boyarin declares that "what drove Paul was a passionate desire for human unification, for the erasure of differences and hierarchies between human beings and that he saw the Christian event, as he had experienced it, as the vehicle for the transformation of humanity."[10] But neither of the two of Paul's own accounts of his "conversion" mentions any notion of his restlessness with Jewish ethnocentrism or his ardor for a universal humanity that was somehow "solved" by a universal Christ (Gal 1:11–17; Phil 3:4–11). The Galatian account particularly speaks of Paul's advancement in Judaism beyond his contemporaries. Previously Paul understood what he was doing in harassing the church as a faithful response to the traditions of his ancestors. He no doubt saw in the church's Christology a fundamental threat to the Torah. But God broke into Paul's life "to reveal (*apokalupsai*) his Son to me, so that I might proclaim him among the Gentiles" (Gal 1:16). It was "a revelation (*apokalupsis*) of Jesus Christ" (Gal 1:12), which caused "a reconfiguration of Paul's convictional world."[11] With Christ in place of the Torah as the center of this new world, he then read the Old Testament differently. He found the inclusion of non-Jews into the people of God in the promise to Abraham ("the gospel [declared] beforehand," Gal 3:8), now fulfilled in Christ. His apostolic vocation was set.

A fourth feature to observe about Paul is that *he wrote as a pastor-theologian*. He spoke to concrete situations in local congregations and reflected on those situations in light of the gospel. Because he did this so well, there is the temptation to draw his thoughts together into a system, and in effect to turn him into a systematic theologian of the likes of St. Thomas Aquinas or Karl Barth.

The "systematic" approach to Paul doesn't work, for at least two reasons. First, we only have seven undisputed documents written by Paul. His understanding of life and reality in light of Christ was likely much bigger than the sources we have. He mentions having written other letters that we do not have available to us (1 Cor 5:9–11; 2 Cor 2:3–4). Robin Scroggs draws a helpful analogy between Paul and a professor whose lectures are aimed at or deflected by the questions and concerns of the students in her classes. She may spend a great deal of time addressing issues that are less important to her own thought world yet urgently significant for her students. If only seven lectures from six of her courses are collected, can we be sure that we have a full grasp of her thought world?[12]

Second, Paul cannot be put in a "systematic" straitjacket because of the pastoral nature of his writings. In most of the letters, modern readers are let in on an ongoing conversation between Paul and his original readers. We are not always told what the issues at stake are or what questions Paul is answering. Scholars often differ in their understanding of what is critical and what is peripheral.

For example, what were the circumstances that provoked Paul to write 1 Corinthians 15? Why were members of the community saying, "There is no resurrection of the dead" (15:12)? Were they embracing an overly realized eschatology that assumed that resurrection had already taken place, or was their problem primarily an antipathy toward a bodily resurrection? Or did both of these factors play into their denial of the resurrection of the dead? In any case, Paul was not writing the Corinthians a treatise on the resurrection. He was dealing with a specific group within the community, who for reasons known to them and to Paul (but not entirely clear to us) denied the resurrection.

A fifth feature to observe about Paul is that *he was an apocalyptic theologian.* Paul's letters hardly resemble apocalyptic literature such as Daniel or Revelation with their bizarre symbols and surreal figures of beasts and dragons and seals to be opened, so how can we say he was an apocalyptic theologian?[13] It may help to recall a bit of history. During the second century BCE, the Jewish people found themselves in dire straits. They lived under the control of the Seleucid Greeks, who under Antiochus IV suppressed their religious practices, even violating the temple by setting up an altar to Zeus and by sacrificing swine's flesh.

One Jewish response to such horror was a guerrilla war, organized and led by the priests. They initially fled Jerusalem and took refuge in the central hill country, from which they raided Judea until they finally recaptured Jerusalem. The temple was reconsecrated in 165 BCE (an event still celebrated today with the festival of Hanukkah), and the Jews enjoyed a century of relative peace and semi-independence. Though it is clearly an oversimplification, the theology of the priests might best be characterized by the expression "God helps those that help themselves."

Another Jewish response to the horrors imposed by the Seleucids was the withdrawal of certain groups from the conflict into apocalyptic communities. One such group gathered at Qumran and gave us the Dead Sea Scrolls. Their theology differed from the militaristic priests. Previously in times of military defeats and economic disasters, the prophets had identified Israel's disobedience and its worship of false gods as the reason for its plight. It was being punished for its sins. But now Israel was eager to practice its religious traditions, yet it was prevented from doing so by a foreign power. The call to repentance the prophets had issued did not seem to fit. Something else was needed to account for their plight. Why had God, who had called Abraham and Sarah and had entered into covenant with them, allowed their descendants to be disenfranchised from the promises?

In spite of all this, these sectarian groups confessed, God would intervene, defeat the forces of Satan, and usher in a new age free of suffering, conflict, and violent oppression. God would establish his cosmic rule not only over the Jews, but also over the whole world. It will be God's doing and happen according to God's timetable. To be sure, there are various depictions of this triumph of God in apocalyptic literature. Sometimes angels lead the forces of God; sometimes a Messiah does; sometimes God does. Occasionally one finds mention of the resurrection of the dead. Other writings depict a rebuilt Jerusalem with a new temple at the center.[14]

Using this apocalyptic rhetoric, Paul boldly announces that God has already acted in Christ to deliver believers from "the present evil age" (Gal 1:4).[15] His death and resurrection have inaugurated a brand-new creation (Gal 6:15; 2 Cor 5:17), providing a radical break with the past. Paul preached a gospel that he did not attribute to any human source, but to an apocalypse of Jesus Christ (Gal 1:12). It is "the power of God for salvation" (Rom 1:16). As we shall see throughout his letters, this divine invasion in Christ, breaking the stranglehold of sin and evil, also looks forward to the final triumph of God over the persistent powers that yet resist God's will.

On the basis of this dualism and the conviction that God has broken the power of the enemy, Paul utilizes a notion of two ages, though he never fully develops this idea. Christians live at the juncture of the new age breaking into the old. It is both a painful and a hopeful time. Some are being saved, and others are perishing (1 Cor 1:18).[16] It is through this somewhat undeveloped theology of history that we consider Paul an apocalyptic theologian.

Finally, Paul was *a theologian of grace* par excellence. To say this is not to speak only of God's disposition toward unworthy people. Many prophets and apostles have testified to the divine graciousness experienced in God's acts of mercy and deeds of love. Hosea, for instance, recounted the amazing tale of God's reaching out to a promiscuous wife and of her restoration, and Jesus told the story of the father who runs out to meet the wayward son and throws a huge party to celebrate his homecoming. Of course, Paul would readily agree with these images of God. When Paul uses the word *charis* (grace), he infers something more than God's merciful disposition to those who do not deserve it. Repeatedly, the word is linked with God's liberating power made known in the crucified and risen Jesus. Paul writes of grace as a "state" in which we are currently standing, but as such it is linked to the apocalyptic event of Jesus and consists in "boast[ing] in our hope of sharing the glory of God" (Rom 5:2).

The Greek noun for "grace" occurs twenty-four times in Romans, and more often than not, it designates the event of Jesus Christ to dispel the power of sin.

> For there is no distinction, since all have sinned and fall short of the glory of God; they are now justified by his *grace* as a gift, through the redemption that is in Christ. (Rom 3:23–24)

> For if the many died through the one man's trespass, much more surely have the *grace* of God and the free gift in the *grace* of the one man, Jesus Christ, abounded for the many. (Rom 5:15)

> Where sin increased, *grace* abounded all the more, so that, just as sin exercised dominion in death, so *grace* might also exercise dominion through justification leading to eternal life through Jesus Christ our Lord. (Rom 5:20–21)

In his own day Paul was accused of preaching a libertine gospel (Rom 3:8). Though we do not know from whom the charge emanated, it may well have come from Jewish Christian readers of his earlier letter to the Galatians. There he insisted that God's righteousness comes as a free gift apart from the law and that any effort to impose legal requirements on Gentile converts (such as circumcision) is to deny grace. He concludes an important section saying, "I do not nullify the grace of God; for if righteousness comes through the law, then Christ died for nothing" (Gal 2:21). The point is that the grace of God and the crucifixion of Christ belong together. To deny either one is to deny the other.

Grace then becomes a very specific term for Paul. It is hard to say that Paul excludes the so-called common gifts that God graciously provides for all humanity (though he does not say much about them), but his concentration is on the particularity of Jesus Christ, even when he writes experientially. In telling of "a thorn in the flesh" sent to him as a messenger of Satan to torment him so as to keep him from being too elated, Paul writes about appealing to God three times for the removal of "the thorn." The answer he receives is "My grace is all you need" (NEB). He interprets this then in terms of his theology of the cross, namely that God's power comes to light in human weakness. "For whenever I am weak, then I am strong" (2 Cor 12:1–10). This discernment that sees God's hand at work in the death of Jesus distinguishes Paul as a theologian of grace.

2

Romans

There is no doubt that the letter to the Roman church is a letter of introduction. Paul had never been to Rome, and in anticipation both of his coming and his hope to enlist the Roman church as a base for his further mission to Spain, he wrote this letter (Rom 15:22–23). Given that a Christian congregation was already established there, it is not surprising that he should send such a letter to pave the way for his arrival.

From chapter 16, however, we learn that Paul had many friends in Rome, some of whom had been his coworkers in Asia Minor and in Greece. He naturally sent them greetings, using very affectionate terms; three are called "beloved," one couple is referred to as "kin" (or perhaps "compatriots"), and one woman is described as "a mother to me." One might ask, "If Paul had so many friends in Rome, why was it necessary for him to write a letter of introduction?"[1] Why did Paul need to present himself theologically to his readers?

In attempting to solve this issue, two features of this letter are worthy of our consideration. First, the apostle admits to considerable anxiety in the face of the trip he must make before going to Rome (Rom 15:24–33). The predominantly Gentile congregations of Greece had taken up an offering to send to the mother church at Jerusalem to assist the saints there in their time of need. It was Paul's job to take this offering to Jerusalem, but he was fearful of doing so for two reasons. Given the highly nationalistic mood of the times (the decade leading up to the first revolt against Rome), he was afraid for his life. As a Jew who once persecuted the church and then claimed to be the apostle to the Gentiles, the Jewish population would have been deeply suspicious of Paul.

Second, Paul was uncertain that the church in Jerusalem would in fact accept the offering he brought. The Jewish Christians there lived under constant pressure from their kinfolk to avoid association with non-Jews. It might be costly for them if they accepted this gift from their Gentile brothers and sisters in Christ. If they rejected the offering from the Gentile congregations, it would be a devastating blow to Paul, who had worked hard for a Christian community in which "neither Jew nor Greek" mattered. To have the church splintered into Jewish and non-Jewish factions would have been crushing. Thus, Paul asked the Roman church for their prayers and support in this trip he must make to Jerusalem before coming to see them.

A second feature of the letter worth considering is the comment in Romans 3:8, which suggests that some are slanderously accusing Paul of teaching libertinism. Who would do this? The most likely answer would be those "false believers" (Gal 2:4–5) who in Jerusalem had urged the circumcision of Titus and had caused problems at Antioch (Gal 2:12). Even though some of them may have shared Paul's vision of the gospel going beyond the boundaries of Judaism, they did so in terms of God's reaching out to Gentiles through the law, not apart from it. What Paul wrote to the Galatians—namely that the law was our "disciplinarian" until Christ should come, but that from now on we are no longer subject to that disciplinarian (Gal 3:24–25)—sounded much like a lawless gospel to them. And if the law was no longer in effect, why not say, "Let us do evil so that good may come" (Rom 3:8)?[2]

If in writing this letter Paul wanted the Roman church's support for his work in Spain and he had one eye on Jerusalem and his mission there, we can understand why he wanted to clear up any misrepresentations or misunderstandings created by his letter to the Galatians. Though in Galatians Paul wrote nothing about Jews qua Jews, in Romans he faced head-on this issue of the failure of Jews to respond to the gospel (Rom 9–11).

Without reneging on anything he wrote to the Galatians, Paul had an important theological task before him then in introducing himself to the Romans. Theologically, on the one hand, he had to make the case that Israel can count on God's being faithful to the covenant promises made to their ancestors. God is both promise keeping and promise making, and so is the one in whom the Jewish people have every reason to trust. On the other hand, God shows no partiality (Rom 2:11). As Paul asked rhetorically, "Is God the God of Jews only? Is he not the God of Gentiles also?" The answer came, "Yes, of Gentiles also, since God is one; and he will justify the circumcised on the ground of faith and the uncircumcised through that same faith" (Rom 3:29–30). God has thus opened the way for Gentiles to be received by faith as descendants of Abraham and Sarah (Rom 4:10–11).

If I am correct in isolating these two features of the letter, then Romans is not primarily a treatise arguing how one is to be saved—whether by works or by faith. Martin Luther's haunting question, "How can I, a sinful person, find acceptance in the eyes of a holy and righteous God?" is not really the burning issue of Romans. The issue is more theological than soteriological. The letter is neither a systematic treatment of Paul's thought nor a compendium of Christian doctrine. Some theological issues important to Paul are wholly missing from or hardly addressed by Romans (e.g., the Lord's Supper).

Rather the letter addresses a specific set of questions. How can a God, who has chosen Israel as a special people, at the same time welcome Gentiles into the fold by the same door? Can God be counted on to honor commitments made to the Jews? How does God's impartiality, expressed by including the Gentiles, not compromise God's faithfulness to Israel? In light of all this, what is God's purpose now for the Mosaic law? Holding together these two characteristics of God—impartiality and faithfulness—is the theological task of Romans.

ROMANS 1:1–17

In form, the letter is undistinguishable. It begins and ends in a fashion familiar to Pauline readers, yet what is occasionally missed is the powerful statement of the gospel with which the letter opens (Rom 1:1–17). In identifying himself as one called to be an apostle to the Gentiles, Paul interrupted the introduction of himself in order to define immediately the gospel of God. The gospel is a reality promised in the Holy Scriptures, centering in his Son (1:2–3a). On the basis of stylistic and formal features, it looks as though Paul here has quoted a confessional formula, possibly even known to his Roman readers, specifying in two parallel couplets what is to be affirmed about the Son, "Jesus Christ our Lord":

- "who was descended from David according to the flesh";
- who "was declared to be Son of God with power according to the spirit of holiness by resurrection from the dead." (1:3b–4)

Already Paul had stated what was critical about the faith he shared with the readers: Jesus, who is "Son of God" and "our Lord." Thus, in the traditional prayer of thanksgiving that follows (1:8–15), Paul wrote of the obligation he felt to preach the gospel to all sorts of people ("both to the Greeks and barbarians, both to the wise and to the uneducated") and to the community at Rome. Readers then know what he meant by the "gospel" he eagerly intended to proclaim.

But the citation of the confessional formula is not the only unusual feature of the opening of the letter. Nowhere else does Paul so clearly map the theme of a letter as he does in 1:16–17. "For I am not ashamed of the gospel; it is the power of God for salvation to everyone who has faith, to the Jew first and also to the Greek. For in it the righteousness of God is revealed through faith for faith; as it is written, 'The one who is righteous will live by faith.'"

Since the rest of the letter elucidates this theme (see especially 3:21–31), commenting on every phrase is not necessary here, but two observations are important. First, Paul's apocalyptic perspective comes to the fore in that he wrote about the gospel using the language of "power." As will become evident at strategic places in the letter (3:9; 6:14; 7:11; 8:2), he understood the tyranny under which humans lived and from which they needed to be freed. In the gospel, divine power was unleashed to liberate those trapped under the malignant forces of sin and death. God invaded the human scene to bring liberation. Karl Barth comments:

> He [Paul] does not say that the gospel *has* such power (as if it might perhaps not have it). On the contrary, he states . . . that the gospel *is* such power. The phrase means that it is God's almighty power, God's omnipotence. It is not a power among other powers, it is not a power to which others could even be compared, it is not a power with which another power could compete, but the power which is over and above all other powers, which limits and governs them all. That is the gospel.[3]

The second observation has to do with the inclusion of "the Greek" but the priority of "the Jew." Paul did not want his Gentile readers to forget that though they, too, are members of the people of God, there is in the divine purpose a certain precedence in order. Later in the letter a reminder of Jewish priority comes specifically directed to Gentile readers who might gloat over their status: "remember that it is not you that support the root, but the root that supports you" (11:18). Though Paul remained the advocate for the Gentiles in the church, Romans maintains a certain tension between the particular and the universal character of the gospel, which Paul never fully works out.

ROMANS 1:18–3:30

Having begun with a clear affirmation of the gospel, Paul turns to the matter of what people are saved *from*. The gospel, which brings salvation to everyone who believes, confronts a dilemma shared by all people, be they Jewish or non-Jewish. The first major block of the letter (1:18–3:20) develops in stark and unmistakable tones Paul's diagnosis of the human condition.

Three features of this section stand out. First, the analysis is remarkably free of moralistic judgments. It begins not with human sins (the noun does not even occur until 3:9 and then only in the singular) but with the revelation of God's wrath (1:18). Humans have had various opportunities to know God, but the response to such evidences of God's "eternal power and divine nature" has been a worship and serving of the creature rather than the Creator. The refusal to honor God *as God* is humanity's fundamental problem. People have preferred the lie to the truth, and this basic distortion has in turn spawned a long catalog of unacceptable activities. Humans' minds are darkened, and their powers of perception are perverted. They not only perform destructive deeds; they also applaud others who do the same things. But at the center lies the failure to glorify and honor God.

Three times the haunting phrase "God gave them up" (1:24, 26, 28) occurs. Some commentators, in order to avoid the image of an irrationally angry God, have taken this threefold expression to imply that God's wrath is impersonal and that God simply lets humans stew in their own juices.[4] Evil brings its own moral retribution, and the retribution comes on like a thermostat when the moral temperature drops below a certain point. Years of smoking bring on lung cancer; driving down a busy street at breakneck speed invariably results in an accident.

But as John A. T. Robinson forcefully argues, "Wrath is essentially the perversion of a *personal* relationship. It is, whether expressed or unexpressed, the wrath of *God*."[5] It need not be thought of as capricious or irrational; rather it "is God's divinity asserting itself where it is not recognized by human beings . . . God's reacting presence in a world over which he remains in charge even when it defies him."[6]

Second, 2:11 plays a pivotal role in the section. God shows no favoritism in judgment. Because of their behavior, Jews and Gentiles prove themselves alike ("without excuse" [1:20]) before God. Gentiles sin apart from the law; Jews sin under the law. The verdict on both is the same. "God shows no partiality."

The rhetoric used leading up to 2:11 is interesting. Paul in 1:18–32 outlined the situation of non-Jews. No mention is made of the breaking of the law; no hint is given of the failure to keep the covenant. Anyone familiar with the Wisdom of Solomon (13:1–9) would recognize the line Paul took. Then at 2:1 he abruptly shifted gears and declared that those who pass judgment on the Gentile sinners are as guilty as they are.

Paul may have set a trap for any moralistic persons who delighted in condemning those more sinful than themselves ("whoever you are"), or he may have specifically had the Jews in mind; in any case all people, whether Jew or Gentile, are eventually included. God's impartiality means "there will be anguish and distress for everyone who does evil . . . but glory and honor and peace for everyone who does good" (2:9–10).

Third, Paul raised two of the fundamental issues of the letter in 3:1–9, issues that he did not immediately answer until later. (Paul often does this in Romans, raising questions, giving partial answers, and then later returning to them again.) The two issues are precipitated by the manner in which the Jews are treated at the end of chapter 2. In pronouncing judgment on the Jews, Paul came perilously close to removing any special status the Jews had. Circumcision as a rite is thoroughly relativized, and secret matters of the heart determine the "real Jew," matters spiritual and not ritual (2:25–29). Given God's long and involved history with the Jews, Paul then had to face the question of whether the Jews had any advantage at all (3:1–5). Had their disobedience caused God to turn his back on them? Had God because of their unfaithfulness decided to substitute Plan B for Plan A? If so, then this action raises serious theological questions and puts in abeyance God's integrity since God had made unconditional promises to the Jews. Can God and God's promises be trusted?

Along with this question comes a second. If God is as gracious as Paul declared, then what about God's capacity to judge evil in the world (3:6–8)? If God shows mercy to sinful people, then how can we count on God to punish a Hitler or a child abuser or a rapist? Don't issues of right and wrong matter? Or do we live in an amoral world?

Romans 3:9 provides the conclusion to the section (beginning with 1:18), namely "that all, both Jews and Greeks, are under the power of sin." As if to indicate that he is not the first person to come up with this analysis of the human situation, he draws together a chain of quotations from the Psalms, Ecclesiastes, and Isaiah to support his position (3:9–20).

ROMANS 3:21–31

Three qualities of God are mentioned in 3:1–9: faithfulness (3:3), righteousness (or justice) (3:5), and truthfulness (3:7). These aspects of God's integrity are called into question by Paul's message of universal grace and by the Jews' rejection of the gospel. Now Paul moved to respond to the questions by returning to the gospel, already set out as his theme in 1:16–17. A free translation of 3:21–26 runs as follows:

> But now, apart from the law, the righteousness of God has been disclosed, although it is witnessed to by the law and the prophets, namely the righteousness of God that comes through the faithfulness of Jesus Christ to all those who believe. For there is no distinction, for all have sinned and are lacking the glory of God. All are being justified undeservedly by God's grace through the redemption that is in Christ Jesus, whom God put forward as a means of atonement, in the light of Christ's faithfulness to God in the shedding of his blood. This was to demonstrate the divine righteousness, because God in his patience

had passed over the previously committed sins. It was to demonstrate
God's righteousness at the present time—that God is righteous and
that God justifies the one who shares the faith of Jesus.[7]

Hays convincingly argues that once we acknowledge Romans 3 as a defense of
God's integrity, it is difficult to see how our faith in Jesus would contribute to
that disclosure. "God has solved the problem of human unrighteousness and
Israel's unfaithfulness by putting forward the one perfectly human being,
Jesus."[8]

It is God then who takes the initiative in rectifying the plight humans got
themselves into, and God does this in the death of Jesus. God remedies the situation, graciously doing for humankind precisely what it cannot do for itself.
Furthermore, the death of Jesus—not his miracles or his teaching—proves
God to be in the right ("the righteousness of God has been disclosed";
"demonstrates God's righteousness at the present time"), and answers the two
specific questions the earlier section raised about God's integrity (3:1–9).

On the one hand, this activity is in clear continuity with the Old Testament
("witnessed to by the law and the prophets"). God is consistent and has not
reneged on the covenant promises made to the Jews. In fact, the death of
Christ is a fulfillment of God's primordial intention to include Gentiles among
the chosen people (to be developed further in chap. 4) and their inclusion does
not modify God's stance toward the Jews (to be developed further in chaps.
9–11). The death of Jesus makes possible the redemption of *all* who have
sinned and lack God's glory. Thus, now there is no distinction before God
between Jew and Gentile.

On the other hand, the question about whether God takes sin lightly and
thus has forfeited any right to judge the world is also answered in the death of
Jesus. The stress on atonement in this text (both in the word "redemption"
and "sacrifice of atonement," NRSV), in which Paul may again have cited a
creedal formula known to his readers, indicates that God has not ignored
human disobedience, but acts responsibly in Christ to justify the ungodly (4:5).

Several rhetorical questions close the section (3:27–31), giving Paul a
chance to affirm that God is the God of the Gentiles just as much as of the
Jews, and that faith upholds the Mosaic law, it does not contradict it—two
important but by now unsurprising conclusions.

ROMANS 4:1–25

Using well-established rabbinic methods of interpretation, Paul called on the
story of Abraham to make several further points. First, citing Genesis 15:6,

Abraham did not earn God's favor, but rather simply trusted in the God who "justifies the ungodly" (4:5). It is not that God came to a good man like Abraham and a good woman like Sarah and confirmed their good qualities; God is not a God like that. Speaking from a Christian perspective, Käsemann puts it sharply, "Faith is constituted by the fact that with the preaching of the gospel the Lord who is the basis of the gospel comes upon the scene and seizes dominion over us. . . . Because as the Lord he does not allow himself to be taken in, we are constantly dependent on his word. Faith is living out of the word which bears witness to his lordship, nothing more and nothing less."[9]

Paul makes a second point in connection with the Abraham story, namely, Abraham's faith mentioned in Genesis 15:6 *precedes* Genesis 17, in which circumcision is made essential for inclusion into the covenant people of God (especially Gen 17:9–14). Paul drew a rather logical conclusion from the order of the text: Abraham's experience of faith occurred before he was circumcised, before he acquired the particular Jewish identity. Paul affirmed then that Abraham is the ancestor and model for non-Jewish people as well as for Jewish people (4:11b–12). Neither has priority over the other.

A third point drawn from the Abraham story concerns the barrenness of Sarah and the old age of both Abraham and Sarah in the face of the promise that they would have a son. Abraham is idealized by Paul to be unwavering in anticipation. "He grew strong in his faith as he gave glory to God, being fully convinced that God was able to do what [God] had promised" (4:20b–21). Abraham and Sarah could only "hope against hope." They had reached the limit of human hope, and yet they continued to believe. As models of faith, they could be taken as heroes and made to be only models for the rest of us, except that Paul attached another liturgical formula to the end of the section. He introduced a new figure into the Abraham-Sarah story, "Jesus our Lord . . . who was handed over to death for our trespasses and was raised for our justification" (4:24–25). The presence of this formula prevents believers from presuming that their own faith justifies them, even if they achieve an extraordinary, unwavering faith like that of Abraham and Sarah. Human faith does not save; the God who raised Jesus from the dead saves.

ROMANS 5:1–8:39

At the beginning of chapter 5, Paul recapitulates the thrust of the previous section ("Therefore, since we are justified by faith," 5:1a), and then shifts gears to make possible a new discussion. We notice the shift primarily in terms of the change of language. No longer do we find "faith," "believing," "the righteousness of God," "Jew," and "Greek" as key topics. Instead we encounter "life," "death," "to live," "to die," and particularly the work of the Spirit. Whereas Old Testament texts were prominent in the first four chapters, only two citations occur between 5:1 and 8:39.

As is often noticed by commentators, 5:1–11 provides a transition to the new discussion. The section is framed by the verb "boast" (5:2, 11), giving the unit a doxological flavor, and can be divided into three subsections. In the first, God's love provides the grounds for hope, even in the face of suffering (5:1–5); the second subsection postulates the extraordinary nature of Christ's death as the supreme expression of God's love (5:6–8); the third affirms the justification and reconciliation experienced in the present as reasons for confidence in the day of final judgment (5:9–11).

Two features of 5:1–11 stand out. First, the particular way in which Christ's death is depicted is striking (5:6–8). It is an unforeseen and unparalleled event that happens as a surprise. There is no preparation for it, no contingency that makes it provisional, no call to repentance to activate the results. As Käsemann has noted, some modern translations misleadingly read "at the right time" (RSV, NRSV), rather than "at that time, then."[10] The point of the text seems to be that the event occurred, according to human reckoning at least, at the most inopportune moment—when we were weak, ungodly, and sinful.

The second feature to note is that at the beginning of the section attention is directed to the future: "we boast in our hope of sharing the glory of God" (5:2). The very reality that humanity has lacked (3:23) becomes both the object of confident anticipation and the grounds for a positive attitude toward the sufferings of the present (5:3). Rather than being the occasion for bewilderment or lament or anger, afflictions are understood as a necessary part of the experience of grace. The implied readers are invited to face tribulations in hope, even exulting in them, not out of a sick masochism, but because they are sure that the present is not the end of the story.

The "therefore" of 5:12 signifies this section (5:12–21) as a development of 5:1–11. How can such weak, ungodly, sinful creatures afford to have confidence in the day of judgment? The answer is, as Achtemeier succinctly puts it, "Christ got us out of the mess that Adam got us into. What Adam did, Christ undid; where Adam failed, Christ succeeded."[11]

Of course, Adam and Christ are more than individuals; they incorporate all people into themselves. Each is the progenitor and prototype of all humanity. Through the one person, death spreads to all people; through the other, life comes to all. But the two are not equal. The one figure dominates the other. Obedience triumphs over disobedience; grace triumphs over sin; life triumphs over death.

Notice the world-embracing character of both Adam and Christ, a reflection of Paul's apocalyptic perspective. Nothing suggests that the actions of either figure (disobedience and obedience) are in any way limited to a few—death to those who disobey and life to those who obey. There are no restrictions. To quote Käsemann again, "Since death is a force which shapes the cosmos, freedom from it, like the justification that underlies this freedom, has to have universal validity if it is to be seriously maintained."[12]

Because the work of Christ rights the wrongs of Adam, Paul was led to a sanguine expression of grace. The arrival of the law, he contended, did not suppress the sinful activities of human beings; it exacerbated the situation. "But where sin increased, grace abounded all the more" (5:20). Once sin exercised its dominion over people through death; now grace exercises its dominion over people by giving life in Jesus Christ.

ROMANS 6:1–7:6

This enthusiastic affirmation of God's grace pushed Paul to face the charge earlier leveled against his teaching (some accused him of saying, "Let us do evil that good may come," 3:8). Thus he raised the obvious question, "Should we continue in sin in order that grace may abound?" (6:1). Paul's response forces readers to recall their own baptism, to remember that baptism is their realistic association with the one whose act of obedience made the many righteous (6:3–11).

On the one hand, the text describes Christ as one who died, was buried, and was raised from the dead. His resurrection was different from a resuscitation of a corpse since we know "that Christ, being raised from the dead, will never die again; death no longer has dominion over him" (6:9). In his tomb lies the broken power of death, the ultimate enemy whose defeat signals the ultimate triumph of God. The death, burial, and resurrection of Christ constitute the decisive apocalyptic event.

On the other hand, the way Paul expounds the association of believers with Christ implies a certain incompleteness for the baptized. In baptism believers are united with Christ in his death and burial, but they *await* resurrection with him.[13] The main verbs in 6:5 and 6:8 are in the future tense. For the present the newness of life to which believers are called is a cruciform life (6:4). In Christ the promised new age has arrived, but the old age is not yet gone. We live at "the juncture of the ages."[14]

The remainder of chapter 6 challenges readers to live out of the new age and not out of the old, to present themselves as agents of righteousness in the warfare against evil, and not to let sin gain a foothold in their mortal bodies. Indicative mood verbs declare that believers are liberated from sin's clutches (6:17–18) and are set alongside imperative mood verbs demanding allegiance to righteousness (6:19).

Between chapters 5 and 6, two significant changes have taken place. First, whereas in 5:6–8 the death of Christ is depicted as an unconditional, noncontingent gift of grace to the ungodly, in 6:1–23 those acknowledging the gift must recognize its demands for a transformed life. Second, whereas the contrast between Adam and Christ in 5:12–21 is presented in universal categories that encompass all of humanity, the union with Christ in baptism in 6:1–11 limits the gifts to the Christian community. The basic paradox of universalism and particularism remain in remarkable tension, as they do elsewhere in the letters. The abandoning of either pole truncates Paul's gospel.

Paul's illustration from marriage law and its application (7:1–6) provide yet another answer to the allegations of libertinism. The death of the husband creates a new situation in which the widow is free to marry another man. Likewise, the death of Christ brings freedom from the law and makes possible union with another—namely, the risen Christ.

ROMANS 7:7–8:39

The apostle's statement in 7:6, "But now we are discharged from the law, dead to that which held us captive, so that we are slaves not under the old written code but in the new life of the Spirit," raises yet another issue for Paul. What then is the state of the law? Or as Paul framed the question, "Is the law sin?" He immediately responds, "By no means!" But then in what follows we wonder whether he has sustained his point or not. Listed below are the things said about the law in 7:7–12:

- It brings the knowledge of sin (7:7).
- It becomes the occasion for sin to act (7:8).
- It leads to the arousing of sin (7:9).
- It offers life but brings death (7:10).
- It becomes the occasion for sin to deceive and to kill me (7:11).

None of these statements gives a very positive picture of the law. But then to the reader's surprise the conclusion drawn is that "the law is holy, and the commandment is holy and just and good" (7:12). How can that be? While the law ends up being a vulnerable partner serving the aims and schemes of sin, sin (and not the law) is the culprit that ultimately brings deception and death. Sin takes up residence in the individual and prevents one from doing the good and entices one to do the evil (7:20). The law is vindicated, but at the same time is shown to be incapable of curbing sin.

While we cannot linger over the complex exegetical matters in this passage, the final verse in the chapter (7:25) warrants special attention.[15] Having uttered the victorious cry of deliverance from "this body of death . . . Thanks be to God through Jesus Christ our Lord!" Paul concludes, "So then, with my mind I am a slave to the law of God, but with my flesh I am a slave to the law of sin" (7:25b). After declaring oneself free through Jesus Christ, how is it possible to admit service to the law of sin? Commentators have made a myriad of suggestions on how to remove the tension between 7:25a and 7:25b. The Revised Common Lectionary even cuts the lesson off in midstream at 7:25a! Dunn's explanation is most helpful. He contends that the coexistence of the two ages lies behind the tension between the two types of service. On the one hand, the new age has broken in; "new life of the Spirit" (7:6) is possible; and service is rendered the law of God. On the other hand, the old age has not yet passed away, the flesh is vulnerable, and service is still given to the law of sin. The cry of freedom in 7:25a is not the expression of a salvation finished or one yet to begin, but of a salvation "under way and still to be completed."[16]

The connection between chapters 7 and 8 is obvious because the law remains a matter of concern, but the emphasis shifts now to the difference made by the breaking in of God's new age—the sending of the Son and especially the gift of the Spirit.[17] Readers hear again the good news that the sending of Jesus means the condemnation of sin and the fulfillment of the requirements of the law in those who live according to the Spirit and not according to the flesh. Lest there be any doubt, readers are reminded that they belong to the new age; "you are in the Spirit" (8:9).

The Greek word for "spirit" is the same word for "wind" and likely carries with it at least two connotations: "breath" (therefore life and vitality) and "gale force winds" (therefore power and energy). In chapter 8 the word is used primarily for God and connotes God's lively activity, God beyond our control. This Spirit comes to dwell in believers (8:9, 11), to deliver them from bondage to the flesh (8:11–13), to enable them to call God "Father" (8:15), and to set them in the family as heirs of the divine gifts (8:16–17).

Romans 8:17, however, ends with an unusual caveat that we are heirs of God "if, in fact, we suffer with him so that we may also be glorified with him" (8:17). What does it mean to "suffer with Christ"? From what Paul has written thus far, it would not only entail union with Christ in the baptismal act (6:3–4) but also the living out of that union in a hostile world where the opposition is fierce and the conflict sharp. Participation with Christ in the here and now cannot help but involve opposition. It may not be a spectacular persecution. It may be a relatively tolerable pressure one learns to live with. In any case, it cannot be avoided.

In fairness to Paul, we should be clear that he did not avoid the issue of suffering with Christ. First there is his important thesis: "The sufferings of this present time are not worth comparing with the glory about to be revealed to us" (8:18). Then, as if to explain how the "heirs of God and joint heirs with Christ" (8:17) do in fact suffer with Christ, he turns his attention away from believers to the suffering of the world, to the predicament of creation and humans within it, whose lives are a perpetual groaning because of the way things are in the world (8:19–22). Hungry, victimized, oppressed, whether enraged or despondent, this earthly choir can only lift up its inarticulate cries of futility and anguish. What the Spirit directs God's family to do is to join its cries with the groaning of creation, to stand in solidarity with those who suffer, to take up the cause of the oppressed, but to do so as those who hope and who eagerly await the completion of the family circle. Even prayer is redefined in terms of "our inarticulate groans" (8:26 NEB) with creation's plight of futility and bondage to decay (8:20–21).

In light of "the glory that is to be revealed," these "groanings" turn out in fact to be labor pains. They are not the cries of despondency and depression but the groans of an eager hope that patiently awaits the birth of new life, and that meanwhile sustains those who wait for "the freedom of the glory of the children of God" (8:21).

To identify so closely with a groaning creation is bound to leave the family of God in an embattled state, susceptible to the same circumstances that creation experiences and in need of divine reassurance. Threats come not only from a shared humanity but also from hardship, distress, persecution, famine, nakedness, peril, and sword, all because the family of God has taken up the cause of the powerless. A citation from Psalm 44:22 depicts the current situation: "For your sake we are being killed all day long; we are counted as sheep to be slaughtered." The final paragraph of the chapter (8:31–39), therefore, eloquently expresses God's commitment to stand by the family in these moments of crisis and to lead them to be "more than conquerors" (8:37).

ROMANS 9–11

Paul has left one aspect of his letter of introduction incomplete. He clarified many misunderstandings that might have been caused by his letter to the Galatian communities. He provided good reasons for welcoming the Gentiles into the people of God. What remains unclear, however, is the Jews' present relation to the promises God made to their ancestors. When Paul affirms, "nothing shall separate us from the love of God," are the Jews excluded from or included in the "us"?

This is precisely the issue that chapters 9–11 address. The heart of the problem for Paul was theological, not historical. He was not interested in why the Jews, for the most part, did not accept the Messiah, but whether God's promises to the Jews were still going to be honored. This involved him in a complex answer, which nonetheless provides a clear conclusion.

The section breaks into three distinct sections. The first section (9:1–29) begins with the recognition of all the special gifts and God-given perquisites that belong to Israel (9:1–5). Then immediately Paul cuts to the chase: "It is not as though the word of God had failed" (9:6). Why? Because God's electing promise, not natural birth or human works, *always* determined descendancy in Israel's past. Isaac was the chosen son of Abraham and Sarah; Jacob was the chosen son of Isaac and Rebecca. In neither case did the human parties have anything to do with it. Furthermore, God's call is not an arbitrary action, but serves the divine purposes in special and unusual ways. Thus, God's word did not fail because both Gentiles (9:24–26) and Jews (9:27–29) are called to be God's people in the very same manner.[18]

The second section (9:30–10:21) confronts the obvious question: why is it that Gentiles are coming into the church and not Jews? Paul responds with "a baffling inversion"[19] of the pattern one would naturally expect. He used the image of a footrace to make the amazing point that the Gentiles, while not pursuing righteousness, arrived at it. Israel, on the other hand, which did strive for righteousness, did not arrive at the law. Though full of zeal, they never reached the finish line. The problem is that God put a stumbling block in their way: God's own righteousness, misunderstood by the Jews as a mark of their distinctiveness, can only be received by faith (9:32–33). As Johnson states:

> To establish one's own righteousness is not simply to grasp after God's righteousness by individual legal perfection, which is neither what Jews do nor what Paul accuses them of doing. To establish one's own righteousness is rather to misunderstand the nature of righteousness, to consider it a human possession rather than divine, to be ignorant (10:3) of its impartiality as well as its faithfulness, to construe God's faithfulness *as* partiality.[20]

In the following verses we learn that the divine righteousness that caused Israel to fall is now "the word of faith" that the apostle proclaims as the story of God's impartiality in Christ. Quoting first Isaiah 28:16 and then Joel 2:32, Paul declares, "The scripture says, 'No one who believes in him will be put to shame.' For there is no distinction between Jew and Greek; the same Lord is Lord of all and is generous to all who call on him. For, 'Everyone who calls on the name of the Lord shall be saved'" (10:11–13).

In the third section (11:1–36), Paul begins by bluntly putting the question again, "Has God rejected his people?" (11:1). He initially answers in terms of Jewish Christians, like himself, who have not been rejected by God. Then he turns to the story of Elijah to recall that there were seven thousand who had not bowed to Baal. But even a large remnant is insufficient for Paul. To be sure, the runners in the race stumbled over the stone of God's righteousness, but their stumbling has led to the inclusion of the Gentiles among God's people. In a remarkable turn, the inclusion of the Gentiles is finally going to lead to Israel's inclusion (11:11–12).

Paul used several different metaphors to express "this mystery" of God's working (11:25), but none more prominently than the olive tree. The natural branches were broken off, and wild olive branches were grafted on. The latter cannot be arrogant about their inclusion, but in light of God's activity should stand "in awe" (11:20). One cannot presume upon grace. In time, however, the natural branches will be regrafted on the tree, or as Paul states unambiguously, "All Israel will be saved" (11:26).

Two verses summarize Paul's points and, in doing so, reiterate the theological character of his argument. First, God's faithfulness to Israel "for the sake of their ancestors" rests on the fact that "the gifts and the calling of God are irrevocable" (11:29). It is not because Israel has demonstrated or will demonstrate particular qualities of fidelity and courage that so please God that God saves Israel. Rather, God does not renege on the gifts and the call given Israel.

Second, the "baffling inversion," rehearsed in 11:30–31, is explained in 11:32: "For God has imprisoned all [people] in disobedience so that he may be merciful to all." The double use of the word "all" is intentional. For both Jew and Gentile, all avenues of escape have been closed off—all doors locked tight, all windows barred, so that God and only God may be merciful to all. As 11:29 affirms the faithfulness of God, so 11:32 affirms God's impartiality.

ROMANS 12–15

In a sense, the powerful doxology at the close of chapter 11 could have ended the letter. Paul has already addressed the major issues of his theology that might have arisen for discussion among his Roman readers: misrepresentations or misunderstandings of his earlier letter to the Galatians, particularly regarding the law, and his stance concerning God's faithfulness to his kinfolk, the Jews. And yet without the last five chapters Romans would be incomplete. Right thinking is not much good without right living. The gospel by nature asks to be embodied in the life of the community and in the lives of the members of the community. Discussion and argument must finally give way to prayer and practice. And so in four of the five remaining chapters Paul writes about the concrete expression of the gospel in human life.

Romans 12:1–2 serves as a theme for the section, much as 1:16–17 did for the first eleven chapters, and from it we can get a good glimpse of the direction in the end of the letter. Several features of Paul's understanding of the embodiment of the gospel stand out. First, the verses are written to a communal Christian context ("brothers and sisters"). They are not addressed to the broader Greco-Roman culture to provide universal, timeless truths for the society. Paul did not intend that they be put up on the walls of public buildings for the instruction of the general populace. Though much of what is said in these chapters is not very specific and even paralleled by similar statements from other literature (e.g., "hate what is evil, hold fast to what is good," 12:9; cf. Ps 34:14; 37:27), Paul clearly aimed his words at those who have read the first eleven chapters of the letter.

Nor are these verses directed to individuals in the community in isolation from one another. Though somewhat foreign to Western instincts, Paul took the communal context seriously and trusted the common gifts of discernment and wisdom given to believers. He later writes, "I myself feel confident about you, my brothers and sisters, that you yourselves are full of goodness, filled with all knowledge, and able to instruct one another" (15:14).

A second striking feature of these verses is the way in which what is said about Christian living grows out of and is related to the gospel. The "mercies of God," spelled out in the previous eleven chapters ("therefore"), call for reordered lives. God's rectifying activity includes a divine claim on believers for what they do and how they live. Imperative mood verbs are more prevalent in these later chapters, but each presupposes the many indicatives of divine grace that have preceded them.

Interestingly, a number of linguistic linkages also connect chapter 12 with the previous chapters of the letter. Particularly, the appeal to "present" your bodies to God recalls the frequent use of the same Greek verb in chapter 6 (6:13 [twice]; 16, 19 [twice]), as well as the noun "body" (6:12; 12:1). Furthermore, the notion of such a presentation as being a "spiritual worship" reverses the choice we noted as so decisive in the earlier section of the letter, to "worship and serve the creature rather than the Creator" (1:25).[21] These linkages reinforce that the embodiment of the gospel encouraged in 12:1–2 is part and parcel of the gospel story itself and not an addendum tacked on at the end.

The third striking feature of this section is its eschatological character. Paul's language here reflects the notion of the two ages drawn from Jewish apocalyptic. Believers are not to be squeezed into the mold of "this age," but to be shaped by the presence and power of the new age. The "mind," once debased (1:28) and given up by God, is now to be transformed by the "new creation" brought by Christ, in which matters like circumcision and uncircumcision no longer count (Gal 6:15) and people are valued in a new way (2 Cor 5:16–17).

The fourth outstanding feature of 12:1–2 is the dimension of discernment issuing from the presentation of themselves as living sacrifices. The end of the transformation of the mind is that "you may discern the will of God." A maxim like "Hate what is evil; hold fast to what is good" (12:9) leaves a lot of room for specific decision making, for sifting the important from the trivial, for determining the genuine from the bogus.

In another letter Paul prayed for the readers that their love might increase more and more with knowledge and insight "to help you discern what is best" (Phil 1:9–10, author's trans.). Discernment has to with drawing a conclusion about the worth of something on the basis of testing and proving. Just as once humans discerned that God was unnecessary for life and God gave them over to an undiscerning mind (1:28), so now through the mercies of God and the responding worship offered to God, the gift of discernment is restored.

For the next chapter or so, Paul describes what the embodiment of the gospel looks like in both the church (12:3–13) and the broader culture (12:14–13:7). Within the context of the Christian community, two features stand out. First, employing a very effective literary device called *paranomasia* (repetition of a root word), Paul warns readers of thinking more highly of themselves than they ought to think, but encourages them to value themselves "soberly," each person doing so according to faith's standards and not according to the world's standards (12:3). Paul was only too aware of the yardsticks used in this age to determine one's successes or failures, often resulting in too high or too low a view of oneself. In his case religious measurements were used (Gal 1:13–14; Phil 3:4–6), but the self-evaluations of the new age are based on God's gift of faith. Such an evaluation leads one to discern the one body, the church, each member having been gifted in a special way (so 12:4–8). As Meyer comments, "Diversities are acknowledged but stripped of their divisive power by being subordinated to the interpretive norm of 'faith.'"[22]

Second, 12:9–13 presents a list of exhortations, the first of which is "Let love be genuine [without pretense]." It is not surprising to find love heading the list since the term is prominent in all of Paul's letters as the primary mark of the embodiment of the gospel (cf. 1 Cor 13; Rom 13:10; Gal 5:6, 22). It clearly has roots in the Old Testament, but Paul's use of the term does not imply some abstract ethical concept. He defines love in terms of the self-sacrifice of Christ, "who loved me and gave himself for me" (Gal 2:20), and warned readers against insincerity or feigning the reality itself. John Calvin saw the issue and wrote, "It is difficult to express how ingenious almost all men [*sic*] are in counterfeiting a love which they do not really possess. They deceive not only others, but also themselves, while they persuade themselves that they have a true love for those whom they not only treat with neglect, but also in fact reject. Paul declares here, therefore, that the only real love is that which is free from all dissimulation."[23]

We have noted a division between the treatment of the embodiment of the gospel within the Christian community (12:3–8) and in the broader society (12:9–13:7). But this is not a hard and fast division. In fact, the hostility, the threat to peace, and the temptation for revenge implied in 12:9–21 might come from within rather than outside the church.

The passage that follows has caused the church such grief through the years that we should pause to examine it more carefully (13:1–7). Often used as the biblical warrant for the support of oppressive governments such as Germany under the Third Reich and South Africa under apartheid, the passage must be read in its original context. Four brief observations about the text follow.

First, the immediate issue that evokes the words of submission to the civil authorities from Paul may well have been a festering tax revolt against Rome. The section culminates in 13:7 with the positive word to "pay to all what is due them," and two forms of taxes are listed in the obligation readers owe. Rather than being a statement on the nature of government in general, it seems to provide directions for the church in a crisis looming before the Roman community in the mid to late fifties of the first century CE.

Second, the notion that citizens owe the authorities an acknowledgment of their rightful place is not a novel proposal for a Jewish community. Both the Old Testament and the literature of Hellenistic Judaism recognize that the authority of God stands above and beyond human rulers and the obligations owed to foreign powers (e.g., Jer 29:7; Prov 8:15–16; 24:21–22; Dan 2:21; Wis 6:1–11; Sir 17:17; Letter of Aristeas 196, 219, 224).

Third, the initial imperative, "Let every person be subject to the governing authorities," demands that the readers take seriously the role of the civil magistrates, but it does not demand obedience to those authorities. One might disobey the government officials, if one thought their demands contrary to God's will, and at the same time be exposed to their discipline or punishment. Civil rights leaders, who violated the segregationist laws and practices of the southern states and who went to jail for their actions, were disobedient to many local magistrates but remained subject to their authority.

Fourth, the broader context, with its strong eschatological presence, cannot be ignored. At the beginning of chapter 12, readers are told not to conform to this age, but to be transformed as their minds are renewed by the new age (12:1–2). At the end of chapter 13, they are reminded of the lateness of the hour and the nearness of the coming salvation (13:11–14), which renders all human institutions ephemeral. Jesus, not Caesar, is Lord, thus relativizing the current governmental structures and putting loyalty to the state into a penultimate position. The state's authority is never final. What remains a constant obligation for believers is their love for another (13:8–10).

The next block of exhortations comes in connection with "the strong" and "the weak" in the Roman church (14:1–15:6). The issues of contention mentioned are the eating of meat (or being a vegetarian, 14:2–3), the observance of special days (14:5–6), and the drinking of wine (14:21), though, frankly, the report of the issues is so vague (particularly as compared to the situation in Corinth) as to leave modern readers uncertain as to the details Paul addresses. Some interpreters are inclined to think he may be reflecting the problems of the house churches of Corinth, from where he was writing the letter to the Romans. What becomes evident is that, because God the impartial judge has welcomed them (14:3), "the strong" are to accept "the weak" and "the weak" to accept "the strong." "Let us therefore no longer pass judgment on one another, but resolve instead never to put a stumbling block or hindrance in the way of another" (14:13).

At 15:7–13 we reach, in some respects, the climax of the book. The injunction to "welcome one another" is aimed no longer at "the weak" and "the strong" but at "the circumcised" and at "the Gentiles." Each is to "welcome"[24] the other, accepting and respecting his or her differences, "just as Christ has welcomed you." Mutual acceptance of Jews and Gentiles then becomes at least one of the indispensable implications of the long and involved argument of Romans, all because Christ has confirmed the promises made long ago to the patriarchs of Israel and because the Gentiles have been included as a part of God's people. The theological direction of the letter finds its practical expression not in an aggressive evangelization of Jewish people but in a profound respect for who they are as people of God's promise.

3

1 Corinthians

Paul's relationship to the Corinthian church was complex. He founded the Christian community there (1 Cor 2:1–5; 3:6; cf. Acts 18:1–11) and in the letter refers to himself as "your father through the gospel" (1 Cor 4:15). Acts indicates that on his initial visit he stayed in Corinth eighteen months (Acts 18:11). Not only was Corinth a cosmopolitan city, but also the Christians there represented a wide spectrum of social and economic classes, including owners of substantial homes as well as slaves.

As was Paul's custom, he moved on to preach the gospel in other urban locales without breaking his ties with the Christians in Corinth. He wrote them at least one letter prior to 1 Corinthians, a letter apparently lost to us today, in which he addressed sexual immorality within the community (5:9) and responded to verbal and written communications he received from the Corinthians. They reported their situation to him and asked for guidance regarding various issues before the church (1:11; 7:1; 16:17).

Because Paul deals with the problems of the church at Corinth in his letters, commentators of the letters often concentrate on these specific issues and the cultural and social diversity behind those issues. In doing so, they leave unidentified any unified theological purpose (more obvious in Romans) in the writing of the letter. First Corinthians has been generally treated as more about ecclesiastical problems, and what the members should do about them, than about theological problems, such as what the readers are to think about God or about the gospel.[1]

It is true that the letter invites the reader's attention to particular topics under debate (notorious sexual immorality, members taking one another to court, marriage relationships, the eating of meat offered to idols, hairstyles, the poor being excluded at the Lord's Supper, the practice of spiritual gifts, and the denial of the resurrection). Yet the way in which the initial problem (factionalism in the church, 1:11–17) is addressed indicates that the letter functions as much more than a problem-solving document.

Essentially, 1 Corinthians is an appeal for ecclesial unity. The way in which Paul deals with the various problems in Corinth reveals an overriding concern for harmony in the church.[2] Furthermore, in helping the church to move beyond its factions to be the one body of Christ, Paul names the seminal problem in Corinth: the church must learn to think differently about both God and its own life together. It needs to develop an epistemology rooted in the crucified Christ.

After a traditional opening to the letter in which Paul is not reticent about commending the Corinthians for the rich spiritual gifts God has given them (1:1–9), we meet the first problem.

1 CORINTHIANS 1:10–4:20

Right off the bat, Paul appeals to the Corinthian community that "all of you be in agreement and that there be no divisions (*schismata*) among you, but that you be united in the same mind and the same purpose" (1:10). Paul received word through Chloe's family of the divisions in the church, apparently centered on a leadership squabble (1:11–17). But the section that follows does not directly mention factionalism; instead, it engages in a lengthy and forceful analysis of human wisdom (1:18–2:16).

How are the two connected? How does the sharp critique of wisdom relate to the problem of division in the church? The Corinthians are chided for their pretentious wisdom (3:18–20), a wisdom that is linked to their boasting about particular leaders (3:21–22). But this relationship is not spelled out clearly and hardly accounts for the extensive reflections on the wisdom and power of God in 1:18–2:16.

We must take seriously the obvious epistemological concern of 1:18–2:16. This section presents readers with a way of knowing God that is radically different from the way that led to factionalism in the church. Human wisdom is bound to misconstrue the character of God and how God works in the world (cf. Rom 1:18–30). A community whose conduct is based on human inclination results, not surprisingly, in jealousy and division among its members (3:3–4). The parties have become so fixed in their own ideologies that a strategy of conflict management, in which the apostle might facilitate a conversation between the groups, seems fruitless. For the communicants to sit down and talk out their differences would accomplish little. The whole community must readjust its vision. It must come to a different way of knowing God and envisioning its life together. Paul thus points to the message of the crucified Messiah not as a statement of atonement, but as the new epistemological focus. The section from 1:10 to 2:16 can be easily divided into five parts:

- 1:10–17 Factions in the community
- 1:18–25 God's foolishness and power
- 1:26–31 The experience of the Corinthians
- 2:1–5   The ministry of Paul in Corinth
- 2:6–16   God reveals the divine wisdom of the cross through the Spirit

Beginning with a forceful affirmation in 1:18, "For the message about the cross is foolishness to those who are perishing, but to us who are being saved it is the power of God," Paul writes of the "foolishness" (1:18–2:5) and the hiddenness of God's wisdom (2:6–16).

Four observations are critical to this section. First, verse 21 offers a reason for God's decision to thwart the wisdom of the "wise." "Since, in the wisdom of God, the world did not know God through wisdom, God decided, through the foolishness of our proclamation, to save those who believe." God's decision to initiate the saving activity through the cross (and not some other way) is set against the backdrop of the world's failure to know God. The problem of the world is that its norms for knowing have proved inadequate and result in not knowing. God simply does not fit the world's criteria and expectations. Thus, over against the sign-seeking Jews and the wisdom-demanding Greeks, Paul set the message of the cross. It provides no new information about God, but effects a decisive act of salvation.

Second, following an invitation to the readers to reflect on their own calling as people of God (1:26–31), Paul offers a reminder of his initial preaching at Corinth (2:1–5). "For I decided *to know* nothing among you except Jesus Christ, and him crucified" (2:2, emphasis added). The choice of the infinitive "to know" is interesting. Why not "to preach" or "to proclaim" or "to declare," any of which might read more smoothly than "to know"? What is at stake is the issue of epistemology, which produces the hearers' perspective on God and on their life together. In the gospel they are invited to put on new lenses and to view life differently.

Furthermore, the message of the cross is not merely a new logic or a new cognitive enterprise; the message entails knowing and doing, living differently as well as thinking differently. Paul's so-called hardship catalog in 4:9–13 is clear evidence that a way of thinking consistent with the scandal of the cross makes people into fools for Christ's sake and spectacles to the world.

Third, the word "power" occurs four times between 1:18 and 2:5. Each case either denotes or connotes divine power. God has decisively invaded the world in the crucified Christ, and thus the foolish message of the cross is the very revelation of God's power (1:18). Those Corinthians engaged in a power struggle over leaders were no doubt startled to discover that God's power is operative in ways very different from competitiveness and the usual practice of jockeying for position. God's power preempts competing factions and authorizes all sorts of ministries for the whole church. Thus, Paul comments at the end of the section, "I will come to you soon, if the Lord wills, and I will find out not the talk of these arrogant people but their power. For the kingdom of God depends not on talk but on power" (4:19–20).

Fourth, the next section (2:6–16) carries the argument further, making the case that the wisdom of God, already defined as the message of the crucified Messiah (1:24), is not an innate property humans possess, but is the gift of God, a self-revelation taught by the Spirit. Six times between 2:6 and 2:16 the two Greek verbs for "know" appear. People not led by the Spirit naturally find foolish the message of the cross.

An insight critical for the rest of the letter unfolds in 2:6–8, where this new way of knowing is given an eschatological cast. The secret and hidden wisdom spoken among the mature is not "a wisdom of this age or of the rulers of this age." Since none of the rulers of this age "knew" this, they crucified the Lord of glory. The repeated use of the phrase "of this age" reflects the perspective of apocalyptic dualism; the wisdom decreed "before the ages" cannot be grasped by "this age." This wisdom is only known through the message of the crucified Christ.

In chapters 3 and 4 the message of the cross is applied to the ministries of Paul and Apollos (3:5–15; 4:1–13) and to the Corinthians (3:1–4, 16–23). Particularly in regard to the Corinthians, the text appropriately stresses the incompatibility between being spiritual (the way of knowing via the message of the cross) and being a fractured community (3:1–4). The divisions in the church prove that their way of viewing God, and their life together, need a radical readjustment.

Theologically, the first four chapters of this letter argue that a new epistemology commensurate with the message of the cross is the only solution to the community's disharmony. In the long run unity in the church can be no more than superficially attained unless the imaginations of the members change, unless their angles of vision are transformed.

If George Kennedy is correct that the New Testament retains an oral quality for its audience, and its books should be read primarily as speeches, then we can assume that Paul's argument is accumulative.[3] The epistemology developed in the early chapters carries repercussions for the rest of the letter. A critical foundation has been laid for confronting the other problems in the community. Even though Paul does not find it necessary to repeat the new epistemology with every issue he faces, at important junctures he continues to prod readers to understand themselves and God differently in order to move beyond division to unity. We note those reminders as we follow the argument of the book.

1 CORINTHIANS 5:1–6:20

This section addresses the problem of a man in the community who is living in a sexual relationship with his stepmother (5:1–13). Paul, somewhat surprisingly, addresses the church first, before pronouncing judgment on the guilty party. The congregation's arrogance, its boasting, and its failure to mourn are appalling. At the heart of Paul's rebuke is an urgent plea for a new, communal self-understanding. Mixing the cultic images of unleavened bread and Passover lamb (5:6–8), the text prods the Corinthians to think of themselves as an unleavened community that demonstrates honesty and dependability—as a community for whom the paschal lamb has been sacrificed. As Hays notes, the sacrifice is not to atone for sin, but marks the setting apart of Israel as a distinct people delivered from slavery. Just as the blood of the Passover lamb distinguished Israel as a special people, set apart by God, so the blood of Christ sets apart the Corinthians as a distinct people of God's care and protection.[4] In the light of this new identity, the community can maintain its unity.

Part of this epistemology based on a new Christian identity involves a new view of the self, and more specifically, of the body. In dealing with the question of extramarital sex, Paul focuses on the body as belonging to the Lord. He reminds his readers that the body is a temple of the Holy Spirit. "You are not your own. For you were bought with a price; therefore glorify God in your body" (6:19b–20).[5] Any thought of sexual autonomy is excluded. The reason to glorify God in the body and not to engage in sexual immorality is rooted in a new way of understanding the self.

1 CORINTHIANS 7:1–40

Chapter 7 advises the Corinthians in various marital situations. Different opinions and practices in regard to marriage were apparently a further source of contention in the church. Throughout the chapter, two basic theological axioms are at work. First, the primary goal of life is to realize one's "calling." God calls people to serve him, and though there are stated exceptions, they should serve God where they are. One should not be preoccupied with altering one's earthly status and missing one's "calling" (see especially, vv. 15, 17–24). Second, the passage sets the whole issue of marriage in an eschatological light. "The appointed time (*kairos*) has grown short. . . . The present form of this world is passing away" (7:29, 31). In light of the coming end, even marriage is penultimate. Both theological axioms clarify the new identity Paul desires for the Corinthians and shapes the responses he gives to their queries concerning marriage.

1 CORINTHIANS 8:1–11:1

In some respects, the issue of eating food previously offered to idols (8:1–13; 10:23–11:1) presents the most intriguing application of the new epistemology to the life of the community. Any first-time reader of 1 Corinthians, upon scanning 8:1–6, would certainly anticipate Paul to side with those who espouse a correct theology (those who have "knowledge") and to settle on the legitimacy of eating the available food. He develops a cogent case for eating food consecrated to idols based on solid theological rationale (8:6). But the "however" of verse 7 moves the argument in an entirely different direction.

At issue is the nature of the community. Is this a community where those with a correct theology can ignore others who are averse to eating the idol-consecrated food? For Paul, what takes precedence is not the principle of superior knowledge, but the realization that those who lack knowledge are those "for whom Christ died" (8:11). In the new community, edification takes precedence over freedom; the other person's concern takes precedence over one's own rights (10:23–24). The christological epistemology of 1:18–2:16, when applied to the controversy over eating food offered to idols, calls for a community of sensitivity and love.

Furthermore, because the community is one body that partakes of one loaf, the worship of idols is forbidden (10:17). The text forges an intriguing link between the sacramental bread, the crucified body of Christ, and the ecclesial body. What results is an affirmation that "participation in Jesus and his body becomes identical with incorporation into the church as the body of Christ."[6] Identifying itself as a people who share in the Lord's Cup and the Lord's Table, the community cannot simultaneously engage in the worship of pagan gods.

1 CORINTHIANS 11:2–14:40

Chapters 11 to 14 address a number of problems with worship in the Corinthian community, all of which contribute to the church's disunity. The difficulties surrounding the practice of the Lord's Supper (11:17–34) derive, at least in part, from social conventions of the broader culture that had become operative at the Corinthians' meals. It was customary for the wealthy to have preferred seating and a better menu than the poor, who often could not arrive on time for the gatherings. Paul gives a practical response, "If you are hungry, eat at home" (11:34), but that is not all he has to say. The specter of some people with too much to eat and drink and others who go away hungry demands a theological response.

Paul rehearses the liturgy of the Lord's Supper and adds a line, clarifying what the church is about when it celebrates communion: "You proclaim the Lord's death until he comes" (11:26). The critical phrase in 11:29 ("without discerning the body") is surely a reference to the ecclesial body. How members of the community view one another is the decisive issue, no matter who they are and on which side of this division they fall. Does the congregation recognize itself as the distinctive body of Christ? Throughout chapter 11 Paul pushes for a new communal self-understanding, consistent with the declaration of the Lord's death.

The issue concerning spiritual gifts runs throughout chapter 14. Paul's primary concern is to correct the notion—apparently held by some members of the community—that speaking in tongues somehow gives one a higher spiritual value than other Christians. Two theological affirmations lie at the center of Paul's response. First, 12:3 presents a new perspective by noting that the baptismal confession, "Jesus is Lord," can be truly confessed only under the influence of the Spirit. The primary activity of the Spirit is to lead to the confession that binds the church together. By linking pneumatology and Christology, Paul develops a fresh understanding of spiritual gifts. The confession, "Jesus is Lord," relativizes all gifts.

Second, Paul confronts the Corinthians with their true character as the body of Christ (12:12–24, 27). The directness of 12:27, with its emphatic "you" ("Now you are the body of Christ"), reinforces Paul's effort to shape the identities of his readers in line with the way of the cross. The implications of that identity are clear:

- The variety of gifts are given by one Spirit (12:4–11).
- The diversity of members contribute to the functioning of the whole body (12:14–31).
- Love is the primary gift (13:1–13).
- Church members are to edify and encourage one another and to speak the word with clarity (14:1–40).

1 CORINTHIANS 15:1–58

Most of the issues arising out of the Corinthian community that Paul has addressed thus far have been behavioral. While Paul does not hesitate to give counsel regarding the problems about which he had heard, or about which the community had sought his advice, it is clear that he pushed them to think differently about God and about themselves. The giving of the crucified Christ, for Paul, was not only God's salvific act; it is the lens through which he wants the readers to view reality. Martin Luther, opposing the scholastics of his day, argued that theologians who believe that the invisible things of God can be perceived from the visible do not deserve to be called theologians. This type of theology can only lead to calling the good bad and the bad good. God can be known only "through suffering and the cross," and even then, as with Moses, we know only the backside of God (Exod 33:23)—that is, God hidden in the revelation.[7]

The issue in chapter 15, however, is not primarily behavioral, but rather theological. Some in the Corinthian community claimed that there was no resurrection of the dead (15:12). Apparently they accepted Jesus' resurrection (at least Paul's argument seems to assume such a belief on their part), but for various reasons (which scholars debate) they are unable to affirm a future resurrection for themselves, their peers, and those who might be alive at the time of the return of Jesus.

Paul begins his response with a traditional statement of the gospel that was preached to them and that they accepted (15:3–5):

- Christ died for our sins according to the Scriptures.
- He was buried.
- He was raised on the third day according to the Scriptures.
- He appeared to Cephas, then to the twelve.

Paul makes two points in 15:12–19. First, with a two-directional logic Paul ties the resurrection of Jesus to the future resurrection of the community. On the one hand, if Jesus is not raised, then there is no resurrection of the dead (15:12). On the other hand, to deny the future resurrection is to deny Jesus' resurrection (15:13, 16). The two resurrections cannot be separated so that one can be accepted while the other is denied. Second, Paul clarified what is at stake for those who deny the resurrection: "our proclamation has been in vain" (15:14); "your faith has been in vain" (15:14, 17); God is being misrepresented (15:15); "you are still in your sins" (15:17); and "we are of all people most to be pitied" (15:19).

Paul then explains in 15:20–28 how this can be: the risen Christ is "the first fruits of those who have died" (15:20). He first states the apocalyptic ordering. Christ is the first installment of the harvest that both inaugurates and pledges the offerings of the total crop. The term "first fruits" signifies both something incomplete (Christ is *only* the first fruits) and something hopeful (Christ assures the final harvest). Then Paul moved to the christological ordering that parallels Christ and Adam (15:21–22). Note the future tense of the verb in 15:22: "all will be made alive in Christ." What happened to Christ has not yet happened, but will happen to "all."

Then in 15:35–58 Paul faces the question inevitably raised when one talks about the resurrection: "What is it like in the future life? What sort of body will people have?" Two features of Paul's answer are significant. First, except for those left alive at Jesus' return, there must be death. "Fool! What you sow does not come to life unless it dies" (15:36). One can only speak of resurrection if there is death. Second, there will be a change, both for those who die before the return of Jesus and for those who are alive at that moment. "We will all be changed!" (15:51). The perishable body will have to put on the imperishable, and the mortal body will have to put on immortality. While the word "body" provides some continuity between the now and the then, the stress in the passage is clearly on the discontinuity.

What 1 Corinthians 15 discloses is an argument for the future resurrection of the dead, based on the traditional gospel that Paul had preached to the Corinthians and in which they had put their trust. The epistemology of the cross construes the gospel as a warrant for something decisively begun but not yet completed. In turn, the present becomes a critical moment: the time when people are perishing or being saved (1:18), when believers live by faith and not by sight, when the inbreaking new age overlaps with the old (10:11).[8]

Appropriately, the chapter is concluded with a charge to the congregation: "Therefore, my beloved, be steadfast, immovable, always excelling in the work of the Lord, because you know that in the Lord your labor is not in vain" (15:58). Chapter 16 includes a word about the collection and then ends with conventions often used to conclude a letter.

What Paul seeks to do in 1 Corinthians is to influence the minds, dispositions, and intuitions of the audience and to do so in line with the message he had initially preached to the community (2:2). He confronts readers with the critical nature of God's saving action in the crucified Christ such that it can become the glasses to refocus their vision of God, their own community, and the future.[9]

4

2 Corinthians

Of all the Pauline letters 2 Corinthians is the most enigmatic, yet in many respects the most fascinating. On the one hand, scholars do not agree whether it is a unified letter or the piecing together of two or three letters. Is 6:14–7:2 a letter fragment, written by Paul or perhaps even against Paul? Are the chapters dealing with the collection (chaps. 8–9) repetitious? Does the sharp change in tone of Paul's defense between chapters 1–9 and 10–13 indicate two separate letters written by Paul but at differing stages of his relationship with the community at Corinth? If so, which of the two comes first? Could chapters 10–13 actually be "the tearful letter" mentioned in 2 Cor 2:4? Since these questions of integrity do not markedly influence our theological probe into the letter, we shall not let them deter us here. Instead, we deal with the final form of the text.[1]

On the other hand, 2 Corinthians is authentically Pauline. Even more than Romans, it serves as a window into the theological mind of the apostle, letting ancient and modern readers view his vigorous defense of himself before detractors, his acknowledgment that the gospel is carried in earthen jars, and his preoccupation with the glory of God. The letter lets us see Paul amid the rough-and-tumble of his ministry, interpreting the Old Testament Scriptures, agonizing over the seduction of the church by forces within and without, all the while writing with forceful and vivid images.

PAUL'S SELF-DEFENSE

The reader becomes quickly aware that Paul has been attacked by a group or groups in Corinth and essentially wrote the letter as a self-defense. His authority and style of apostleship are being challenged. He is accused of writing weighty letters but of being a poor speaker. He has no charisma and no sense of presence, so his detractors claim (10:10). But unlike Galatians, it is not critical that modern readers discover exactly who his opponents were in Corinth or even what they were advocating. They appear in the letter only as a contrast to him, his intentions, and his mission. As Young and Ford declare, "What the text is about is Paul, not his opponents, and its thrust is discernible without precise knowledge of the situation."[2]

What is the character of Paul's defense? First, he roots his ministry in the divine initiative. The Greek word for "God" appears seventy-nine times in the letter and as the subject of most of the actions that are related. For example, Paul is accused of vacillating and of talking out of both sides of his mouth because he had departed from his announced itinerary. He made his decision not to revisit the Corinthians "according to human inclinations" (*kata sarka*), so his opponents contend. Paul responds that God does not say "yes" and "no" but always "yes." Paul asserts, "It is God who establishes us with you in Christ and has anointed us, by putting his seal on us and giving us his Spirit in our hearts as a first installment" (1:21–22).

Another key text for affirming the divine initiative is 2:14. Beginning to write about his ministry, Paul paints a picture of a parade following a battle, with the captives as prisoners being led by their captors through the streets of the city. Though the metaphors are mixed, the prisoners then spread the decisive aroma of Christ everywhere they go. "But thanks be to God, who in Christ always leads us in triumphal procession, and through us spreads in every place the fragrance that comes from knowing him" (2:14). Again, when Paul's ministry appears to encounter hard times, he defines the hard times as reminders that "this extraordinary power belongs to God and does not come from us" (4:7). Always, God is the initiator and the source of his ministry (cf. 3:4–5).

A second feature of Paul's ministry is its connection with the crucified Christ. The epistemology that he urges in 1 Corinthians he embraces for himself in 2 Corinthians. Having given a litany of the mishaps that had happened to him in the service of the gospel, he interprets them: "Always carrying in the body the death of Jesus, so that the life of Jesus may also be made visible in our bodies. For while we live, we are always being given up to death for Jesus' sake so that the life of Jesus may be made visible in our mortal flesh" (4:10–11). Association with Jesus necessarily means association with Jesus' death. Had Jesus been some other sort of figure, such as a conquering ruler, association with him would be different. But Jesus went the way of the cross; Paul thus interprets his ministry in the light of a crucified Jesus.

Four brief notes concerning this connection of Paul's ministry with the crucified Christ: First, the message and the messenger are drawn together in a remarkably tight relationship. Twice the word "body" and once the words "mortal flesh" occur in 4:10–11, underscoring that the locus for the crucified and risen Jesus is the concrete life of the apostle, not some mystical or ecstatic realm. Schütz rightly comments, "Paul appropriates to his entire ministry this close relationship to the gospel. In a sense all that Paul does is a reflection of what the gospel does; all that he is is a reflection of what the gospel is."[3]

Second, the identification with the crucified Jesus leads to Paul's paradoxical conviction that God's power is most evident in weakness, that is, real human weakness. The Greek word for "weakness" pertains to some sort of debilitating state, such as a physical illness, a disability, a feeling of inadequacy, or the experience of poverty, all of which were viewed stigmatically by the classical culture.

In the intensely polemical section of the letter, where the argument is full of self-parody and irony, Paul gives what is sometimes called the "fool's speech" (11:21b–12:10). In it he makes three moves. Initially he provides another catalog of hardships, not to display them as a badge of courage, but as marks of weakness (11:21b–29). Then he relates his failure in standing down the governor of Damascus, from whom he escaped by means of abandoning the city—hardly a brave act for a true apostle (11:30–33)! Third, he tells of his thorn in the flesh, which he interpreted to be "a messenger of Satan sent to torment me, to keep me from being too elated," presumably about the visionary experience he had fourteen years previously. Though he prays for freedom from this thorn in the flesh, he receives an unusual answer, "My grace is all you need; power comes to its full strength in weakness" (12:9 NEB). Then he concludes, "Therefore I am content with weaknesses, insults, hardships, persecutions, and calamities for the sake of Christ; for whenever I am weak, then I am strong" (12:10). This paradoxical claim lies at the heart of Paul's theology of the cross. Christ "was crucified in weakness, but lives by the power of God" (13:4).

Finally, the purpose of this association with the crucified Christ then is that the *life* of Jesus might be evident and visible and in the same realm of existence as the *dying* is made evident and visible. Paul explains how this happens in 4:14: "We know that the one who raised the Lord Jesus will raise us also with Jesus, and will bring us with you into [God's] presence." Though the hardships and trials of apostolic mission are realistically depicted, the text offers reasons for hope. The hardships become the occasion that makes Christ's risen power visible, both in Paul's life and the lives of his readers.

THE NEWNESS OF THE GOSPEL

In the ancient world, letters of recommendation were widely used to commend friends and to introduce trusted strangers to other people. Using this common imagery (perhaps because his opponents actually practiced it?), Paul cleverly points out that the Corinthians, as an enfleshment of the gospel, were his commendation, that is, "a letter of Christ, prepared by us, written not with ink but with the Spirit of the living God, not on tablets of stone but on tablets of human hearts" (3:3).

But then Paul offers a disclaimer regarding his own competence and instead declares that God was responsible for making him a servant of "a new covenant, not of letter (*gramma*) but of spirit; for the letter kills, but the Spirit gives life" (3:6). Here, Paul alludes to Jeremiah 31:31–33, where the prophet anticipates the time when a new covenant will be written on the hearts of people, and "I will be their God, and they shall be my people." By claiming to be a servant of "a new covenant," Paul affirms that the new age had come in Christ. While the glory on Moses' face, once he has seen God, is transitory, "the light of the knowledge of the glory of God" is seen "in the face of Jesus Christ" (4:6). The apostolic preaching of the gospel takes on immense significance because it becomes the medium for the revelation (apocalypse) of God.[4]

This newness of the gospel is highlighted again in 5:14–6:2. Paul continues his "defense" of his ministry, beginning with a statement of the gospel: "For the love of Christ urges us on, because we are convinced that one has died for all; therefore all have died. And he died for all, so that those who live might live no longer for themselves, but for him who died and was raised for them" (5:14–15). Something earthshaking (apocalyptic) has taken place in the cross, with sweeping implications for human history.

The text then underscores several features of this inclusive nature of Christ's death. First, Paul returns to a theme he developed in a previous letter to the Corinthians (1 Cor 1:18–2:16): the cross opens a whole new way of knowing. "Worldly standards have ceased to count in our estimate of anyone" (5:16 NEB). The usual categories, such as race, gender, and social status, have become obsolete for judging people. The old standards of decision making and the rigid systems of perception are now ephemeral and powerless. People, including Christ, must be viewed in a different light.

Second, the death of Christ in fact entails "a new creation" (5:17). It is critical that the expression not be reduced to a statement about the change within the individual—that in Christ a person becomes a new woman or a new man. The use of "all" in 5:14–15 and "world" in 5:19 indicates the cosmic character of Paul's thinking. The long-promised new order is inaugurated in the cross. Such a declaration does not deny that human lives are lived in the midst of a broken and disoriented world, rather it affirms that the old order is ultimately powerless to effect changes; the new world alone provides meaning.

The third feature of Jesus' death concerns God's reconciling activity. The stress falls here on both the subject and objects of the action. Regarding the subject, God is supremely the actor, the one who has broken through the alienation and hostility to win over the enemy (5:18a). It is a divine activity that transforms and renews the divine-human relationship. The remarkable phrase "not reckoning their trespasses against them" recalls Psalm 32:2 and God's gracious stance toward an antagonistic people who often do not recognize their own antagonism.

Regarding the objects of God's reconciliation, Paul specifies two entities, "us" (5:18) and "the world" (5:19). Both are helpless to deal with their own estrangement. Since the passage occurs in the context of Paul's discussion of his own ministry and mission, this common plight of "us" and "the world" becomes significant. Solidarity between the two protects the "us" from ever assuming a superior stance toward "the world."

A fourth feature of the passage is the commission to be engaged in God's ministry of reconciliation. The above distinction between "us" and "the world" also provides the dynamic for mission. The church declares to the world that, unlike everyone else, God is not angry on account of their sins. Paul saw himself among that group through whom God makes his appeal, entreating the world to be reconciled to God (5:20).

GOD'S GENEROSITY

The world of the first century CE operated out of a notion of scarcity, an economy of limited goods. Those in the villages and in the preindustrial cities perceived that there was only so much to go around. Bruce Malina comments, "In their social, economic, and natural universes—their total environment—all the desired things in life, such as land, wealth, prestige, blood, health, semen, friendship and love, manliness, honor, respect and status, power and influence, security and safety—literally all goods in life—exist in finite, limited quantity and are always in short supply."[5]

Furthermore, a person could not hope to rise above his or her situation, except at the loss and expense of others. Any change in situation, whereby one improved his or her financial position, was a threat to the stability and order of the community. Interestingly, Paul's strategy in dealing with churches in such a culture was not to provide a set of rules that would govern the lives of the Christian community as they accommodated themselves to the situation, nor did he advocate the radical overturn of the economic and social order. Instead, what appears in 2 Corinthians is an affirmation of the immense generosity of God and what this implies for Christians.[6]

Though numerous places in the letter speak of the (over)abundant grace of God, three passages particularly highlight the generosity of God.

1. In the initial blessing (1:3–11) readers are told of God's engagement with human suffering, out of which comes divine consolation. It is a remarkable mutuality, but one that overflows. "Just as the sufferings of Christ are abundant for us, so also our consolation is abundant through Christ" (1:5). No matter how great the suffering, there is more than enough comfort to go around.

2. Chapters 3 and 4 depict life in the new covenant and use the rhetoric "how much more" to convey the extravagance of God. "For if there was glory in the ministry of condemnation, much more does the ministry of justification abound in glory!" (3:9). The Greek verb *perisseuō*, meaning "be more than enough; be present in abundance; abound," appears ten times in 2 Corinthians, out of proportion to its appearances either in other Pauline letters or in the New Testament generally. "Everything is for your sake, so that grace, as it extends to more and more people, may increase thanksgiving, to the glory of God" (4:15).

3. The appeal for the collection in chapters 8 and 9 most evidently offers this notion of divine generosity. Paul begins by setting up the churches of Macedonia as a model for responding to God's bounty to them. Though poor and without adequate resources, they gave "even beyond their means" (8:3) in response to God's goodness. At the heart of the appeal is the christological statement, which expresses divine grace: "Though he was rich, yet for your sakes he became poor so that by his poverty you might become rich" (8:9). The use of economic terms to describe the incarnation is striking. The economics of abundance ("that *by his poverty* you might become rich") results in a new set of relationships with God's people. The Macedonian churches got the point: out of poverty comes abundance.

The intention of the collection, as Paul stated it to the Corinthians, is to bring about equality and fairness among the congregations. "At the present time your plenty will supply what they need, so that in turn their plenty will supply what you need. The goal is equality" (8:14 TNIV). Will the Corinthians trust God's generosity in a time of scarcity? The proof that they will lies in their willingness to share with fellow Christians in Jerusalem who are in need.

"We say it takes money to make money; Paul says it takes poverty to produce abundance. . . . Paul ends his stewardship letter by quoting Exodus 16: 'And the one who had much did not have too much, and the one who had little did not have too little.'"[7]

5

Galatians

Galatians stands out among the Pauline letters for its passionate—some would even say harsh—affirmation of the gospel. The history of the interpretation of the letter reveals a variety of readings that range from second-century Jewish Christian documents that contend that the apostle is preaching a lawless and thus false gospel; through Marcion, who placed Galatians at the beginning of his Pauline canon and stressed its freedom from the law; to Luther, with his anti-Judaic reading of the story of Sarah and Hagar (4:21–31); and to many modern commentators who either disdain Paul's sharp rhetoric or, in light of 3:28, argue for an egalitarian church.

Who were the Galatians? What did they do to evoke such a severe response from Paul? The story begins with a visit Paul made to the area of Galatia in Asia Minor, where he became ill and remained for some time. The people in the towns of Galatia welcomed this stranger in their midst and showed him gracious hospitality. Though Paul's illness may have given them reason to scorn him, they instead extended to him a notably warm welcome ("as an angel of God, as Christ Jesus" [4:13–14]). What sort of sickness might have offended the Galatians? The text gives us few hints. More important, however, is that Paul's illness gave him the occasion to preach and teach the gospel to the Galatians, which they received enthusiastically. The people experienced an extravagant outpouring of the Spirit accompanied by miracles (3:5), and communities of faith (house churches?) were formed. The membership of these communities would have been primarily Gentile, though some may have been previously proselytes to Judaism. The relationship Paul established with these believers was such that he could call them "my little children" (4:19).

Shortly after the first (or perhaps second) visit to Galatia, a group of

47

itinerant evangelists arrived in the area. They were Jewish Christians like Paul, who held an ecumenical openness toward non-Jews. They apparently called for faith in Jesus as Messiah, but advocated that God reaches out to non-Jews through the law, not apart from it, which meant that in order to be a member of God's covenant community, all males had to receive circumcision (so the law argued in Gen 17:9–14). Apparently some of the non-Jews in Galatia found the message of these Jewish Christian teachers persuasive. Paul at least took their teaching with utmost seriousness (1:6–7; 5:2–4, 7–8; 6:12–13).

In response, Paul penned this forceful letter to address specifically the arguments posed by the Jewish Christian group (probably, from Paul's perspective, best labeled "agitators") and to reaffirm the singularity of the gospel. He immediately goes on the offensive, attacking both the motives and the message of these itinerant missionaries. According to Paul, they distort the gospel and, so, actually pervert it (1:6–7; 5:2).

GALATIANS 1:1–10

An initial reading of the letter's beginning indicates that Paul is dealing with an urgent issue. The twofold denial of a human source for his apostleship (1:1), the terse depiction of his readers (1:2b), the extensive greeting, which undoubtedly contains a confessional formula (1:4), and the omission of the usual prayer of thanksgiving in favor of a statement of astonishment and rebuke (1:6–9) immediately attract the reader's attention.

In the letters of Paul, the prayer of thanksgiving normally sets the agenda by telegraphing themes to be developed later. This prayer, however, is omitted in Galatians, and the confessional greeting (1:4) serves its function, providing a theological base for the argument of the letter. Martyn judges that Paul takes what is a traditional atonement formula ("Grace to you and peace from God our Father and the Lord Jesus Christ, who gave himself for our sins") and gives it an apocalyptic interpretation ("to deliver us from the present evil age").[1] He writes, "The genesis of Paul's apocalyptic lies in the apostle's certainty that God has invaded the present evil age by sending Christ and his Spirit into it. There was a 'before,' the time when we were confined, imprisoned; and there is an 'after,' the time of our deliverance. And the difference between the two is caused not by an unveiling, but rather by the coming of Christ and his Spirit."[2]

As horrible as the crucifixion was (and Paul recognizes it as such), it did not occur outside of the divine will. Paul shows no interest in tracking down the perpetrators of the crime nor does he assign blame to any one group. Rather, he is interested in picturing the event on a broader canvass of God's purposes for human life and history. That broad canvass is apocalyptic.

The statement of astonishment and rebuke (1:6–9), which follows the greeting, highlights the authority and uniqueness of the "gospel." The noun or verb ("gospel" or "preach the gospel") occurs five times in these verses. In following the "agitators," the men of Galatia who submit to circumcision are turning away from the grace of God. It is not Paul and his apostleship that they abandon, but rather it is God, the God who called them to be a new creation in Christ. By embracing the message of the "agitators," they reject the gift of newness.

GALATIANS 1:11–24

An issue involved in the reading of the first two chapters of the letter is whether they are primarily written as a defense of Paul's apostleship or whether Paul takes the offensive. Did these "agitators" who had come into the Galatian community attempt to undermine Paul's authority by contending that he was not a proper apostle, or did Paul immediately go on the offensive, making his case for the power and uniqueness of the gospel? Less than honorable things were no doubt said about the apostle, perhaps charges were even leveled against him, but the chapters read much more smoothly without the presupposition that Paul is carrying on a self-apology or a defense of his apostleship. The theme of the chapters is Paul's claim concerning the singularity of the gospel, not concerning his apostleship.

The structure and translation of 1:11–12 are significant, especially since the verses represent "the initial thesis of the letter."[3] "For I want you to know, brothers and sisters, that the gospel that was proclaimed by me is not of human origin; for I did not receive it from a human source, nor was I taught it, but I received it through a revelation of Jesus Christ" (1:11–12). The contrast is between the gospel as a human matter (*kata anthrōpon*) and the gospel as received through a revelation of Jesus Christ (*dia apokalupseōs*). The preposition (*kata*) denotes quality rather than source. Lategan comments, "The gospel does not conform to human criteria, does not take human considerations into account. It does not function in a human way, does not honor human preferences. This is what distinguishes it from the 'other gospel.'"[4] As an apocalypse, the gospel is more than pulling back a veil or curtain to reveal something that has been there a long time; rather, it is "an invasion" (Martyn's preferred phrase) to "deliver us from this present evil age" and bring something entirely new, a brand new world (6:15). Paul then describes his own experience of the gospel.

Three features of Paul's personal testimony of Christ's encounter with him which, although in one sense are obvious, nevertheless shape the rest of the letter (1:12–24). First is the substance of his transformation itself. Again, the apostle refers to this as a "revelation" or apocalypse. The infinitive used in 1:16 (*apokalupsai*) is cognate to the noun in 1:12 (*apokalupsis*), which underlines the eschatological character of the experience. Apparently Paul was at least content with his situation in Judaism, he certainly was not tortured with anxiety or apprehensive about his religious standing—until God, at God's own pleasure, revealed his Son to him.

Second, the transformation has an immediate purpose, "that I might proclaim him among the Gentiles" (1:16). The one long sentence that runs from 1:15 to 1:17 makes plain that the experience of transformation also involves commissioning. It is further reinforced by the use of language derived from the call stories of two Old Testament prophets: Jeremiah (Jer 1:5) and the Servant (Isa 49:1–6). Each story includes the phrase "to the nations," which in Paul's story parallels the phrase "among the Gentiles." Paul does not undergo a period of growth and preparation following his conversion before he is given the task of being a missionary. Rather, his transformation includes his commission to go to the Gentiles. The two cannot be separated.[5]

The third notable feature of Paul's testimony is the response of the Judean churches (1:22–24). Since Paul preached in Syria and Cilicia, the Christians in Judea would not have recognized him if they saw him, and yet their worship confirms the power of the gospel to change people, even an antagonist like Paul.

GALATIANS 2:1–10

The autobiographical section of the letter continues in this section as Paul relates his visit to Jerusalem. Two questions arise in connection with the report of the trip. First, historically, why did Paul go to Jerusalem? Given the forceful argument he has made, it seems totally out of character for Paul to lay before the Jerusalem leaders his message for their approval or disapproval. Yet he writes that he went "in response to a revelation" and that "in order to make sure that I was not running, or had not run, in vain" (2:2).

It is likely that Paul was seeking an expression of the unity and solidarity of the people of God. The singular gospel he so vigorously contended for in chapter 1 demands a singular people of God. It was time for Paul to seek the endorsement of the Jerusalem leaders lest the church splinter into two groups, one basically Jewish and the other non-Jewish. Though called to work among the Gentiles, Paul remained a Jew and cherished connections with the mother church and, through her, continuity with Israel for the churches he established as well as for himself.

The second question regarding Paul's visit to Jerusalem is why he included it in this letter to the Galatians. What function does it play in his case for the singularity of the gospel over against the agitators who insist on circumcising the Gentiles? The critical event in the recounting of the visit to Jerusalem is the refusal to yield to the "false believers" who wanted to have Titus circumcised (2:3–5). This decision led to the conclusion that "the truth of the gospel might always remain with you" (2:5). The inclusion of the Titus incident in the narrative then puts Paul and his cohorts clearly on the side of the Gentiles in Galatia and puts the false believers on the side of the agitators.

GALATIANS 2:11–21

Paul proceeds to recount the incident at Antioch in which he confronted Peter face-to-face over Peter's withdrawal from table fellowship with the Gentile Christians. It seems that it was Peter's habit when in Antioch to eat with the community (likely a mixed group of Jews and non-Jews) until a group "from James" arrived, after which he no longer ate with them.

We wish we knew what this group said or did to cause Peter's change in practice. "Fear of the circumcision" is ambiguous. Since this was a McCarthy-like era, in which relations with non-Jews were threatening, "the circumcision" could refer to the Jews in Judea who were pressuring their Christian kin to abandon association altogether with Gentiles, or the pressure could be coming from the false believers (2:4) who, for theological reasons, opposed the mingling of Jews and Gentiles. In any case, it was a critical issue, in that Barnabas and other Jewish Christians were also persuaded and joined Peter, leaving Paul and the Gentile Christians "at the table." Paul, however, sharply differs with Peter and his friends in their withdrawal from eating with the Gentiles, saying that they were no longer "acting consistently with the truth of the gospel" (2:14).

In the midst of this confrontation, Paul shifts from a combative, "How can you compel circumcision on these Gentiles?" to a first-person-plural style.

> Peter, you and I are Jews by birth and not "Gentile sinners"; yet we know that a person is not set in a right relationship with God by doing what the law prescribes but only through the faithfulness of Jesus Christ. We also have come to believe in the faithfulness of Christ Jesus, so that we might be set right with God through Christ's faithfulness and not by doing what the law prescribes, because, as Psalm 143:2 says, "No one will be set right with God by the law's prescriptions." (2:15–16, author's translation)

It is difficult to know exactly where the "we" in this passage ceases to be Paul and Peter and takes on a more inclusive connotation—that is, the Gentiles in Galatia and even modern readers of the text. The shift is subtle, but very effective in engaging the audience. The uncircumcised Gentiles in Galatia who listened to this story could not help but be moved by Paul's identification with them.

The final verse in chapter 2 (2:21) discloses the heart of Paul's theological argument throughout this section. If being rectified or set right with God comes through law, then Christ's death was useless. The crucified Jesus then becomes the norm against which all other theological proposals are measured. Any proposition that renders the crucifixion unnecessary—the demand for circumcision—negates the true gospel.

GALATIANS 3:1–5:12

Paul then turns to a series of arguments to support the gospel he previously preached and currently re-preaches to the Galatians. The arguments consist of various strategic appeals, some forcing the readers to reflect on their own experience in receiving the gospel (3:1–5; 4:12–20), others inviting their attention to particular texts of Scripture (3:6–29; 4:21–31). The intent is to convince the Galatians of the freedom given in Jesus Christ, in the hope that they may be seized once again by the power of the gospel and reject the overtures of the agitators. The section closes with strong, personal admonitions from the apostle that warn of the dire consequences of succumbing to the attraction of circumcision (5:1–12). Clear distinctions are drawn between the old age, in which circumcision and uncircumcision are critical matters, and the new age, in which believers, awaiting God's righteous verdict, engage in ministries of love.

The first section of appeals (3:1–5) includes five rhetorical questions that force the readers to reflect on their beginnings as a community of faith. How can those who heard the gospel of the crucified Christ allow themselves to be charmed by the agitators' magic? "Are you so foolish? Having started with the Spirit, are you now ending [or seeking to attain perfection] with the flesh?" (3:3).

In addition to the rhetorical dimension of the text, we meet, for the first time in this letter, the contrast between "Spirit" and "flesh," to which the apostle returns in chapters 5 and 6. "Flesh" gets a distinctive treatment by Paul. Sometimes it takes on a religious significance (as a word naturally associated with circumcision, 3:3); sometimes it refers to a human being or the human · sphere without any negative connotation (1:16; 2:16, 20). But when contrasted with Spirit, "flesh" becomes the epitome of the old age and produces destructive and divisive actions that upset its adherents (5:19–21) and lead to corruption (6:8). This sort of negative connotation certainly also hovers over its use in 3:3. Circumcision, though a religious rite, becomes the opposite of God's lively activity.

The second set of appeals Paul offers comes from Scripture (3:6–4:11). That chapters 3 and 4 are so heavy with Old Testament citations in a letter directed to Gentile Christians suggests that Paul is probably dealing with texts used by the agitators to draw their exegetical conclusion that circumcision is the essential doorway to the people of God. After all, circumcision began with Abraham. Paul responds by citing Gen 15:6 and concluding that people identified by faith are members of Abraham's family.

The NRSV, in its translation of 3:7 and 3:9, turns the Greek noun for "faith" (*pistis*) into a verb ("those who believe"), implying that those who believe as Abraham believed are his descendants. But such a rendering ignores the heavy freight that the noun carries in the argument of the letter. As Howard notes, three aspects of faith are "temporally and causally antecedent to the Christian's faith,"—namely, God's faithfulness to the promise, Abraham's faith, and the faith of Christ. "People identified by faith" in 3:7 and 3:9 is thus a shorthand expression for those whom God justified on the basis of the faithfulness of Christ and in response to the promise of Abraham.[6]

Employing several Old Testament texts in 3:10–13, Paul affirms that something has happened to the law: its curse is removed. How could the law, which came on the human scene 430 years after the ratification of the covenant with Abraham, change anything? No longer does it possess the power to suppress and restrain as once it did, as jailor (3:23) and as guardian (3:24–25). Christ's death has freed humanity from such bondage so that "There is no longer Jew or Greek, there is no longer slave or free, there is no longer male and female; for all of you are one in Christ Jesus" (3:28–29). It is as if the law has accomplished its primary job, performing its condemning function ("curse") at the cross. It has exhausted itself so that it now ceases to be a threat and an enslaving power.

It is true that Paul engages the Old Testament in ways that appear strange to our modern sensibilities. For example, between an analogy of an irrevocable will (3:15) and the application of the analogy (3:17), he quotes a familiar phrase from Genesis (12:7; 13:15–16; 17:7–8; 24:7) to characterize Abraham's descendants as the recipients of God's promises: "and to your offspring [or seed]" (3:16). In the Genesis context, it is clear that the singular noun is to be read as a collective, that is, an implied plural. Paul, however, plays on the singular noun ("seed" or "offspring") and contends that it is not to be understood as a plural. It does not refer to those who are biological descendants of Abraham and are his natural progeny (so identified by circumcision). Instead, it refers to one seed, Christ, in whom the promise of Abraham is fulfilled.

By identifying the "seed" as Christ and by pointedly rejecting the plural reading of the word, Paul essentially redefines the marks that characterize Abraham's family. No doubt the agitators in Galatia linked the covenant promises with the law and thereby found a warrant for circumcision. In response, Paul drives a sharp wedge between promise and law and contends that no matter how sacred the law is it cannot modify God's promise to Abraham.

The argument of 3:6–29 is in a partial sense recapitulated in 4:1–7, but with the metaphors of trustees, stewards, slaves, and family members (instead of jailor and custodian). Moreover, 4:1–7 employs two striking "sending statements" that parallel one another:

- "God sent his Son . . . in order to redeem those who were under the law, so that we might receive adoption as children." (4:4–5)
- "God has sent the Spirit of his Son into our hearts, crying, 'Abba! Father!' " (4:6–7)

Both statements depict the apocalyptic story of salvation, and both include the much-debated language of "the elemental spirits" (4:3, 9). The life of the Galatians prior to the coming of Christ was a bondage to appearances, to entities that masked as gods but in reality were not gods (cf. Jer 2:11). Christ has freed them from these ancient powers. To submit to circumcision would be to return to their control, like the released prisoner who, unable to tolerate his freedom, cannot live outside the walls of confinement.

In the third set of appeals (4:12–20) Paul returns to the personal relationship established with the Galatians. In this section, we learn of Paul's previous visit to Galatia and the warm manner with which he was greeted. How could the situation change so quickly from extravagant hospitality to exclusion and rejection? Paul admits to being perplexed by the change that has taken place in the Galatians.

The fourth set of appeals (4:21–31) returns to Scripture, giving Paul's rendition of the story of Sarah and Hagar, drawn primarily from Genesis 16 and 21. Two different experiences of birth underlie the apostle's interpretation of the story (4:23). Hagar was much younger than Sarah, and the birth of her son is depicted in Genesis 16 as happening in the normal course of events. The birth of Isaac, however, was extraordinary because of Sarah's age. Paul compares the births through contrasting prepositional phrases: "according to the flesh" and "through a promise." "Flesh," of course, signifies circumcision (3:3), opposes the "Spirit," and produces all sorts of destructive "works" (5:16–21). On the other hand, the "promise" comes to fulfillment only in Christ, which renders those who belong to Christ (even Gentiles) true descendants of Abraham and Sarah (3:22, 29).

Martyn notes a significant change in Paul's use of the verb for "begetting" or "giving birth." In the Old Testament (the Septuagint) birth narratives of Isaac and Ishmael, the verb *tiktô* ("bear, give birth to") is exclusively used. Paul, however, studiously avoids *tiktô* in Galatians (except in citing Isa 54:1) and in its place employs in 4:23–24, 29 another verb for birthing (*gennaô*). The change in verbs is more significant when we discover that Paul regularly uses *gennaô* to denote the genesis of Christians and Christian communities through the gospel (e.g., Phlm 10; 1 Cor 4:14–15). "Paul speaks of two different ways in which churches are being begotten among Gentiles at the present time, and thus of two different Gentile missions."[7] The "birthing" alludes to two different ways in which the gospel is understood and Gentiles are evangelized, not to two different religions, Judaism and Christianity.

Galatians 4:28–31 pointedly draws the implications of Paul's reading of the Sarah-Hagar story. Readers are to identify themselves with the Sarah-Isaac-free line, "Now *you* (emphatic 'you') are children of promise like Isaac" (4:28). As also in 4:31 ("So then, friends, we are children, not of the slave but of the free woman"), the tone is affirmative and distinct. Gentile believers need not take second-class or inferior roles in God's family. As Paul reads it, the law itself makes this clear (4:21).

Galatians 5:1 then functions as a transition, ending the argument of 4:21–31 and at the same time introducing the next section of the letter (5:1–12). Using several different images (a yoke, walking, indebtedness, running a race, and leaven in the dough), Paul indicts the agitators who have come into Galatia and urges the rejection of circumcision by the Gentiles.

GALATIANS 5:13–6:10

Following a vigorous polemic against circumcision and the law (5:1–12), Paul moves in this final section of the body of the letter to a positive statement of what it is like to live as free people. How does the community cope with the realities of human existence in the old age? What does it mean to live as people of the "new creation"? How is newness embodied and expressed amid the old?

First, the apostle deals with the thorny question of the law. Thus far in the letter, the law has been cast in a negative light. It carries a temporary function as a jailor or as a custodian who has a role to play, but only until the child reaches a designated age. Then the child is no longer subject to the control of the law (3:23–25).

The good news about the law, however, is that it "has been fulfilled (brought to completion)." Unfortunately the NRSV and NIV, leaning heavily on Rom 13:8–10, translate the verb in 5:14 as "is summed up." But the more natural rendering of the Greek verb *peploretai*, like a promise realized or a prayer answered, is "has been brought to completion." The perfect tense and the passive voice of the verb indicate that something has happened to the law, an event in the past with lingering effects for the present. As Hays puts it, the agitators "were urging the Galatians to be circumcised and to do what the Law required in order to bring order and moral security to their lives. Paul proclaims, however, that a new reality has come on the scene 'in Jesus Christ' (cf. 5:6)."[8] The meaning of the law is brought to completion by the one "who loved me and gave himself for me" (2:20), the one who absorbed the curse of the law on our behalf (3:13).

The command in 5:13 ("Through love become slaves to one another") is then authenticated and made plausible by the affirmation of 5:14. Jesus has done what he did both in his teaching and in his sacrificial death, and having thereby fulfilled the law, makes it possible for God's people to serve one another in love.

Beyond the law, believers are reminded that they "live by the Spirit" and thus are protected from the desires of the flesh. In 5:16 Paul writes, "Live by the Spirit, and *you will by no means* gratify the desires of the flesh" (author's trans.). There is truly a war going on between Spirit and flesh; they are avowed enemies. But being led by the Spirit yields the "fruit" of the Spirit (5:22–23) as well as the bearing of one another's burdens (6:1–5). And bearing one another's burdens leads to the fulfillment of "the law of Christ" (6:2). Paul has in mind not a different code, but rather the law that Christ has brought to completion by his life of love and his sacrificial death (2:20).

GALATIANS 6:11–18

Paul takes the pen at this point (6:11) and adds his own conclusion—much like the rest of the letter—in a daring fashion. He boldly pits himself against the agitators: "They compel you to be circumcised" and by so doing avoid persecution for the cross (6:12). For Paul circumcision and uncircumcision do not matter at all (6:15), and he bears in his body the marks of Christ (6:17). They seek to make a good showing in the flesh (6:12–13), whereas Paul boasts only in the cross of Christ (6:14). The real difference between the two is that "the world" with its sacred categories of Jews and non-Jews, males and females, slaves and free people is now passé by the arrival of the "new creation." As Hays puts it, "Paul is not speaking here about the establishment of a new religion or the spiritual rebirth of an individual. He is claiming that God who created the world has come to reclaim and transform it."[9]

6

Philippians

An initial reading of Paul's letter to the Philippians suggests an immediately warm and mutually accepting relationship between writer and audience. The apostle expresses a deep and genuine affection for these believers, who, during his imprisonment, sent him a gift and shared in the spread of the gospel. Whereas in Corinth Paul defends himself in the face of his attackers and in Galatia he contends with agitators who preach a distorted and perverted message, in Philippi his relationship with the recipients has gone well. Though he warns them against antagonists of the faith, there is no indication of a personal attack on Paul or a wholesale departure on the part of the Philippians from their initial calling.

Then why did Paul write the letter? Four reasons are apparent. First, he expresses gratitude to the Philippians for a gift, carried to Paul by Epaphroditus, a member of the Philippian community. Epaphroditus became ill in the process and is now returning home. Thus the letter is really a thank-you note to the congregation (4:10–20) for the gift they have given. Second, for some reason Paul felt it necessary to commend Epaphroditus, explain his illness, and urge the readers to receive him back with honor (2:25–30). Third, Paul takes the occasion to call attention to false teachers in their midst, referred to as "dogs . . . evil workers . . . those who mutilate the flesh" (3:2) and "enemies of the cross of Christ" (3:18). Fourth, the Philippian believers either had been persecuted or were soon to be persecuted (1:29–30), and Paul urges them to "stand firm" and to maintain unity in the face of external aggression (1:27–30) and internal disagreement (4:2–3). Of course, not all of these reasons for writing carry equal weight. The letter suggests that the first and the fourth intentions really led Paul to write and, having decided to do so, he also urges the acceptance of Epaphroditus and adds warnings about the false teachers.

Yet the letter, in spite of these various reasons for writing, exhibits an amazing cohesiveness, which has led many recent interpreters to contend that Paul employs an ancient letterform as a model for Philippians, and that it is "a hortatory letter of friendship."[1] It exhibits a number of the conventions of friendship, such as the present-absent motif (1:19–26; 2:12), the expression of affection and the desire to be with the recipients (1:7–9; 4:1), the reciprocity between writer and readers (1:7, 30; 2:17–18; 4:14), the pattern of giving and receiving (4:10–20), the importance of mutual participation (*koinōnia*, 1:5; 2:1; 3:10; 4:15), the necessity of agreement and equality (1:27–2:4; 4:2), the need for a single mind (2:2, 5; 4:2), and the sharing of common enemies (1:27–30; 3:2, 17–19).

The friendship between writer and readers, however, does not fully describe the character of the letter. What emerges as dominant and pervasive throughout is the figure of Jesus Christ. It is the mutual sharing in the gospel that binds writer to readers and undergirds the calls to unity and community. Groups are common enemies of Paul and the Philippians because in various ways they are in opposition to the gospel.[2] The strong christocentric focus of the letter provides the foundation for the friendship between Paul and the Philippians.

Paul Schubert, in his study of the prayers of thanksgiving in the Pauline letters, indicates that the apostle telegraphs themes in the opening prayers that the reader can anticipate reappearing later in the letter.[3] This is especially the case with Philippians. The following is a partial list:

- joy (1:4, 18, 25; 2:2, 17–18, 28: 3:1; 4:1, 4)
- sharing/participation (*koinōnia*) (1:5, 7; 2:1; 3:10; 4:14)
- gospel (1:5, 7, 12, 16, 27; 2:2; 4:3, 15)
- thinking/mind (1:7; 2:2, 5; 3:15, 19; 4:2, 8)
- imprisonment (1:7, 12–14, 16–17, 19–26, 30; 2:17; 4:14)
- compassion/love (1:8, 9, 16; 2:1–2, 12; 4:1)

The list itself speaks against several modern interpreters who contend that Philippians is actually a composite of three letters (due to the abrupt seams at 3:2 and at 4:10–20). The list, however, argues against a composite theory since these themes run right through the whole letter and signal its unity. (This, of course, does not preclude taking the Christ hymn of 2:5–11 as pre-Pauline.)

PHILIPPIANS 1:1–11

It is clear from the beginning of the prayer of thanksgiving that this letter evidences a deep affection on the part of the apostle for the Philippians. For one thing, he gives thanks for their "partnership in the gospel" (author's trans.)

from the initial moment when they heard and received it up to the present. He bears in mind more than the gift carried by Epaphroditus to Paul in his imprisonment; he addresses their active engagement with him in the proclamation of the Christian message. He later mentions members of the community who "have struggled" with him and with his cohorts in the work of the gospel (4:3). Second, Paul is confident of the reliability of God, who will see to the completion of what has been started among the Philippians. Third, Paul is thankful for the mutuality and intimacy between him and his readers. They hold him in their hearts during his imprisonment, and he vows before God that he yearns for them (1:7–8). The expression "with the compassion of Christ" (1:8) is unusual and gives reason once again for seeing the mutuality between Paul and the Philippians as a three-way relationship. Writer and readers are drawn together by their common connectedness to Christ (1:7).

PHILIPPIANS 1:12–26

Ancient letters of friendship, like familial letters, are usually structured so that following the opening conventions the writer reports his situation, reassuring the readers that all is going well, before turning to inquire about the circumstances of the readers.[4]

What Paul writes is therefore striking. Instead of first reporting details about his personal circumstances during imprisonment, he stresses the "progress of the gospel" (1:12, 25), which has even penetrated the Roman guard (1:1–14). Although some preachers declare the gospel for the wrong reasons, like envy, partisanship, and pretense, the gospel is nevertheless preached, and Paul rejoices.

The central paragraph begins with a word of rejoicing (1:18b) and concludes with an anticipated joy Paul will share with the Philippians (1:25–26). In between the apostle wrestles with his upcoming trial. If the verdict is death, then it will bring him more of Christ. If he is freed, then he will have the opportunity to participate more fully with the Philippians in their ministry of the gospel. Since Paul clearly anticipates being released (1:25), this is in no sense a soliloquy on suicide. The joy motif that surrounds the paragraph would make such a notion highly implausible.

PHILIPPIANS 1:27–2:18

In this section Paul turns to his audience, saying he wants to hear about them and their whereabouts (literally, "about your affairs," "about the things concerning

you," 1:27). More than being merely solicitous, Paul spells out exactly what he
wants to learn about the Philippians, namely, how they are unified in their
advocacy of the gospel in the face of opposition. Fee notes the chiastic structure that links the various parts of this section.

A. Appeal to steadfastness and unity in the face of opposition (1:27–30)
   B. The appeal to unity based on their common life in Christ (2:1–4)
      C. Christ, the expression of humility and the one to be worshiped
      (2:5–11)
   B' Application of the appeal, based on their mutual relationship
   (2:12–13)
A' Further application: unity in the face of opposition (2:14–16)

"Just one thing! Live as citizens worthy of the gospel of Christ, so that,
whether I come to you myself or not, I might hear of your affairs: that you
stand firm like good soldiers in the one Spirit, contending side by side for the
faith of the gospel as good athletes do" (1:27, author's trans.). In the Greek,
three images are used for the readers: citizens, soldiers, and athletes. In its own
way each image connotes the conflictual character of the faith. Inevitably the
gospel evokes enemies, who are offended by the good news of God's breaking
into the human scene in Christ.

Who are these "opponents" of the Philippians (1:28)? There is no reason
to connect them with the other religious groups mentioned in the letter (as in
3:2 or 3:17), who hardly pose a physical threat to the believers. More likely the
opposition comes from the civil authorities. The most telling piece of information comes in 1:30, where Paul connects his struggles with that of the readers. The Roman authorities imprisoned Paul for preaching the gospel, and a
similar group apparently threatens the Philippians for the same reason. Paul
counsels the church not to break ranks, to stand firm and maintain a unified
front. If they suffer, they suffer for Christ's sake (1:29–30).

This passage (especially 1:29–30) sounds strange, even morbid, to the
Western world. ("For he has graciously granted you the privilege not only of
believing in Christ, but of suffering for him as well.") Three things need to be
said to clarify Paul's position. First, it is critical to delineate Paul's word about
suffering from the tragic and often meaningless suffering caused by natural
disasters, ravaging disease, or the premature ending of life. Paul writes rather
about a form of suffering that one could avoid if one chooses to live a different style of life. His suffering comes from a life lived in relation to Christ and
that invariably results in vulnerability and openness.

Second, Paul is never surprised nor does he ever complain to God and ask
why this suffering should happen to him. He knows why. The gospel lived out
in the midst of a world that cannot tolerate divine grace and the word of the

cross inevitably evokes opposition. Religion in general may be accepted or even revered by society, but the gospel of the cross inevitably provokes opposition. As Käsemann put it, "Hostility to the cross is the leading characteristic of the world."[5]

Third, such suffering can be spoken of as a gift of grace because it binds one to the crucified Christ. Later in the letter (3:10; cf. 2 Cor 4:10–11), Paul writes of wanting to share Christ's sufferings by becoming like him in his death, which is actually a component of knowing the power of his resurrection. This is not a masochistic trait of Paul's nor does it evidence a lust for martyrdom, as was the case with many saints of the second century. Suffering for Paul comes as an inevitable result of fidelity to the gospel and becomes a means of sharing fellowship with the crucified and risen Christ.

The appeal for unity repeated so often (2:1–3) is marked by the characteristic of humility. Humility is a prominent theme throughout the letter (2:3, 8; 3:21; 4:1) but an odd topic in Greco-Roman ethical discussion. In that context it tended to specify that which is lowly, mean, trivial, and insignificant. A meek person tends to take on a servile disposition and to become an obsequious flatterer.[6] In the Judeo-Christian literature, however, humility becomes a positive characteristic, both in relation to God and to one's fellow human beings. It depicts the proper response to God, to whom service and obedience are owed. The christocentric stress of Philippians draws the two together. Christ "humbled himself and became obedient to the point of death" (2:8). In practical terms this means moving beyond a preoccupation with one's own concerns to a consideration of the needs of others. So Karl Barth writes:

> The reason why we are to see the other person's point of view, to let ourselves be enticed out of our own hut and over into his, is not that that were a holy place, but it is only when men [and women] thus come together, when they take a joint view of things, when they bow jointly before him who is greater than both my neighbor and myself—it is only then that the really holy, true and helpful One comes into my field of vision at all. It is not until I see the other person's point of view that I myself really see. . . . Always my neighbor is the barrier, but also the door. There is no road that passes by him.[7]

At Philippians 2:5–11 one reaches the center of the letter. Paul may or may not have personally composed this hymn or liturgical formula, but the way he employs the hymn in the letter is critical and complex. The hymn divides itself neatly into two strophes. The first declares Jesus' humiliation, culminating in his death by crucifixion (2:6–8). The second announces God's exaltation of Jesus, making him the object of worship (2:9–11). What complicates the interpretation of the hymn is that the context is clearly parenetic. Paul is not addressing a christological confusion that may have existed in the Philippian church and needed attention. The hymn instead explicates the imperatives in 2:2–5 and especially the term "humility" (2:3). Christ is the subject who humbled himself and became obedient unto death. But the hymn doesn't stop with 2:8.

What does the interpreter do with the second strophe, which sings of God's climactic act in exalting Christ above all the principalities and powers (2:9–11)? How does it connect with the parenetic context of the hymn as a whole? Those to whom the exhortation is addressed are not asked to be humble simply because Christ is a model of humility. Rather they live in a world that is being transformed by what God is doing. They are told to live humbly with one another in a context in which God is subjecting the demonic powers to Jesus and where ultimately "every knee will bow and every tongue confess" his lordship.

The first strophe (2:6–8) pictures the self-emptying Christ whose act of humiliation underlies the exhortations regarding oneness and humility (2:1–4). The second strophe (2:9–11), in which the story of God's act of vindication of the self-giving Christ is completed, ensures the ultimate victory of God in exalting Christ above all the principalities and powers. The second strophe is essential for the community's living out of the exhortations. Therefore, Christ is not simply a model of humility to be followed, but the Lord to be worshiped by the whole creation.[8] As Käsemann writes, "He reveals obedience but does not demonstrate it as something to be imitated. To put it succinctly, he is *Urbild*, not Vorbild; archetype, not model."[9]

The two paragraphs that follow are linked to the hymn by the consequential particle "therefore." In light of the drama of the self-giving and exalted Christ, the community is exhorted to "work out your own salvation with fear and trembling" (2:13). Two items are to be noted. First, the word "salvation" apparently refers to the integrity, well-being, unity, and wholeness of the community, and not primarily to the individual's eschatological destiny. The context of the letter certainly supports this communal understanding. Second, Paul leaves the readers with a tension between working out their own problems and God's being at work in and among them to bring about the wholeness and unity God demands. While the readers struggle to keep a united front in the face of opposition, God remains the empowering presence, working to assure that the divine purpose and plan will be accomplished.

PHILIPPIANS 2:19–30

Often in the letters of Paul the inclusion of future travel plans does more than provide necessary or interesting information. For example, in his letter to Philemon Paul encourages Philemon to receive Onesimus back no longer as a slave but as a brother. The mention of his coming visit thus serves as both a carrot and a stick. It functions as an enticement to Philemon to do what is right and simultaneously serves as a warning that he intends to follow up on this matter.

Here Paul indicates his plans to send Timothy to Philippi soon and to commend Epaphroditus, who is apparently the bearer of the letter (1:19–30). His comments about Timothy are so enthusiastic that one suspects that he is being set up as a model to be followed. "I have no one like [Timothy] who will be genuinely concerned for your welfare. Like a son with a father he has served with me in the work of the gospel" (2:20, 22). In effect, Paul writes, "Take Timothy as a model for how to live in humility. He is a paragon of what is right and good in the Christian life."

The same thing might be said for Epaphroditus, except that Epaphroditus is one of the Philippians himself, who in bringing the gift to Paul from the Philippians became ill and in his illness became something of a burden to Paul. In sending him back home, Paul wants to be sure that he receives a proper welcome. In fact, Epaphroditus had risked his life for the gospel. (The Greek expression *mechri thanatou* (to the point of death) occurs only one other place in the Pauline corpus, and that is in connection with Christ in 2:8.) The added phrase "and honor such people" (2:29) lifts him and others like him to an exemplary role.[10]

PHILIPPIANS 3:1–4:3

The text moves from the travelogue back to the readers and their immediate situation, to exhortations and examples, both negative and positive. The basic intent is to encourage the Philippians in their effort to live as citizens worthy of the gospel, especially when under pressure and in the face of opposition.

The initial warning regards "the dogs . . . the evil workers . . . those who mutilate the flesh" (3:2). Exactly whom these terms designate is difficult to determine. The expression "those who mutilate the flesh" (*katatomē*) seems to be an ironic twist on the word "circumcision" (*peritomē*), suggesting that maybe the warning is against Jewish Christian missionaries who, like Paul, reach out to the non-Jewish world but do so through the law and thus contend that circumcision is an essential badge for membership in the people of God. In light of the pun on circumcision, "dogs," a term used by Jews as a derisive label for unclean Gentiles (cf. Mark 7:27–28), is turned back on its users.

No further comment is made about this group, its theology, or its activities, suggesting that it is not likely much of a threat to the Philippians. In fact, the word rendered in the NRSV as "beware" might best be translated "consider" or "take note of." The matter is not to warn the Philippians about a menace

that the church should be wary of (as in Galatians), but simply to call attention to the identity of a group that clashes with the church's identity. The context is more hortatory than polemical.

Paul then refers to himself in contrast to these "dogs." He claims a pedigree
as royal as any of them. Both by heritage and by accomplishments, he depicts
himself not as an outsider but as a loyal Jew (3:4–6). The shift comes at verse 7.

> Yet whatever for me were assets, these things I have counted as loss
> because of Christ; and what's more, I am counting all things as loss
> because of the surpassing value of knowing Christ Jesus my Lord.
> Because of him I have undergone the loss of all things and am count-
> ing them as rubbish, in order that I might gain Christ and be found
> incorporated into him, with no righteousness of my own, i.e., a righ-
> teousness based on law; rather with the righteousness that comes
> through the faithfulness of Christ, a righteousness from God based on
> faith. (3:7–9, author's trans.)

In this passage Paul basically depicts two slants on righteousness. One
comes via the law, and of which he, Paul, stands as an exemplar. The other
comes through the faithfulness of Christ. Using the commercial language of
the day, he declares the former as loss, and the latter as gain. He then underscores the epistemological side of Christ's righteousness. "What I want is to
know Christ, the power of his resurrection and the participation in his sufferings, being conformed to his death, so that I might attain his resurrection of
the dead" (3:10–11, author's trans.). Knowing Christ is not a matter of more
information about his life nor is it a matter of developing a proper attitude
toward him. Knowing Christ is a matter of *participation* in Christ. In baptism
one publicly declares her or his inclusion in Jesus' death and resurrection, and
the present participle "becoming like him" (3:10) implies continuous con-
formity to the crucified Christ. As it is put elsewhere, "always carrying in the
body the death of Jesus" (2 Cor 4:10).

Thus far in the letter Paul has pointed to Christ (2:5–11) and, by association, to Timothy and Epaphroditus (2:19–30), as paradigms for the readers.
Paul now goes so far as to say that his own story should also be read as an example to be followed (3:15–17). While this seems a bit arrogant to Western readers, this is typical of students in the ancient world who would be expected to
imitate their teachers.

Two footnotes might be added to this section. One has to do with the
unusual imperative in Greek, "join in imitating me" (3:17). This implies that
the readers should be bound together in imitation, and be so led to a common
mind. Second, "observe those who live according to the example you have in
us" broadens the number to include those others whose stories parallel the stories of Paul, Timothy, and Epaphroditus.

Finally, Paul sets two antithetical models over against one another; one serves as a dark backdrop for Paul's story and for the church (3:18–21). Moreover, the associations with other paradigms in the letter are striking. While this group is depicted as "enemies of the cross" (3:18), Christ is obedient to death on a cross (2:8), Epaphroditus comes close to death for the work of Christ (2:30), and Paul seeks to share Christ's sufferings and to be conformed to his death (3:10). By contrast, for this group the end is destruction, whereas Christ's end is his universal lordship (2:9–11), and Paul's goal is "the heavenly call of God in Christ Jesus" (3:14). Finally, the "mind" of this group is oriented toward earthly things (3:19), whereas the community's "mind" is to be shaped by Christ's story (2:5) and by Paul's story (3:15).

The eschatological depiction of the church ("our citizenship is in heaven; and it is from there that we are expecting a Savior, the Lord Jesus Christ" [3:20]) has a subversive character to it and no doubt represents a challenge to the empire. Since the titles "Savior" and "Lord" were used by and for Emperor Augustus and many of his successors, the church, through this confession, stands under Jesus rather than the Roman authorities. Furthermore, the future to which the church looks is not an escape to heaven, but a transformation of "the body of our humiliation," and an expression of the power by which God will "make all things subject to himself" (3:21). Paul's concern, however, is not primarily political, but is an effort to reconcile two parties in the Philippian community, led by former colleagues of Paul, who are apparently at odds with one another. Paul invokes the eschatological community to help them reach a common mind.

PHILIPPIANS 4:4–23

Following some traditional exhortations, Paul specifically acknowledges the gift brought by Epaphroditus (4:10) and the Philippians' earlier gifts, which supported his work (4:15–16). Sometimes the thanksgiving has been read as a begrudging expression of gratitude ("a thankless thanks") since Paul plays down his need (4:11–13) and makes it clear that he did not seek the gifts (4:17). What is at work here are the social conventions of friendship. Marshall rightly concludes:

> Paul is drawing upon familiar notions of friendship to acknowledge the recent gift and to express his gratitude. Rather than pointing to tension or embarrassment, on Paul's part over the gift, the language implies the opposite. It reflects a warm and lasting relationship. He not only receives the gift gladly as a sign of their continuing concern, but also recalls the mutual exchange of services and affection that they

had shared in the past. Though he himself cannot reciprocate in kind, he is confident that God would more than make good the gift out of, and in a manner befitting, his boundless wealth in Christ Jesus.[11]

The closing words follow the pattern of conventional letter endings, yet two features stand out. First, Paul returns to the theme of "joy," a theme that resounds throughout the letter (1:4, 25; 2:2, 17–18; 3:1; 4:1, 4, 10). The Philippians are urged to "rejoice" (4:4), and Paul does so himself (4:10). Because they share a common commitment to the Lord they are able to rejoice together.

Second, Paul makes a striking statement about his own situation, "I have learned to be content with whatever I have" (4:11). Then he follows the statement with examples (4:12). The Greek word translated "content" (*autarkēs*), frequently used by the Stoic philosophers, denotes a self-sufficiency, a detachment from the world, a contentment for one who lives not at the ups and downs of life. Seneca writes, "The wise man is sufficient unto himself for a happy existence."[12] Verse 13, however, roots Paul's contentment in Christ rather than in himself. While Paul does not cut himself off from the world, he trusts God to provide whatever he needs.

7

Philemon

Every letter has a story behind it. Often the plot hinges on the relationship between the writer and readers, the past encounters they have had, the issues they confront, and the particular matter that has provoked the letter. Then the letter becomes an important item in the story. Unfortunately, with the New Testament letters we are not always able to determine precisely what lies behind the letter and thus are left to reconstruct the story, as best we can, with insufficient or ambiguous evidence.

This is certainly the case with the short letter of Paul to Philemon. Storywise, we can be confident that it comes as genuine communication from the apostle Paul, who is himself in prison. The letter regards a slave named Onesimus, which means "useful" (v. 11). Onesimus "belongs to" Philemon, Paul's friend and a prominent Christian in Colossae. That he owned a house big enough for the church to meet in, and that he had slaves indicate that Philemon was a fairly wealthy person.

Onesimus for some reason leaves home, comes under the influence of Paul, is converted to the Christian faith, and becomes very useful to Paul in his ministry. Paul, however, is hesitant about keeping Onesimus and giving him greater responsibility until he is reconciled to Philemon. This letter is thus written to support and commend Onesimus to Philemon. Paul hopes that Philemon will welcome Onesimus "as you would welcome me" (v. 17), "no longer as a slave but more than a slave, a beloved brother" (v. 16). Paul likely wanted Philemon to send Onesimus back to assist him in his work.

This sketch of the basic story leaves us, however, with several unanswered questions. First, was Onesimus actually a slave? Allan Callahan, reviving a theory proposed by abolitionists during antebellum days, has contended that the word "slave" appears only a couple of times in the letter and is used as a term of honor. As the hymn in Philippians 2:5–11 puts it, the ultimate is attained only by a slave in its dreadful, common, sense. "Perhaps this is the reason he was separated from you for a while, so that you might have him back forever, no longer as a slave but more than a slave, a beloved brother—especially to me but how much more to you, both in the flesh and in the Lord" (vv. 15–16). In fact, Callahan proposes that Onesimus and Philemon were (blood) brothers, that Apphia (v. 2) was their (blood) sister, and that the issue that separated them was a family matter. Onesimus likely caused a disruption that divided the brothers, and Paul offers to pay any costs incurred in the disruption.[1]

The difficulty with Callahan's thesis is the projection of the family language ("brother," "sister") as literal, but the language of "slave" as metaphorical. Only twice does Paul speak of "the brother(s) of the Lord" (1 Cor 9:5; Gal 1:19) in such a way that implies blood brothers. More often, Paul employs the term "brother" (or "brothers and sisters") for fellow Christians.

Second, did Onesimus flee because he had taken some of Philemon's money? Was then Onesimus a fugitive from justice? The offer on Paul's part to repay any debt caused by Onesimus's departure (vv. 18–19a), as well as the reminder that Philemon was in debt to Paul for his whole life (v. 19b), suggest that Onesimus might have absconded with some of his master's funds. The repeated mention of debt is prominent in the letter.[2]

The problem, however, is how Onesimus met up with Paul. Perhaps Onesimus knowingly fled to the place where Paul was imprisoned. But why would he seek out a friend of his own master? The likelihood that, by chance, Onesimus ended up incarcerated in the same jail cell with Paul seems highly unlikely. Or, might Onesimus have gone to Paul's place of imprisonment to seek a friend who would intervene for him with Philemon? Peter Lampe has discovered from Roman legal proceedings that when a slave got into some difficulty with his or her owner the slave was free to seek out a third party to be an advocate for the slave in dealing with the master.[3] The slave was not seeking to escape his or her owner, but rather to return under different conditions. Onesimus then would not have been a runaway slave, but a slave who sought Paul, the friend of his owner, for counsel and advocacy with Philemon. When Onesimus in fact became a Christian is not clear, but apparently at such a time that Paul developed considerable trust and confidence in him, enough to send him back to Philemon (contradicting Deut 23:15–16), with the subtle suggestion that he be received as a brother "in the flesh" as well as "in the Lord." This third option seems the most plausible of the three. Onesimus could have sought out Paul because he knew he was a good friend of his master. The debt possibly owed Philemon could easily have been incurred over his absence from regular duties.

Paul's appeal in behalf of Onesimus is sensitive and subtle. For example, Petersen identifies the roles played by each of the principal actors in terms of their titles.[4] Onesimus's roles in relation to Paul are brother and child; in relation to Philemon, slave, brother, and debtor; in relation to God (or Christ), child and slave. Onesimus plays two social roles in relation to Philemon: as his slave in the world and as his brother and son in the church. The implied issue is "Can Philemon continue a master/slave relationship with Onesimus when Onesimus is also his brother, and the brother and child of Paul?"

While Paul claims to withhold his apostolic authority (vv. 8–9), he nevertheless makes it clear that he wants and perhaps even expects Philemon to welcome Onesimus. In addition to the titles, his rhetoric throughout the letter is forceful. Two examples suffice. First, verse 22 reads, "One thing more—prepare a guest room for me, for I am hoping through your prayers to be restored to you." His forthcoming visit functions as both a stick and a carrot. It encourages him to act responsibly and, at the same time, warns him that Paul will soon hold him accountable for his decision. Second, though the issue is primarily a personal one, he addresses the letter not only to Philemon, but also to Apphia, and "to the church in your house." This opens the door to the positive influence of others in the Christian community, who might support and encourage Philemon in his reception of Onesimus.

How does this story end? Does Onesimus gain his freedom? Does he return to work with Paul, as apparently Paul wants him to do? Does Philemon do the decent thing and change the master-slave relationship and receive Onesimus as a brother? Unfortunately we do not know the end of the story of Onesimus.

Did Philemon do the same for all other slaves under his care? N. T. Wright suggests that the manumission of Christian slaves would have made life harder for them. Had all the Christians of Paul's day who owned slaves have suddenly released them, it is difficult to wonder what would have happened to this large mass of unemployed people.[5] It is more puzzling, however, to contemplate "why Paul did not express more clearly the anomaly of Christian slave ownership, particularly the ownership of fellow Christians."[6] There may have been practical reasons why Paul was hesitant to do so, but the matter (like the treatment of women in the household codes) leaves one disappointed and puzzled as to why he did not attack the institutionalized social evils of his day more than he did.

8

1 Thessalonians

The first letter to the Thessalonians has a warmth and intimacy matched only by the letter to the Philippians. Paul demonstrates his affection and pastoral capacity in the way in which the letter praises the church there (1:6–10). The believers have been tested and found trustworthy (1:5); they are commended as an example to others (1:7). In response to Timothy's report on his visit there, Paul writes to the Thessalonians, "How can we thank God enough for you in return for all the joy that we feel before our God because of you?" (3:9).

Interestingly, there is no hint in the epistle of the conflict recorded in Acts (17:1–15). There we read that Paul's evangelistic efforts in Thessalonica began in a synagogue but were received with a mixed response. "A great many devout Greeks and not a few of the leading women" (17:4) were persuaded, but some of the Jews became jealous, organized a group of hoodlums, and incited a mob assault against Paul and Silas. While Jason, one of Paul's hosts, was being harassed by the mob, Paul and Silas were hustled out of town and sent to Beroea, where they received a more sympathetic hearing. Luke's account of the early church presents the readers with a dramatic narrative, but he writes several decades after Paul's stay in Thessalonica. Since the letter implies that the church is primarily Gentile in character ("how you turned to God from idols" [1:9]), we are inclined to give historical precedence to the letter for factual information and to draw on Acts only when the narrative does not conflict with Paul. If opposition developed to Paul and the community in Thessalonica (and it certainly did), it more likely came from Roman-backed civil authorities than from Jews. The identification of the opposition in 2:14

71

as "your own compatriots" (in contrast to the Jews of Judea) would clearly indicate a non-Jewish group.

While these Gentiles at Thessalonica were the results of Paul's earlier evangelistic efforts, they were much more than that. They themselves had become ministers by virtue of their conversion. Paul writes, "You became an example to all the believers in Macedonia and Achaia" (1:7). Other believers find their lives influenced by the Thessalonians. They have become genuine models of faith.

As far as we know, 1 Thessalonians is the earliest letter written by Paul, who was the first theologian of the church. Paul had no Christian predecessor as a letter writer, no model for adapting and transforming the existing patterns of the Greco-Roman letterform. Thus 1 Thessalonians breaks new ground and becomes the first in a line of letters written by Paul or in his name to nurture and instruct the early Christian congregations.

1 THESSALONIANS 1:1–10

Following a traditional beginning (senders, recipients, and greetings), the apostle launches into a prayer of thanksgiving that commends the readers highly, not merely because of their faithfulness to God, but because of their chosenness by God as objects of divine love. The theme of election is an essential component of the letter. "For we know, brothers and sisters beloved by God, that he has chosen you, because our message of the gospel came to you not in word only, but also in power and in the Holy Spirit and with full conviction" (1:4–5a). The Greek verb *kaleō* ("call") and its cognates appear frequently throughout the letter, reminding the readers of their election as Christians and of their obligation to live out that calling in the world.

The familiar triadic formula then expresses their obedience to God: "work of faith," "labor of love," and "steadfastness of hope" (1:3). Three accompanying verbs suggest active responses to the gospel: "turned to" (*epistrephō*), "serve" (*douleuō*), and "wait for" (*anamenō*). The first half of the statement (1:9–10) relates how the Gentiles turned to the only true God from their service of false gods. Rather than the usual pitting of faith over against works, "the work of faith" is grounded in the faithfulness of God, who "will do this" (5:23–24). Timothy is sent to the Thessalonians to check on this very thing, that is, how faithful to the gospel they are under the pressure of opposition, 3:1–5. Douglas Harink comments:

> From beginning to end in the letter, Paul thoroughly inscribes the walk of the Thessalonians within the faithful action of the Father, Son, and Holy Spirit, so that while their walk in holiness is always genuinely

their own, it is always also wholly the work of God. Paul is surely as clear here as anywhere that the Thessalonians are what they are in Christ solely through God's grace and Spirit.[1]

The love they demonstrate emerges from the fact that God chose them in Christ (1:4). In fact, the specific love they are to show one another is God taught (4:9–10), a peculiarly Pauline expression in which the apostle "is continuing to place the life of this church in the hands of God—noting God's vengeance, calling, giving of the Holy Spirit, and now God's teaching."[2]

The second half of the sentence (1:10), however, is cast in eschatological language. Those in the Christian community affirm that the one whom God raised from the dead will return again as a part of God's final triumph over evil. The readers have come to know the newness of the gospel, which is "not in word only, but also in power and in the Holy Spirit and with full conviction" (1:5). At the same time, they await God's consummation.

1 THESSALONIANS 2:1–12

Paul recalls his previous visit and the visit of his colleagues to Thessalonica. The report of the visit has sometimes been read as if Paul were under vicious attack and were defending himself and his friends. The clarification of his ministry as not having originated from deceit or base motives (2:3) may suggest that charges have been brought against him and, in Philippi, even physical abuse. At the same time, it should be noted that Paul concludes the section with a word of thanksgiving for the way in which the gospel has been received in Thessalonica (2:13–16).

Two things stand out in this recollection of his previous visit to Thessalonica. First, Paul always spoke and lived to please God, and he encouraged the believers there to do likewise (2:3–8). Greed, flattery, deceit, trickery, and impure motives were simply not a part of his presentation of the gospel. Though he had a certain right to pull out his apostolic status and make demands on the church, he repeatedly chose not to do so.

Second, Paul employs very intimate family terms to describe his ministry among the Thessalonians. In addition to the familiar "father" (2:11), and "brothers and sisters" (2:1, 17; 4:1, 13), there are numerous expressions of affection and thanksgiving for his readers. The phrase "we were gentle (*ēpioi*) among you, like a nurse tenderly caring for her own children" (2:7) might even be rendered "we were infants (*nēpioi*) among you, like a nurse tenderly caring for her own children." Gaventa proposes this alternative reading and comments, "The apostles were not 'heavies,' making much of themselves through various demands (2:7a), but we were as unassuming among the Thessalonians as infants."[3]

1 THESSALONIANS 2:13–3:13

In the prayer of thanksgiving Paul declares that accompanying the preaching and reception of the word in Thessalonica was the genuine character of the apostles. "You know what kind of persons we proved to be among you for your sake" (1:5). He earned his own living and refused to be a burden to anyone. Paul and his colleagues demonstrate a high degree of integrity in their visits and in their dealings with the readers and anticipate the same from them.

In the remainder of chapter 2 and all of chapter 3, in various ways the closeness of Jesus and the believers in Thessalonica becomes evident. Timothy was sent "to strengthen and encourage" them, lest the persecutions, both those that happened to Paul and to the Thessalonians, had been too great a temptation for them (3:2–5). He employs the metaphor of being made "orphans" to depict the anguish he feels in being cut off from them (2:17).

Furthermore, Paul senses in a profound way the eschatological flavor of all of this. "We longed with great eagerness to see you face to face. . . . [C]ertainly I, Paul, wanted to again and again—but Satan blocked our way. For what is our hope or joy or crown of boasting before our Lord Jesus at his coming (*parousia*)? Is it not you? Yes, you are our glory and joy!" (2:17–19). As Paul does in later letters, he presents the believing communities as evidence of his apostleship and his standing before God in the final day.[4]

Alongside the closeness between Paul and his readers, he celebrates in the letter what Abraham Smith calls "the Word's relentless power."[5] The word invaded the Thessalonian community, who received it in conjunction with the Spirit (1:6) and who has been the agent of its dissemination not only in Macedonia but as far away as Achaia (1:8). By "word," Paul means the "gospel of Jesus Christ," the good news that his readers embraced and preached and taught (cf. also 3:2). The word is persistent in creating a community in which sisters and brothers love one another, behave properly toward outsiders, and reject the temptation to be dependent on one another.

1 THESSALONIANS 4:1–12

Following a brief prayer-wish (3:11–13), Paul jogs the memories of his readers to invite them to recall the apostles' teaching when they were initially present at Thessalonica (4:1, 2, 6). The focus here falls on their sanctification (or holiness), a word that with its cognates occurs six times in this brief letter. It names that quality of life that distinguishes the Christian community from the world. The "saints" (or "holy ones") are the people chosen and set apart by God, who at the coming of Jesus will be blameless. Two ambiguous Greek words in 4:4 leave us with an uncertain rendering of the verse; however, it is clear that the Thessalonians made a good start of demonstrating their love for one another and need only to press on, to "do so more and more" (4:1).

1 THESSALONIANS 4:13–5:11

The concluding section of the letter consists of three subsections, each introduced in the Greek text by the same preposition (*peri* (concerning), 4:9–12, 13–18; 5:1–11). They well may be questions that have arisen within the community and asked of Paul by letter or communicated through Timothy. The initial question arose out of the expectation that Jesus would return soon. Christian family members and friends have died. What is their situation now? Will they be disadvantaged because they did not live until Jesus' return?

Paul does not chide the Thessalonians for grieving; grief is natural enough. What he wants is that they understand their loss in a way different from those who have no hope. The foundation for an answer lies in a double affirmation in 4:14. First, "we believe that Jesus died and rose again." The statement has a confessional tone about it and may well have been a creedal formula. The second is the parousia. Jesus' resurrection is not the end of his earthly sojourn; the apocalyptic drama continues and has a future. "Even so, through Jesus, God will bring with him those who have died."

What has or will happen to family members or friends who have already died? This seems to be an anxious question, troubling the Thessalonians. There will then be a meeting with the Lord, with those who have died preceding those who are still alive, and it will be a perpetual meeting ("always"). This apocalyptic scenario is not intended to frighten anyone. Rather, Paul wants it disseminated as an encouraging word, a means of consolation to those who have suffered grief (4:18; 5:11).

"The day of the Lord" (5:2) has a long history in Jewish literature. In Amos 5:18–20 the people who long for the "day" are warned that it is a day of darkness and not light. In Joel 2:31–32 the "day" is "great and terrible." Likewise, in 1 Thessalonians 5:2–3, the description of the "day" is grim and foreboding, "like a thief in the night" (5:2), like a hostile intrusion at the most inopportune moment—until the readers are reminded that they are children of the day, and God destines them for salvation and not destruction (5:9–10). Jesus' death and resurrection make all the difference. An emphatic "you" sets the readers apart from those who will be surprised by the "day." They need not anticipate the end time as a threat. Yet they are to "keep awake and be sober" (5:6) and to mind their own business (4:11–12).

1 THESSALONIANS 5:12–28

The letter closes with a series of exhortations. While we know little of the specific situation in the church that evokes them, we can note three interesting features about them. First, there is a specific call to a life of worship. Rejoicing, praying, and giving thanks are not designated as only Sunday activities, but are characterized by the repeated adverbial emphasis: "always," "without ceasing," "in all circumstances." And the verbs used are those of worship and not verbs like "obey," "serve," "submit to." The manner of life is characterized by delight, by gratitude, by confidence.

Second, there is a specific call to discernment. Readers are told not to quench the Spirit, but to test everything (5:19–22). The words of the prophets should be studied in order to sift and prove the will of God. Even the more particular directives Paul gives, such as "respect those who labor among you," "admonish the idlers," "help the weak," are fairly general in scope. Readers are told to make their own judgments, to sort the critical from the trivial, the important from the unimportant, in a word, to "discern" by means of the Spirit.

Third, there is a specific call to a life of holiness, a theme encountered earlier in the letter (4:3–8). To live a "holy" life is to live a life in distinction from the world. The call to holiness comes in the form of a prayer to God. "May God . . . sanctify you entirely." God alone can enable the community to stand blameless in the day of judgment. The concluding benediction, having asked God's blessing on the community, ends with the assurance that God "is faithful, and he will do this."

Then comes a somewhat surprising ending, "I solemnly command you by the Lord that this letter be read to all of them" (5:27). No other undisputed letter of Paul's demands the public reading of the text (cf. Col 4:16). The command might be obvious if there were factions in the church, and if Paul were eager to make sure all the readers heard what he had to say. But the letter does not reflect internal division at all. He likely then is simply urging that the whole community hears, and not just a few of the church's leaders. Gaventa rightly comments about the command, "It is a positive theological claim about the character of his letter rather than a strategy for plastering over the cracks that are beginning to etch their fine lace into the walls."[6]

PART TWO
The Pauline Tradition

9

Introduction to the Pauline Tradition

Thirteen canonical letters are written in the name of Paul, and we have thus far dealt with seven. The other six bear his name, but serious doubts are raised about whether he wrote or even could have written them. Each letter has its own set of issues—contents, style of writing, historical setting, and so forth.[1] No question is raised about their canonicity or their being authoritatively a portion of the Christian Bible, only about their authorship and thus their historical setting.

Sometimes these books are dubbed as "forgeries," and in a sense they were. Though bearing his name, someone other than Paul wrote them. In another sense, however, we recognize that there were no copyright laws in the first century to raise a host of moral and legal questions. Pseudonymous writing, which was fairly widespread, could be done for ulterior motives, such as profit or malice, or it could be done in order to contemporize a particular tradition. The latter seems the primary reason for the six disputed letters of Paul.

After the death of the apostle, a disciple who knew and revered his message would seek to answer the question, "What would the apostle say if he were living today and facing the problems of this community or that community?" The actual writer may not have put the question that precisely, but, standing within the Pauline tradition, he or she sought to let the tradition speak to the new and different moment in the life of the communities.[2] Each writer has his or her own voice, some more in tune with Paul than others, but all drawing on the apostle to enrich the church.

Among the disputed letters, two types of literature emerge in the Pauline corpus. First, a letter is written that almost copies identically an undisputed letter, and the differences are subtle. Clearly the undisputed letter serves as the source for the historical setting projected in the second letter. The prime example in the canon is 2 Thessalonians, where the author uses 1 Thessalonians as a model to deal with a crisis in the post-Pauline church. The two letters show remarkable similarities, and yet at the same time 2 Thessalonians affirms a very different eschatology from 1 Thessalonians. Whereas the first letter views the return of Jesus as imminent, the second letter tends to slow down the church's expectation and to say to the readership that numerous events have to take place before the end comes (2 Thess 2:1–12).

Second, some letters clearly project a later date and setting than the undisputed letters and, rather than mimicking a genuine letter of Paul's, exhibit their own individuality. They often bear telltale marks that indicate that they were in fact written after Paul's demise. The so-called household codes (Eph 5:21–33; Col 3:18–4:1; Titus 2:1–10), the diminished status of women (Eph 5:22–24; Col 3:18; 1 Tim 2:8–15), the development of a clearly defined ecclesial order (1 Tim 3:1–13), and the groups the writer engages (Col 2:20–23; 1 Tim 4:1–4; 6:3–10; 2 Tim 2:14–26) all tend to reflect a time after Paul's death, as the church faces a different set of problems and issues. Moreover, the stress on church order, godliness, and sound teaching replace the primary Pauline themes of righteousness and faith, and yet each letter has its own distinctive flavor that marks it out from all the rest.

10

Ephesians

Karl Barth once wrote that when the angels go about their official task of prais-ing God, they play only Bach. But when they get together as a family with the door closed, they play Mozart, and "our Lord listens with special pleasure."[1] In a similar way, when the church goes about its official task of doing theol-ogy, it leans heavily on the letters to the Romans and to the Galatians. But in the quiet moments, when it wants to praise God with joy and delight, it reads aloud Ephesians, and "our Lord listens with special pleasure."

Ephesians is lyrical from beginning to end. Written as if to be prayed or sung rather than studied, its mood exudes adoration and gladness. There are a few warnings in the latter three chapters, but they remain vague and unspe-cific. Unlike other letters, it is impossible to reconstruct from the letter what the situation is in the church to which the letter is written.

Furthermore, the phrase in 1:1 "in Ephesus" is missing from several early and trustworthy manuscripts. Most English translations either put the phrase in brackets or add a note at the bottom, indicating its uncertainty. This textual anomaly, plus the general nature of the letter, has precipitated a number of hypotheses about the origin and reason for writing. Colossians (4:17) men-tions a letter from Paul to the Laodicians. Could Ephesians be that letter? Could it have been a circular letter intended to be read in several churches along the Lycus River valley (Colossae, Hieropolis, Laodicea)? If so, its asso-ciation with Ephesus, the largest city in the region, could account for its name.

Lincoln has examined the rhetoric of the letter and has concluded that the first three chapters represent an effort to reinforce the Christian identity of the readers, to recall "the privileges and status they enjoy as believers who are a part of the church."[2] These chapters have a celebrative tone, and through the language of worship (thanksgiving and prayer) and the language of anamnesis (recalling the past), their self-understanding as the people of God is supported and strengthened.

The last three chapters are essentially deliberative rhetoric, where the writer is calling the readers to live in line with their status as members of God's family. When the two types of rhetoric are read together, Ephesians is "an attempt to reinforce its implied readers' identities as those who have received a salvation which makes them members of the church and to underscore the necessity of their distinct role and conduct in the world."[3]

EPHESIANS 1:3–14

This blessing defies careful grammatical analysis, just as do the prayers in *The Prayerbook*. Some Greek testaments place no punctuation in 1:3–14, making it one long sentence (followed by another, 1:15–23). Eduard Norden is reputed to have labeled it "the most monstrous sentence conglomeration I have ever met in the Greek language."[4] The only structural clue is the change in pronouns that occurs at verse 13 (from "we" to "you"), highlighting the contrast between "we Jews who first hope in Christ" and "you Gentiles who also came to believe."

The section, however, is rich in its theological message:

1. For one thing, the emphasis falls strongly on God's activity. Vigorous verbs are used. God *has blessed* us; God *has chosen* us; God *has destined* us; God *has lavished grace* upon us. Humans can do nothing to warrant or merit this gracious activity of God. Even faith is conspicuously not mentioned until 1:13–14. This is not a matter of God's choosing those who believe; rather God chooses in Christ "before the foundation of the world" and carries out in history the redemptive plan, and only then does faith enter the picture. "Faith" consists of hearing the truthful word that God has already destined us to be his family. "Faith" does not actualize or release what is otherwise potential or latent.

2. The text also affirms who the God is who is acting the way God acts: a particular God, "the God and Father of our Lord Jesus Christ." The language is relational, not mechanistic or philosophical. This God is not Aristotle's "first cause" nor Tillich's "ground of being," but the God who is known in Jesus Christ.

3. God carries out the activity of election "in love." This appears repeatedly in the passage. Even if the phrase "in love" is taken with 1:4, nevertheless "the Beloved" (1:6) is a term used for Jesus, and the word "grace" occurs three times (1:6 [bis], 7). Of course, behind the whole notion of election lie the stories of Abraham and Sarah, of Jacob and Esau, of Joseph and his brothers, all instances of God's gracious choosing.

4. The christocentric character of God's election is prominent. Eleven times in these verses the phrase "in Christ" or its equivalent occurs (note especially 1:4, 7, 11). Actually Christ is the one elect person, and we receive our election by our inclusion in him.

5. The purpose of election is in one sense that we might be "holy and blameless before him in love" (1:4). Here the quality of life the readers are summoned to live is spelled out by two closely related terms. Since the word "holy" derives from the same word as "saints," whom the writer has already addressed (1:1), the readers are called to live out what has already been given. But that calling is set in a larger context: "to the praise of his glorious grace" (1:6, 12, 14).

EPHESIANS 1:15–23

At 1:15 the blessing becomes a petitionary prayer of thanksgiving in which Paul prays that the readers receive the Spirit of wisdom and revelation to the end that they may discern the gracious gifts that God has given them. Strikingly, the word "power" appears several times in this section. It is the petition in 1:19 that is picked up and elaborated in the succeeding verses. God's power is made known in the raising of Jesus from the dead and in his exaltation (unlike 1 Cor 1:18, where God's power is made known in the preaching of the crucified One).

Here the writer is guided by an exegesis of Psalms 8:6 and 110:1 and concludes with the remarkable statement in 1:22–23. God's power is available to all of God's people. Readers are not left to the mercy of the hostile forces that surround them, whether political, social, or cultural. Rather Christ has been given to the church as the head over all things.

Lincoln has pointed out that because Christ is filling "all in all," there is a promise of continuity between the realms of creation and salvation, between world and church. The readers "are to take their bearings in the cosmos from their relationship to Christ . . . They [i.e., readers] have not hereby been removed from life on earth or from the sphere of conflict, as the writer's closing exhortation will make clear, but in the continuing fierce battle against the still active evil powers in the heavenly realms, they will be able to stand their ground and resist, because they are fighting from a position of victory (6:10–17)."[5]

EPHESIANS 2:1–22

"Salvation" is a word rarely used in mainline church circles today, or if used, then used with some apology. It has been associated with revivalism, with getting one's ticket punched in order to gain entrance to heaven, and has lost the richness of its biblical heritage. The Letter to the Ephesians can help in our understanding of the term.

Chapter 1 ends with the exaltation of Christ; chapter 2 draws on the implications of such exaltation for the people of God. It keeps the discussion of salvation in the context of worship and praise.

The second chapter divides into two parts: 2:1–10 and 2:11–22, though the two parts have similar movements: then/now movements, which are especially helpful in "remembering" (2:11). At the beginning the readers are set in a situation of total depravity of the direst sort. Three images depict humanity's plight: the helpless state of the corpse (2:1); the indentured slave ("following the ruler of the power of the air" [2:2]); and the condemned prisoner ("children of wrath" [2:3]). Each portrays the powerlessness humanity experiences, even when it wants to change. There is no finger pointing. The "you" of 2:1 and the "we" of 2:3 make the situation universal. The Jews are included in the corporate sin, but, as we shall see in 2:11–13, the Gentiles are pictured in even darker hues.

Then in 2:4 we meet the transitional word, the divine reversal, and the announcement of God's remedy, "*But* God . . ." The language is particularly strong: "But God, who is rich in mercy, out of the great love with which he loved us even when we were dead through our trespasses . . ." God loves the unlovely, and God's actions include making us alive together with Christ Jesus, raising us up with him, and seating us with him in the heavenly realms.

Note that the eschatological timing is different in this text from what we have seen in Romans. We are already seated in the heavenly places in Christ, whereas in Romans 6 (which is also strong on participation with Christ), we have died with Christ and believe that we *will also live* with him (6:8). This "eschatological reservation" in Romans marks a major distinction between the undisputed Pauline letters and the disputed letters.

The spotlight is turned in Ephesians 2:8–10 on the self-awareness and the activity of those who are saved. Two features mark these verses: a sense of grace and a doing of good works. Gratitude is marked by activity, not passivity. Salvation means doing what one is intended to do. The writer is not against works, nor does he pit works over against grace. The doer simply recognizes that the works he or she does are the works of God. "For we are what he has made us, created in Christ Jesus for good works, which God prepared beforehand to be our way of life."

A dark picture of the Gentiles is painted in 2:11–12. They are depicted as being without Christ, being alienated from Israel, strangers to the promises, without hope, and without Yahweh in the world. Again comes the great reversal, this time specifically for the Gentiles: "*But now* in Christ Jesus . . ." Following a reflection on Isaiah 57:19, six statements are made to clarify Christ's action and to support this new status of the "uncircumcised."

1. He has made the two (i.e., Jews and Gentiles) one.
2. He has broken down the dividing wall of hostility.
3. He has abolished the law with its commandments and ordinances.
4. He has created in himself one new humanity in place of the two.
5. He has reconciled both groups to God in one body through the cross.
6. He has put to death the hostility existing between the two.

Two observations regarding this section of Ephesians (2:11–22) are pertinent. First, the statements affirming the unity of Jews and Gentiles into one new humanity do not reflect the heat of Galatians (6:12–18), where Paul struggles for a place for the Gentiles and concludes that "there is no longer Jew or Greek, there is no longer slave or free, there is no longer male and female" (Gal 3:28). Nor are these statements comparable to those in Romans where the wild olive branches are grafted onto the natural olive tree (Rom 11:11–24). Here in Ephesians the community (no doubt largely composed of Gentiles) of which the readers are a part is a new third entity, in which Jewish and Gentile components have long been dissolved. The new humanity replaces the two divisions. "The admission of Gentiles into the church on equal footing with Jewish Christians, over which there had been so much struggle and over which Paul had expended so much energy, is taken for granted by this writer. It is not an issue for which he has to argue."[6]

Second, the church as the household of God, established on the foundation of the apostles and prophets, with Christ as the chief cornerstone, clearly denotes the universal church and no longer a local gathering of Christians. A variety of images are used for this new people of God: God's family (2:19), the new temple (2:20–22), Christ's fullness (1:23; 4:13), the bride of Christ (5:23–33), and the body of Christ (1:23; 2:16; 4:4, 10; 5:23). All of the uses of the word *ekklēsia* in the letter carry a universal connotation. While there is no developed polity, as we encounter in the Pastoral Letters (e.g., 1 Tim 3:13), in Ephesians the church is clearly identified as a community of God's people with a role and a mission in God's cosmic plan.

EPHESIANS 4:1–16

If the first three chapters of Ephesians, in the context of worship and prayer, serve to remind the readers who they are as God's children, then chapters 4–6 appeal to them to demonstrate their identity in the church and in the world. The church is not set over against the world, nor is there any hint that the church has major problems that need to be straightened out. There are enemies out there to be engaged (6:10–17), but a writer with as much of a realized eschatology as this one has will naturally maintain a positive stance toward the issues.

This section begins with a reminder of the unity of the church, which in fact it already possesses (4:1–6) and is witnessed to by citing the seven bases for unity. In the course of affirming the church's unity, the writer speaks to the practical functioning of the church—that is, particular gifts are given to people "to equip the saints for the work of ministry" (4:12). The oneness of the church expresses itself in its common life, and it is through the church that God's plan, so long hidden, is fully revealed. "So that through the church the wisdom of God in its rich variety might now be made known to the rulers and authorities in the heavenly places" (3:10).

EPHESIANS 4:17–5:20

Lincoln comments, "The writer of Ephesians clearly has a vision of the Church as one, holy, catholic, i.e., universal, and apostolic."[7] It is in this latter portion of the letter that the challenge to holiness comes. Actually the writer prefers the language of newness. Readers are told to discard their old humanity, like they would an old coat. The "old" is of course associated with living under the power of the old dominion, with its corrupt and deluded ways. "Putting on" a new garment, then becomes the positive action of taking on the life of the new age and of being continually renewed in and by that gift of newness. The change-of-clothing imagery is frequent in the New Testament, sometimes connoting baptism; however, there is little reason to read baptism into the Ephesians texts.

From 5:21 to 6:9 the inclusion of the so-called household codes has raised a number of problems. The rules are closely paralleled by a similar list for the household found in Colossians 3:18–4:1. In Ephesians they are prefaced by a general call to mutual submission, which tends to relativize the otherwise hierarchical relationships within the family. Certainly relationships are structured differently if the mutual-submission clause is taken seriously, and yet this does not solve many of the problems of interpretation for the contemporary reader.

EPHESIANS 6:10–24

In a letter as buoyant and lyrical as Ephesians, it is arresting that one finds the paragraph 6:10–17, often labeled "The Whole Armor of God." The text recognizes that there is still a war going on, involving not simply human actors but a war against "the cosmic powers of this present darkness, against the spiritual forces of evil in the heavenly places" (6:12). One might hope that the struggle would have been over, but despite the "realized" dimension of the writer's eschatology, the struggle continues. The verb "stand" or "stand firm" (6:11, 13, 14), used three times, accentuates the church's engagement in the conflict.

The language of warfare of course can be misread to justify something like the Crusades or modern-day nationalism. Here it is critical to recognize that the language is metaphorical. One is not to be armed with live bullets and the latest weapons of mass destruction, but with prayer, peace, and perseverance. God's troops in the midst of conflict are to preach the good news of peace (6:18–20). To wear "the whole armor of God" is to be equipped with the divine story and to live the life of holiness and truth.

11

Colossians

Ephesians was written to support a group of Christians in their sense of calling and in their effort to walk worthy of the gospel. We know very little about their life and struggles either within or without the church. Colossians, on the other hand, faces identifiable issues within a community of faith, and the disputes addressed in the letter are more transparent (even if we cannot put an official label on them). Though pseudonymous, the two letters share the name of Paul as writer and share the same perspective and theological outlook. Some commentators even contend that there are literary ties between the two letters.

The writer learns from Epaphras (1:7–8; 4:12–13), probably the founder of the church at Colossae and certainly one of its supporters, of threats to the faith of the Colossian readers. The main threat is labeled a "philosophy" (2:8), a term used to describe a teaching based on "human tradition, according to the elemental spirits of the universe," rather than on Christ. These cosmic powers apparently exercised control over humans and their destinies (2:8). Some of the Colossians thought that the way to gain freedom from and mastery over these forces was by worshiping angels (2:18), by mystical experiences that inflated the ego (2:18), and by adopting a rigorous and ascetic lifestyle (2:18), including the strict observance of ritual obligations (2:16) and world-denying regulations (2:16, 20–22).

The letter seeks to challenge these demands in the light of a cosmic Christ. Whether a group actually existed at Colossae that advocated these positions or whether the believers are merely under the pressures of a pagan environment, perhaps coupled with pressures from Jewish Christians, is difficult to determine.[1]

The opening of the letter reads much like other Pauline letters. The writer begins with a prayer of thanksgiving (1:1–8), which is, not surprisingly, followed by a prayer of intercession (1:9–14). The long thanksgiving (vv. 3–8 are one sentence in Greek) is bound together by the familiar triad of faith, love, and hope. Unlike other places where the three terms appear together, hope serves as the foundation of the other two. Faith describes life from the vantage of Jesus Christ; love depicts the manifestation of faith in relation to the saints; hope is rooted in the gospel and is oriented to the future (1:4–5).

The intercessory prayer seeks for the readers both knowledge and strength, two realities particularly needed in light of the threats they are experiencing. While they are being challenged by "plausible arguments" (2:4) and are faced with "philosophy and empty deceit" (2:8) and "an appearance of wisdom" (2:23), the author prays that they will "be filled with the knowledge of God's will in all spiritual wisdom and understanding" (1:9) to the end that they live lives that please God.

The prayer closes with three forceful statements of God's action on behalf of sinful humanity. First, God has qualified us "to share in the inheritance of the saints in the light" (1:12). As MacDonald has noted, this is the language of belonging, of establishing space between the community of faith and the outside world, which is made even more explicit in the second statement: God "has rescued us from the power of darkness and transferred us into the kingdom of his beloved Son" (1:13).[2] The introduction of "power" language serves as a reminder that the conflict is an apocalyptic one. As the writer of Ephesians puts it, "Our struggle is not against enemies of blood and flesh, but against the rulers, against the authorities, against the cosmic powers of this present darkness, against the spiritual forces of evil in the heavenly places" (Eph 6:12). Third, the saints "have redemption, the forgiveness of sins." While "redemption" is a frequent Pauline expression (Rom 3:24; 8:23; 1 Cor 1:30; cf. Eph 1:7, 14), the use of "sins" in the plural is unlike Paul, who usually writes of sin as a power that enslaves rather than as a wrongful deed one commits.

The writer then cites what is apparently a hymn or creed celebrating the preeminent role of Christ in creation and in the church (1:15–20). We really know very little about hymnody of the early church, certainly not enough to classify hymns, except perhaps by content. This hymn, however, is neatly composed of two strophes, each beginning with a relative pronoun and the verb "to be":

- "who is the image of the invisible God, the firstborn of all creation."
- "who is the head of the body, the church." (author's trans.)

"All this suggests that we have here a two-part poetic unit, the two parts formed in deliberate parallelism with each other and echoing each other. The first half of the unit celebrates the role of Jesus in the creation of the world, the second his role in the redemption of the whole created order."[3] Another reason for taking 1:15–20 as a hymn is the large number of *hapax legomena* in these few verses—seven.

The first unit (1:15–18a) of the hymn seems bound up with the notion of Jewish wisdom (along the lines of Prov 8:22–30; Sir 24:9; Wis 7:25–27). The depiction of Christ has been the topic of serious debate throughout the church's history. The phrase "the firstborn of all creation" (1:15) was taken by the Arians to portray Christ as a creature, the first created being. And yet it is more likely that the prefix *proto-* ("first") denotes precedence in rank rather than in time. It becomes the foundation of the writer's argument in affirming Christ's power and authority over all creation, especially the evil forces that are threatening the faith of believers and are seeking to control the universe. Ultimately they are powerless before this one who is the image of the invisible God. "He himself is before all things, and in him all things hold together" (1:17).

The second strophe of the hymn centers on Christ as the head of the church, who through the cross (1:20) and resurrection (1:18b) brings about God's activity in rectifying "all things."[4] As Christ was preeminent in the "old creation," so now he occupies first place in the new creation. While the first strophe declares Christ's preeminence over all the untoward forces in the universe, the second strophe announces that in Jesus God in his fullness was pleased to dwell and that through the death and resurrection of Christ those same cosmic powers are reconciled to God.

The hymn then is an appropriate reading for Christ the King Sunday, the last Sunday in the liturgical year. It encourages confidence in the reconciling God, who will make all things right. Furthermore, in a later section of the letter (1:20–2:6) the readers are offered an interpretation of the hymn, particularly in terms of its application to the community of faith. This interpretation carries with it both a warning against human fascination with the cosmic powers and their enticements and at the same time an implicit warning against demonizing the powers as if they were unredeemable. In the verses that follow, the verbs used to describe God's stance toward the cosmic powers are more militant and vigorous ("disarm the rulers and authorities," "made a public example of them," "triumphed over them" [2:15]).

The demand to live a unique life (3:8–17), grounded in Christ, is stated in the language of dressing and undressing. Readers are told to set aside "the old self" and to clothe themselves "with the new self, which is being renewed in knowledge according to the image of its creator" (3:10–11). As in Galatians, "In that renewal there is no longer Greek and Jew, circumcised and uncircumcised, barbarian, Scythian, slave and free; but Christ is all and in all" (3:11; Gal 3:28).

One doesn't read very far in the letter without confronting a critical eschatological problem and one that makes the claim to Pauline authorship highly uncertain. No longer is there an expectation of an impending return of Jesus, no longer a sense of urgency because the end is near. The passages that relate the story of Jesus' death and resurrection and even his ascension (and believers who by their baptisms are united with him in these events) are taken to be completed (2:12; 3:1). Baptism symbolizes the believer's participation not only with the crucified Christ but also with the risen Lord, who now reigns at the right hand of God (2:26; 3:1). If Christ has been raised and has gone to be with God, then so have all those whom he represents.

In technical terms, the eschatology of Colossians is more fully "realized" than the eschatology of the undisputed letters of Paul. Believers have not only been rescued from the power of darkness but have already been transferred "into the kingdom of [God's] beloved Son" (1:13). This eschatological shift appears to be not so much a correction of Paul's thinking as a logical development of a later period and an answer to the needs of the Colossians.[5]

And yet in an odd way the eschatological perspective of Colossians may also account for the presence of the household codes (3:18–4:1), which also appear in Ephesians (5:21–6:9). A second generation of Christians, without the sense of urgency stimulated by the prospect of Jesus' return, resorts to a conventional model of household relationships. The assumption is that the household is structured and governed as a microcosm of society, with the condition and motivation to "do everything in the name of the Lord Jesus, giving thanks to God the Father through him" (Col 3:17).

12

2 Thessalonians

A good case can be made for the Pauline authorship of 2 Thessalonians. The unusually close relationship between 1 Thessalonians and 2 Thessalonians leaves the modern reader with one of two options. Either Paul wrote the second letter so soon after the first that it reflected the situation and language of the earlier one or a Christian from a later time employed 1 Thessalonians as a model to address the context of a post-Pauline period. On the one hand, many expressions of 1 Thessalonians appear in 2 Thessalonians, and in some instances they appear nowhere else in Paul's writings. On the other hand, 2 Thessalonians contains an apocalyptic scenario hard to mesh with the situation of 1 Thessalonians. Thus, it seems more likely that 2 Thessalonians was written at a later time, when the apocalyptic speculation was running rampant and when brakes were needed to be put on the speculation.

Two features are striking about the community to which 2 Thessalonians is written. First, it is a community that has suffered considerable persecution. Presumably the civil authorities have generated the suffering, though little in the letter itself identifies the cause. What is most prominent is the "steadfastness and faith" (1:4) exhibited by the church members, whose endurance has made them "worthy of the kingdom of God" (1:5).

The writer reassures them that God will repay with afflictions those who afflict them (1:6) and that their oppressors will experience the ultimate punishment, namely separation from the presence of God (1:9).

Second, the Thessalonian community had undergone considerable confusion regarding the return of the Lord. Apparently the source of their perplexity was the receipt of a letter, purporting to be from Paul, to the effect that the day of the Lord had already come (2:1–2). Could this letter have been

1 Thessalonians, which the readers misinterpreted to imply the return of Jesus? Or was this a letter sent by someone else in Paul's name? To be sure, 1 Thessalonians was written, in part, to respond to the questions raised in the community about the deaths of loved ones. Were they to have any part in the coming end time? Were their family members excluded from salvation? If one reads 1 Thessalonians carefully, however, Paul still awaits the return of the Lord. Whereas 1 Thessalonians was written to encourage church members who are grieving over their deceased loved ones and to assure them that the day of the Lord will come, 2 Thessalonians was aimed at discouraging a premature eschatological celebration.

To clear up the confusion, the writer of 2 Thessalonians seeks to calm the apocalyptic enthusiasm that had become evident in Thessalonica. Several signs must take place before the Day of the Lord comes. The rebellions, the lawless one, the restrainer, the mystery of lawlessness . . . all are apocalyptic events that must take place before the advent of Jesus ultimately destroys the lawless one (2:3–12).

Meanwhile, church members are to keep at their daily tasks (1 Thess 4:9–12). Those who are caught up in the apocalyptic fervor, quit their jobs, and depend on the generosity of others for sustenance are to be dealt with forthrightly. If they do not work, they should not eat (2 Thess 3:6–14). It is as simple as that.

13

The Pastoral Letters:
1 and 2 Timothy and Titus

Since the early eighteenth century 1 and 2 Timothy and Titus have been known as the Pastoral Letters. They are often grouped together because they are written as directions from "Paul" to a younger generation of church leaders, giving guidance concerning pastoral oversight in the congregations. The letters provide support for the recipients as to how they should cope with false teaching, what characteristics they should seek in church leaders (bishops, elders, and deacons), what should be done to maintain a healthy life among various groups (the young, the elderly, the slaves, the widows), and how the wealthy should share their resources.

In many ways the three letters, though purporting to be from Paul the apostle, reveal sharper differences in content, vocabulary, and style from the undisputed letters than do 2 Thessalonians, Ephesians, and Colossians. The development of church polity and the suggestions about coping with false teaching place the Pastoral Letters closer to Clement (c. 95 CE) and Ignatius (110 CE) than to the New Testament.

We shall look closely at four aspects of the life of these young congregations that are addressed in the Pastorals: church organization, false teaching, the role of women in the church, and the style of life commended in the letters.

CHURCH ORGANIZATION

The usual argument has been that the early church leaders were members who were given charismatic gifts of the Spirit to carry out special functions within the life of the church (1 Cor 12:4–11; Rom 12:3–8). Among the undisputed letters of Paul, only at the beginning of Philippians is mention made of "bishops and deacons." (Phoebe is identified as a deacon of the church at Cenchrae in Rom 16:1.) Later toward the end of the first century the church became preoccupied with organizational structures and with officers, such as bishops, elders, and deacons. From the writings of Ignatius of Antioch (115 CE) we discover the pattern of a single bishop (monarchical episcopate) at the head of local Christian communities.

Margaret Y. MacDonald, on the basis of a sociological study of the letters, has modified this traditional assessment by arguing that institutionalization was present from the church's beginning.[1] In Paul's letters it is *community-building institutionalization* (for example, Paul's devoted coworker Timothy [Phil 2:19–24]). In the time of Ephesians and Colossians, it is *community-stabilizing institutionalization* (for example, those who work to equip the saints for the work of ministry [Eph 4:11–14]). In the time of the Pastoral Letters it is *community-protecting institutionalization* (for example, those who struggle to maintain the purity of the faith in the face of outside challenges [Titus 3:9–10]). As the years passed, it became necessary for the churches to delineate more carefully their criteria for leadership.

In 1 Timothy (3:1–7), one finds specific qualities designated for one who is to be a bishop. He must be experienced not only in the faith but also as a manager of his own household. He must be respected by people outside the church, be sensible, and above reproach (1 Tim 3:1–7). Deacons are also to be respectful, not greedy nor given to much wine (1 Tim 3:8–13).

Unlike Paul, who never uses the expression "the household of God" for the church (though he does write to "the church in your house" [Phlm 2; Rom 16:5; 1 Cor 16:9]), the writer of 1 Timothy refers to the church as "the household of God" (1 Tim 3:15) and develops the metaphor even further by calling the church "the pillar and bulwark of the truth." Of course the family of the first century developed beyond that of the contemporary nuclear family. It included slaves, former slaves, and many who were beholden to the paterfamilias beyond being blood relatives.

Young makes the case that church officials are too often understood in the light of later developments and not enough in terms of their present situation.[2] For example, the "bishop" in the Pastoral Letters is paralleled by bishops in the second century and are not interpreted sufficiently in terms of the family. Since the prominent image for the church is the household of God, Young defines the roles of officers in terms of the Greco-Roman household. A bishop is God's household manager. The elders are the seniors in the family, respected for their wisdom and carrying the corporate memory of the group. They form a governing council authorized to appoint and advise the bishop. The deacons offer guidance and reproof but also function in various serving roles. "Here the ministry of the church is still only in embryo, but the stress on authoritative teaching and on proper hierarchical relations modeled on a typical Greco-Roman household, laid the foundations for the development that would later gather pace through the second century."[3]

FALSE TEACHING

Timothy is directed to admonish people in the congregations who are preoccupied with "myths and endless genealogies that promote speculations rather than the divine plan given by faith." They pay attention to the teaching of deceitful spirits and to the instruction of demons (1 Tim 1:4; 4:7).

Apparently, what Timothy and Titus are up against is an early expression of gnosticism, highly ascetic, even to the point of forbidding marriage (1 Tim 4:3). Rather than enjoying God's good gifts, these people "forbid marriage and demand abstinence from foods, which God created to be received with thanksgiving" (1 Tim 4:3). Not at all unlike the opponents of Paul in Corinth, one group contends that "the resurrection has already taken place" (2 Tim 2:17–18).

Considerable speculation has surrounded the connection between these proto-gnostics and Judaism. The author describes them as "desiring to be teachers of the law" (1 Tim 1:7), as ones who "[pay] attention to Jewish myths or to commandments" (Titus 1:14), even as those attentive to the "commandments" (Titus 1:10). There is nothing, however, that defines the relationship more closely or that indicates that the Mosaic law had a prominent role in the conflicts.

THE ROLE OF WOMEN

It may be in connection with what the Pastorals say about the role of women that we more fully understand the nature of the false teaching. In 1 Timothy 2:8–15 a contrast is drawn between men who are to pray "without anger or argument" and women who are to dress "modestly and decently in suitable clothing," avoiding "expensive clothes" and extravagant jewelry made of gold and fine pearls. Instead women are to do good works. Then the writer shifts from the language of persuasion ("I desire") to that of command.

> Let a women learn in silence with full submission. I permit no woman to teach or to have authority over a man; she is to keep silent. For Adam was formed first, then Eve; and Adam was not deceived, but the woman was deceived and became a transgressor. Yet she will be saved through childbearing, provided they continue in faith and love and holiness, with modesty. (1 Tim 2:12–15)

The writer has employed the rules governing wives, which are found in the standard household codes and has applied them to all women, whether married or not. How is one to account for such a command, in light of what Paul had earlier written in Galatians 3:28? What do we do with this conundrum?

Dennis R. MacDonald has made the proposal that the Pastorals in part were written amid oral stories and legends about Paul that circulated among celibate women in Asia Minor. These women were strongly influenced by the narrative that appears in the apocryphal book called "The Acts of Paul and Thecla." Thecla was a young woman who was converted to Christianity through the preaching of Paul on the eve of her wedding. She was infatuated with what Paul had to say about chastity and virginity. When her fiancé failed to win her back on the eve of her wedding, her mother solicited the help of the governor, who had her taken naked to be burned at the stake. She was miraculously saved through a thunderstorm, later baptized herself, and persuaded Paul to ordain her to preach. The "Paul" of the story elevates sexual chastity to a high level, urging women even to abandon their families and become celibate.

MacDonald proposes that the Pastorals were written in part to show, among other things, that the radical "Paul" of the legends was a distortion and to silence those who were repeating the stories.[4] The radical "Paul" apparently taught that women should not marry, or if they marry they should live celibate lives, whereas the Pastorals state that only bearing children will save women. Timothy is told to avoid "old wives' tales," referring to the legends and stories that had grown up around Paul (1 Tim 4:7).

What is intriguing is that the basic strategy for dealing with the false teaching and with the radical stance of the women is to forbid it (1 Tim 1:3; Titus 1:11), to avoid it (1 Tim 4:17; 6:20; Titus 3:9), to guard the sacred tradition (1 Tim 6:20), and to abstain from wrangling over it (2 Tim 2:14, 16, 23). There is little theological engagement with the issues, as in Galatians, Corinthians, and others. All three Pastoral Letters are hortatory documents, filled with instructions, commands, and personal examples of good and bad behavior. At only one point does the writer actually debate with the false teaching or counter the attitude toward women: "For everything created by God is good, and nothing is to be rejected, provided it is received with thanksgiving; for it is sanctified by God's word and by prayer" (1 Tim 4:4–5).

THE CHRISTIAN LIFESTYLE

While on occasion the leadership of the church, particularly those holding offices, are singled out as needing to demonstrate certain Christian virtues, such virtues are expected of all Christians. Two theological bases are given as a rationale for the living of such a life: one is past (the appearance of the grace of God); the other is future (the manifestation of the glory of Jesus Christ, Titus 2:11–14). Not so much is said about the future hope as is written about the past. "When the goodness and loving kindness of God our Savior appeared, he saved us . . . according to his mercy, through the water of rebirth and renewal by the Holy Spirit" (Titus 3:4–5). God is our Savior (cf. 1 Tim 3:16), "who desires everyone to be saved and to come to the knowledge of the truth" (1 Tim 2:3). "Salvation" is the gift as well as the attainment of the perfection that will inherit eternal life. God desires that this gift become effective for all humanity.

What are the prominent virtues to be demonstrated in human life? Often particular qualities are singled out for particular people or groups of people. Two passages make more general references to the quality of life that is to be lived before God. In 1 Timothy 2:2, the writer offers an intercessory prayer for the political leaders "that we may lead a *quiet* and *peaceable* life in all *godliness* and *dignity*." In Titus 2:12, we read that we are "to renounce impiety and worldly passions, and in the present age to live lives that are *self-controlled*, *upright*, and *godly*." The Greek root word *euseb-* (from which "godly" and "godliness" are translated) appears in the New Testament some twenty times, eleven of which are found in the Pastoral Letters and none in the undisputed letters of Paul.

The life Christians are to live is not derived from christological insights (as Phil 2:5), nor is there any injunction to love one another (Gal 5:13; Rom 13:8). Collins notes, "The Pastorals' emphasis on godliness reflects, nonetheless, the Jewish and Christian covenantal notion in which responsibility toward God is inherently linked to responsibility toward others within the community."[5]

One specific moral issue that comes for attention in the Pastorals is wealth. An acknowledgment of God, the generous provider, sets the context for warnings against arrogance and a false reliance on riches (cf. 1 Tim 6:11–16). The readers are not asked to give up what they have or to divest themselves of their possessions, but "to rid themselves of their reliance on them and to use God's rich generosity to enable a rich generosity of their own."[6]

PART THREE

Jesus, the Gospels, and Acts

14

Introduction
to the Synoptic Gospels

The Gospel is a second genre of Christian literature quite different than the letter. The first four books of the New Testament are labeled "Gospels," though there exists a marked difference between the first three and the fourth. The fourth has personnel and events that do not exist in the first three, whereas the first three contain and share among themselves material not found in the fourth. We shall take a careful look at the Gospel of Mark and then take note of distinctive features of the Gospels of Matthew and Luke. The Gospel of John will be treated with the three letters of John as the prominent document of the Johannine tradition.

The earliest example is the Gospel of Mark, written about 65–70 CE, and circulated widely within approximately two decades after its composition.[1] Matthew and Luke clearly borrow material from Mark, and yet they do not displace Mark because they remain distinct stories (and thus the phrase "Synoptic Gospels"). That is, Matthew and Luke do not reproduce Mark's story or dialogue in such detail as to render Mark or either of them redundant. In addition, there is a considerable amount of material that obviously Matthew and Luke share. This is called Q (from the German word for "source," *quelle*). Not all scholars accept the hypothesis of Q, but its presence (or lack thereof) will make no difference to our study since we are dealing primarily with the material in its canonical form. Toward the end of the twentieth century, redaction criticism and, following it, literary criticism have made it clear that each Gospel is more than a collection of isolated units of material but tells a consistent and comprehensible story.

The Gospel tradition seems to have gone through several stages of oral transmission between the time when Jesus lived and taught and the time when the Gospels were written. Most of the disciples, as well as Jesus, spoke Aramaic, though undoubtedly there were a few Greek-speaking Jews mingled in the various communities. Since Greek was the lingua franca of the day, it rapidly took over as the prominent tongue for preaching and teaching the faith, especially for an urban person like the apostle Paul.

After Rome routed the Jewish rebellion in 70 CE, the churches became increasingly Gentile and less Jewish. In fact, Jews who were Christians were dismissed from the synagogues and subjected to considerable persecution.

While the Gospels were primarily written for and circulated among Christian communities, there is increasing recognition that they had a missionary function as well and were read by non-Christians. Particularly in the second century, various apologists suggested that non-Christians read the Gospels. The critic Celsus's (180 CE) attack on Christianity reveals an acquaintance with the Gospels,[2] and Justin states that Trypho learned of the Christian faith by having read "the so-called Gospel."[3] A careful crafting of the literary narratives further suggests that a wider dissemination was intended than the small congregations for which they were written.

15

The Gospel of Mark

The evangelist Mark took the tradition that came to his hand, and without dispensing with his original sources, fashioned a powerful new voice to proclaim the good news, the story of the gift of God's newness. He creatively molded his sources into a comprehensive whole. The questions are: what is that whole, and what does it say to its implied audience.

MARK 1:1–3:6

Mark has no story of Jesus' birth, no account of his childhood. Instead we first meet Jesus as an adult figure, receiving the baptism of his cousin John. Four items are significant about the beginning of the Gospel:

1. The use of the expression "the beginning of the gospel" (or "good news," 1:1) elicits the uses of the word in Isaiah (cf 40:9; 52:7; 61:1). The "beginning" implies not merely the start of the narrative, but its basis or foundation, which continues to be preached, even in Mark's story (13:10; 14:9). In the early church, the term "gospel" had taken on special significance from its frequency in the Pauline letters, where it denotes the church's preaching of Jesus as the source of salvation. Stanton has made the case that the word "gospel" is heard against the backdrop of a rival set of "gospels" in the ancient world and thus is a risky word to use in light of the imperial cult of Rome.[1]

The titles attached are appropriate: "Jesus Christ, the Son of God." "Christ"—that is, Messiah—appears in Mark regularly as an honorific or messianic title (8:29; 12:35; 13:21; 14:61; 15:32), while at other times it appears as a regular name for Jesus (9:41). "Son of God," on the other hand, is used only at pivotal moments—at his baptism (1:11), on the mount of transfiguration (9:7), and at his trial (14:61).

2. Mark's reference to Jesus' baptism is terse but striking (1:9–11). As John leads Jesus up from the water and the Spirit descends on him, the heavens are torn asunder, and the voice speaks from the skies, "You are my Son, the Beloved; with you I am well pleased." Whereas in Matthew's and Luke's accounts of the baptism the expression is simply "the heavens *opened*," Mark uses a different (and more violent) verb, suggesting a translation such as "he saw the heavens *torn apart*."

Don Juel has called attention to the parallel between the tearing of the heavens in 1:9–11 and the rending of the temple curtain in 15:38–39. "The elimination of a barrier between God and creation, clearest in the tearing of the temple curtain, may be suggested in the baptismal scene as well." The implications are that we have a new access to the Father, because "the protecting barriers are gone, and that God, unwilling to be confined to sacred spaces, is on the loose in our own realm. If characters in the story find Jesus' ministry threatening, then they may have good reason to be frightened by his resurrection."[2]

3. The story begins abruptly and assumes a fast pace. Following the description of John, we read immediately of the baptism of Jesus (1:9–11), the temptation of Jesus (1:12–13), the beginning of Jesus' ministry in Galilee (1:14–15), the call of four of the disciples (1:16–20), and in rapid-fire succession, the healing of a man possessed of a demon (1:21–28), the healing of Peter's mother-in-law (1:29–31), a summary account of Jesus' exorcism (1:32–34), a brief report of Jesus' preaching tour throughout Galilee (1:35–39), and Jesus' cleansing of a leper (1:40–45). This frequent succession of events continues throughout the entire story. Nothing slows the pace of the narrative, as in Matthew (e.g., a genealogy and three chapters of the Sermon on the Mount) or in Luke (e.g., lengthy birth narratives and a genealogy). The rapidity of Mark heightens the urgency of the story.

4. The declaration of Jesus' preaching the gospel (1:14) and his announcement that the time has been fulfilled and that the kingdom of God has come near (1:15a) are paramount. The termination of the old age and the inbreaking of the new age are proclaimed, calling for repentance and an act of faith. At each baptism the believer would hear "this announcement of cosmic juncture as a promise that they might now enter the dominion of God . . . and as a call to bury the moribund world in the water and to rise from it to view, through the eyes of faith, God's new creation."[3]

Next follows a series of events that disclose the authority and power of Jesus—in calling disciples to leave behind their work, in exorcizing demons, in healing the sick, in cleansing a leper. As the astonished crowd puts it, "What is this? A new teaching—with authority! He commands even the unclean spirits, and they obey him" (1:27b). God's sovereign power has come near. The radical *novum* is at hand.

The second chapter of the Gospel discloses the opposition that begins to build against Jesus. Mark relates a series of controversy stories (2:1–12, 15–17, 18–20, 23–27), culminating with a plot on the part of the Pharisees and Herodians to destroy Jesus (3:6).

At the center of this section, people question Jesus: "Why do John's disciples and the disciples of the Pharisees fast, but your disciples do not fast?" (2:18). Jesus responds that the wedding guests do not fast as long as the bridegroom is with them. Only during the days when the bridegroom is taken from them will they fast.

Then Jesus relates two brief parables. "No one sews a piece of unshrunk cloth on an old cloak; otherwise, the patch pulls away from it, the new from the old, and a worse tear is made. And no one puts new wine into old wineskins; otherwise, the wine will burst the skins, and the wine is lost, and so are the skins; but one puts new wine into fresh wineskins" (2:21–22). What we have seen in the narrative is the conflict between the dynamic of the new era and the inherited religious practices of the old age. The evangelist makes clear that Jesus cannot really be understood, except by embracing the new era and by abandoning the old. "The old order, then, must sooner or later take away Jesus' life, because he has violently disturbed it with his new teaching, which tears at its very fabric."[4] So we encounter the build-up to 3:6, where the conspiracy to destroy Jesus begins to take shape.

MARK 3:7–8:26

This section also strongly defines who is an insider and who is an outsider. The crowds follow Jesus from all over Galilee "in great numbers" (3:7–8). But Jesus selects and appoints twelve disciples to be with him and to be sent out to exorcize demons, to heal the sick, and to preach the good news. Pretty soon, they begin to encounter opposition themselves; and at the same time, Jesus faces two charges: one made by the religious authorities of his joining into a confederacy with the demons ("He has Beelzebul" [3:22]); and the other made by his family ("He has gone out of his mind" [3:21]).

First, Jesus responds to the criticism of his family, who ironically end up being on the outside. He looks at those who are sitting around him and says, "Whoever does the will of God is my brother and sister and mother" (3:35).

In two brief parables Jesus responds to those who accuse him of being in league with Satan by raising the question of a house being divided against itself ("That house will not be able to stand" [3:25]). Moreover, if one wants to plunder a person's house, he has to tie up the person first and then he can thoroughly ransack the house. The exorcisms and healings are the plundering of Satan's house by the "more powerful" one (1:7). Jesus is currently doing just that—that is, tying up the strong man and raiding Satan's kingdom.[5]

Mark now draws together several of Jesus' parables, which represent the major unit of teaching in the Gospel. The parables in the fourth chapter have to do with the complexities and variations of hearing the word of God. Note that at the beginning and ending of the first parable the reader is strongly advised to "listen" (4:3, 9).

1. Mark begins with the parable of the sower (4:2–9) and its interpretation (4:13–20). While the sower sows seeds that fall on the path and on the rocky ground and amid the thorns, nevertheless, one-fourth of the seed yields a surprising crop. Jeremias has noted that a tenfold yield was considered a good harvest.[6] Here the yield is extraordinary . . . thirty, sixty, and a hundredfold! The one who proclaims the word of God is bound to be encouraged by such results.

2. The secret of the kingdom (4:10–12) represents one of the most difficult of the New Testament interpretive problems and one we will not solve here. Citing Isaiah 6:9–10, the saying seems to summarize the purpose and not the result of the preaching of the kingdom, though it is particularly vulnerable to a deterministic reading. For those on the inside the parables reveal the mystery of the kingdom, whereas for the outsiders, the parables only hide and do not reveal.[7]

3. The symbol of light (4:21–25), with its inherent revelatory character, encourages the reader, whereas the word about "the measure you give will be the measure you get," tends to issue a warning about the risks of discipleship.

4. The parable of the seed growing secretly (4:26–29) stresses the mystery of growth and the reality that God's critical times occur spontaneously, independent of human activity and contributions. "The earth produces of itself" (the Greek: *automatē*, 4:28).

5. The parable of the mustard seed (4:30–32) offers a promise: from small beginnings the kingdom of God will emerge to become cosmic in scope, as the largest of all the bushes in the garden. The birds of the air will rest in the branches of the tree, where they are protected, as promised (Ezek 17:23; 31:6; Dan 4:12, 21).

Mark then extends Jesus' ministry as a worker of mighty deeds by presenting a number of dramatic events in which he stilled the uncontrollable storm (4:35–41); he exorcised the demon who had plagued the Gerasene man and had left him stranded in the tombs (5:1–20); he healed the woman who had been troubled by perpetual hemorrhaging (5:21–34); and he raised Jairus's daughter (5:1–20, 35–43).

This section of mighty deeds done by Jesus ends not with an acknowledgment or acceptance of his works by his townspeople, but by a total rejection by his relatives, heightened by the narrator's comment, "And he was amazed at their unbelief" (6:1–6a). Such a negative reaction to Jesus foreshadows the death of John the Baptist (6:14–29). Moreover, Herod's misuse of power (6:20, 26) anticipates a similar misuse by Pilate (15:6–15).

The two feedings of the multitudes, initially five thousand (6:30–44) and then four thousand (8:1–9), remind readers of the provision of manna in the wilderness (cf. Exod 16:13–35; Num 11:1–35) and foreshadow the supper Jesus will eat with his disciples in the upper room (taking, blessing, breaking the loaves). Jesus' further care for individuals, such as the Syrophoenician woman (7:24–30) and the deaf mute (7:31–37), characterizes his ministry.

The most striking feature of this section comes in the closing incident when Jesus heals a blind man at Bethsaida (8:21–26). Rather than being an instantaneous event as most of Jesus' healings were, this blind man was cured in two stages. First, Jesus put saliva on his hand and touched the man's eyes. He was able to see "people as if they were trees walking." But then Jesus repeated the process, "and he saw everything." Intriguingly, this passage does not appear in the Common Lectionary, though in many respects it reflects the more normal experience of those who come to see the gospel at first but only gradually.

MARK 8:27–10:45

A significant change in the narrative occurs at 8:27, with the stress falling on Jesus' upcoming suffering, the disciples' misunderstanding, and Jesus' instruction in discipleship. Peter's confession of Jesus as Messiah (8:29) contains no new information for Jesus; however, the implied readers of the Gospel begin to learn something new that had only been hinted at previously—namely, that suffering and death are critical to who Jesus is as Messiah. Three times they are told of his upcoming rejection, death, and resurrection (8:27–31; 9:31; 10:32–34). Tannehill calls these passion predictions "antithetical aphorisms."[8] By that he means that prior to this time the implied reader has been allowed to form an understanding of the author's view of Jesus in which suffering and death have had no major role. Only hints here and there have been given. Furthermore, the story of the Messiah the readers know—that is, the Davidic Messiah—was not a story of rejection and death. But now the contrast is sharp, the dissonance is harsh, even paradoxical.

> They assert a necessary connection between opposite terms. The attempt to save one's life will lead to the opposite; the goal of being first can only be achieved by its opposite. The clash of words in each of these antithetical aphorisms emphasizes the conflict between this

vision of life and the normal view, in which people assume that they can directly achieve the goals that their anxious self-concern sets for them. These paradoxical words intend to shake the assumptions that normally control our thinking and planning.[9]

Furthermore, on this journey from Caesarea Philippi to Jerusalem, the disciples are taught the ABCs of what it means to follow Jesus. For example, the disciples argue as to who is the greatest, and Jesus settles the dispute by placing a little child in their midst and directing them to welcome such a one (9:33–37), and soon thereafter Jesus receives and blesses little children (10:13–16). In contrast to the role of the little child, the rich young man is unable to be freed of his wealth and thus is unable to follow Jesus (10:17–22). These demands of discipleship ("antithetical aphorisms"?) are all set in an eschatological context. At the final judgment those who suffer unjustly will be vindicated, and those who reject and are ashamed of Jesus and his teaching will be rejected and unknown (8:38).

MARK 11:1–16:8

Martin Kähler's famous comment that "one could call the Gospels passion narratives with extended introductions" is both inadequate and at the same time highly revelatory with respect to Mark.[10] Kähler's quote is inadequate in that events in the first thirteen chapters of Mark are not merely preliminary or introductory. In Mark, the events from the time of Peter's confession of Jesus as Messiah at Caesarea Philippi (8:29) up to the triumphal entry into Jerusalem are heavy laden with themes and predictions of the future. The three passion predictions and their implications for discipleship dominate the Gospel from at least its midpoint to the end. And yet Kähler's quote reveals the heavy emphasis placed on the passion narrative. Bartlett writes:

> More than any of the other Gospels, Mark's Gospel shows us how the crucifixion wounded God; how in Jesus Christ the suffering of God joins the suffering of humankind; how from now until all eternity God bears in God's heart that suffering and loss, like a scar, like a tree. If the great puzzle of Mark's Gospel is that Christ's death is the sign of Christ's sonship and God's love, the smaller puzzle is like unto it, human life is most alive when we, too, follow in the way of the cross. [11]

Following the cleansing of the temple at Jerusalem, the text lists a number of stories of conflict, all taking place within the context of the temple. The list begins with a challenge to Jesus' authority (11:27–33). After all, Jesus has just run the moneychangers out of the temple and disrupted their business. What right did he have to do this? He first toys with them regarding the source of his authority by raising the issue of John's baptism, but then tells the parable of the Wicked Tenants (12:1–12), where "they" get the point but are trapped by the crowds and cannot make a move against him (12:12). Again, with his answer to the question about paying taxes to the emperor, they have no comeback (12:13–17).

When the Sadducees raise the foolish issue concerning whose wife will this childless widow be, they are exposed as people who do not believe in the resurrection in the first place (12:18–27). The conversation with the scribe turns out in a positive way, as Jesus confirms his response and commends him personally (12:28–34). In fact, Jesus' "praise of the scribe is Mark's way of acknowledging Christianity's debt to Judaism. Its most basic commands are the same."[12]

Jesus, having been queried by individuals and by groups, now takes the opportunity to question the scribes and, using Psalm 110:1, to declare the relation of the Messiah to the Son of David. "This incident reflects the theology of the Markan church that, while affirming Jesus' Davidic origin and messianic mission, rejects popular messianic expectations and redefines them in terms of the exaltation of Jesus above his enemies."[13]

The events that have occurred in and around the temple reach their climax with the prediction of the destruction of the temple (13:1–2) and the apocalyptic instruction that follows (13:3–31). Throughout the chapter the reader is faced with various warnings ("Beware!"). First, there is a group of the warnings spoken to those in the community who must face the false prophets and messiahs who say, "I am he!" Mark declares, "But the end is still to come. . . . This is but the beginning of the birthpangs" (13:5–8).

A second group of warnings is also directed at the community, but in terms of its mission and life (13:9–13). "Beware; for they will hand you over to councils; and you will be beaten in synagogues. . . . The gospel must first be proclaimed to all nations. . . . The one who endures to the end will be saved." The church's mission is carried on but always in the light of the cross.

A third set of warnings comes in the parable of the Doorkeeper, who is assigned the responsibility of watching for the return of the landlord (13:33–37). "Keep alert; for you do not know when the time will come. . . . Keep awake!" Vigilance and accountability are essential characteristics of faithfulness to the gospel and its mission.

Despite these warnings about apocalyptic enthusiasm and eagerness, chapter 13 reaffirms an apocalyptic expectation.

> So, too, God's hour comes unimpeded. He made the decisive beginning, the seed has been sown. He leaves nothing undone. . . . His beginning ripens to its fulfillment. Till then it behooves man [and

woman] to wait in patience and not try to anticipate God but in full confidence to leave everything to him.[14]

Chapters 14 and 15 relate the last few days of Jesus' life. The pace of the story slows dramatically as Mark describes the anointing at Bethany, the extensive plots to do away with Jesus, and the various trials he has to undergo.

Four events, prior to the crucifixion, are most critical for our understanding of the passion story. The first is Jesus' anointing at Bethany by the unnamed woman (14:3–9). When her extravagance was questioned by some of the bystanders, Jesus defended her by saying that she "had anointed his body" ahead of time for his burial. Jesus did not deny that the poor were present in the world and needed food. Jesus would not need anointing at the normal time—namely, after he had died—because God would raise him from the dead. Moreover, "wherever the gospel is proclaimed in the whole world, what she has done will be told in remembrance of her" (14:9).

The second critical event is the Passover meal, which Jesus shared with his disciples, and at which he instituted the Lord's Supper (14:12–25). The verbs ("took," "blessed," " broke," "gave") are reminiscent of the two feedings previously reported in the Gospel (6:30–42; 8:1–10); however, the imagery points forward as well as backward. The vow Jesus spoke over the cup puts it clearly, "I will never drink again of the fruit of the vine until that day when I drink it new in the kingdom of God" (14:25). This future of the kingdom of God stands in tension with the programmatic announcement at the beginning of the Gospel, "The time is fulfilled; the kingdom of God has come" (1:15). Or as William Manson put it, "There is a realized eschatology. There is also an eschatology of the unrealized."[15] The adjective "proleptic" has come into common use to describe this predicament.[16] Jesus is troubled and distressed and even prays that the cup might be taken from him. "Abba," he calls to his Father, "yet, not what I want, but what you want" (14:36).

The word "Abba" is probably not to be understood as the intimate term "Daddy,"[17] but it certainly represents a distinctive and therefore remembered term (cf. Gal 4:6; Rom 8:15). Mark 14:36 is the only use of the term by Jesus. Jesus' prayer is set in the context of God's power to accomplish what God wants and of Jesus' obedience to the Father's will. What ensues is the mystery of human suffering met by the mystery of divine faithfulness and love.

Jesus' final expression in Mark's Gospel prior to his death is the cry of dereliction, "My God, my God, why have you forsaken me?" (15:34). Taunted by his enemies, abandoned by his disciples, and mocked by the soldiers, he resorts to his mother tongue and to the Scriptures (Ps 22:1).

Is this a cry of despair, a loud cry of one who in his death struggle with evil fears he is on the brink of defeat? Or is it a confession of faith in God's power to overcome the forces of darkness and evil, even when things look bleak? Could Jesus have had in mind the rest of Psalm 22, with its positive ending? Countless scholars through the years have debated these questions, arriving at differing conclusions.[18] Brown, having tracked the arguments both pro and con, offers a fitting conclusion. Jesus naturally feels forsaken. "It was not in rage but in prayer that Jesus screamed his loud cry, even as the martyrs in Rev. 6:10 shouted with a loud cry their prayer for God to intervene."[19]

> His "Why?" is that of someone who has plumbed the depths of the abyss and feels enveloped by the power of darkness. Jesus is not questioning the existence of God or the power of God to do something about what is happening; he is questioning the silence of the one whom he called "My God."[20]

Martin Hengel has done a thorough study of the practice of crucifixion in the ancient world. Interestingly, he chose as the study's title the three Latin words used first by Origen, *mors turpissima crucis*, (the utterly vile death of the cross).[21] Not only was the pain hideously intense, but also the death carried with it shame and humiliation. A crucified Messiah, that seems to be a contradiction in terms, lies at the heart of Mark's Gospel.

Mark's depiction of the crucifixion, however, is realistic and to the point. It is not overdone. There is no glorification of suffering, as if Jesus had to endure the most pain of any individual ever if he were to bear humanity's sin. The atonement is not built on a quantitative notion, that the more one suffers the better she or he will be.

Mark articulates two responses to the crucifixion that are highly instructive. First, the temple curtain that separated the Holy of Holies from the outer court was ripped (the same violent verb Mark used for the tearing of the heavens at Jesus' baptism, 1:10) from top to bottom. The ripping of the curtain symbolizes the climax of the anti-temple strand that has run through the Gospel. The tearing of the curtain symbolized "the end of the exclusion from the place of God's presence of all who were not priests, of all who were not Jews."[22] Moreover, the tearing of the curtain also symbolized the end of the protection one had from dangerous encounters with God, who is no longer limited to sacred spaces and who radically changes those whom he encounters.

Mark describes a second response to the crucifixion from a Roman officer, who stood observing the scene and confessed, "Truly this man was God's Son!" (15:39). If there had been any doubt before, there need be none now. Jesus' death opened the door for non-Jews as well as Jews.

Furthermore, the confession says something about God as well. Jesus qua Son of God is the one who reveals God, and this happens at his death, not in his exaltation or glorification. "The narrative seems to be emphasizing starkly that God is to be seen in this figure of powerlessness, weakness, and death."[23]

The final chapter of Mark has perplexed and intrigued scholars since it was written. The best manuscripts available to us testify that the Gospel ends with 16:8 and the account of the women leaving the tomb in terror and amazement, saying nothing to anyone, for they were afraid. The so-called shorter ending as well as the longer ending that includes 16:9–20 is missing from the earliest and most reliable manuscripts. The textual evidence as well as strong internal considerations argues in favor of verse 8 as the conclusion to the Gospel.

Interpreters must wonder: Was an ending torn off the manuscript at an early stage and lost? Did Mark intend to conclude the story with this some-what bizarre finale? What is implied by an ending, which turns out not to be an ending at all? The best alternative is to acknowledge the problem and to read the Gospel ending at 16:8.

There have been a number of interpretations, the most plausible being that of Andrew Lincoln, who insists that verses 7 and 8 be taken together. In verse 7 the young man in white by the tomb makes a promise: "Go, tell his disciples and Peter that he is going ahead of you to Galilee; there you will see him, just as he told you" (cf. 14:28). The "terror and amazement" that overcame the women with the result that "fear" kept them from carrying out their assign-ment is a clear statement of disobedience. The divine messenger had com-manded them to tell, but they said "nothing to anyone." And yet "the double irony is that they are to tell a promise that failure is not the end, but then *they* fail to tell and it *is* the end of the narrative."[24]

The promise, however, turns out to be "a promise of restoration after fail-ure." The silence of the women, caused by their fear, was overcome by Jesus' word of promise. The sequence of promise, failure, and restoration becomes a powerful symbol in that it accounts for human disobedience and yet offers hope beyond failure.

Juel reminds us that the narrative cannot contain the promise. Mark for-bids closure.

> The doors in Mark's Gospel are emphatically open: The curtain of the temple is rent asunder (as is the curtain of the heavens at Jesus' baptism) and the stone is rolled back from the tomb. There is surely disappoint-ment as the women flee dashing hopes that at least one group of follow-ers will prove faithful. But Jesus is out of the tomb: God is no longer safely behind the curtain. . . . The end is not yet, but the story gives good reasons to remain hopeful even in the face of disappointment. The pos-sibilities of eventual enlightenment for the reader remain in the hands of the divine actor who will not be shut in—or out.[25]

16

The Gospel of Matthew

The Gospel of Matthew appropriately appears as the first book in the New Testament. It serves as a bridge connecting the two major divisions of the canon, and though there is a sharp division expressed between Matthew's community and the Pharisees, nevertheless, the text recognizes the necessary fulfillment of the Torah and functions as a fitting point of contact with Israel and Israel's history. In the first four chapters, there are five biblical citations introduced by the stereotypical formula, "This was to fulfill the words spoken through the prophet" (1:22; 2:15, 17, 23; 4:14). Furthermore, the Sermon on the Mount is headlined by Jesus' declaration, "Do not think that I have come to abolish the law or the prophets; I have come not to abolish but to fulfill" (5:17). God has achieved in Jesus those saving purposes previously recorded in the Jewish Scriptures. As Son of Abraham, as Son of David, as well as Son of God, Jesus is rooted in Israel's history and the fulfillment of Israel's heritage. He insists that "until heaven and earth pass away, not one letter, not one stroke of a letter, will pass from the law until all is accomplished" (5:18).

What can we say about the community to which Matthew wrote? It was likely a Jewish Christian group for whom the Scriptures were sacred. Alongside the fulfillment motif noted above, however, there is also a wholesale denunciation of the scribes and Pharisees (chap. 23), as well as an occasion in the Sermon on the Mount, when Matthew's readers are told that "unless your righteousness exceeds that of the scribes and Pharisees, you will never enter the kingdom of heaven" (5:20). Furthermore, when the parable of the Wicked Tenants is recorded in 21:33–44, the narrator comments, "When the chief priests and the Pharisees heard his parables, they realized that he was speaking about them. They wanted to arrest him, but they feared the crowds, because they regarded him as a prophet" (21:45–46). Likewise at the end of the parable of the Wedding Feast, the Pharisees are particularly singled out by their angry response to Jesus.

These attacks on the Jewish leadership likely reveal a Christian community shortly after the parting of the ways between Judaism and Christianity toward the latter part of the first century. Whether or not one can locate this split in relation to the curses pronounced on deviates at Jamnia remains to be seen, but at least one can catch a definite struggle between Matthew's community and "the synagogue down the street."

Yet one must also note the three negative notes regarding the Gentiles in the Sermon on the Mount (5:47; 6:7, 32). Plus, in the missionary sermon, as well as in the apocalyptic discourse, the disciples are told to expect rejection from Gentiles (10:18, 22; 24:9; cf. 18:17). These derogatory references, combined with the harsh comments regarding the Jews, supports the notion that "Matthew's community was a rather beleaguered sect," suggesting that "the evangelist and the readers were very much at odds, not only with contemporary Judaism but also with the Gentile world."[1]

The structure of the book indicates that it is intended to be read as a historical narrative beginning with the birth of Jesus that takes the reader through his ministry, his final journey to Jerusalem, and his death and resurrection. As with Mark, Matthew gives evidence of a line of tension that runs through each portion of the narrative and that blossoms into conflict at key points, culminating in the crucifixion and its resolution, the resurrection.

In relation to Mark, Matthew has expanded the narrative both at the beginning and at the end. At the beginning we have a lengthy genealogy that in stereotypical fashion ("fourteen generations," 1:17) traces Jesus' family tree back to Abraham. Then we read of Jesus' conception and birth (1:18–24), the visit of the magi (2:1–12), his escape to Egypt (2:13–15), the story of the slaughter of the infants in and around Bethlehem (2:16–18), and the return of the holy family from Egypt to Nazareth (2:19–23). At the end we hear of the women's encounter at the tomb with the man dressed in white who announces Jesus' resurrection (28:1–10), the rumor that the guards had stolen the body and hidden it (28:11–15), and the commissioning of the disciples to declare the gospel to all the nations (28:16–20).

Furthermore, the book is marked by five sermons or speeches made by Jesus, which provide a substructure (or some would contend, the structure) of the Gospel. Each sermon ends with the expression, "Now when Jesus had finished saying these things . . ."

5:1–7:29	The Sermon on the Mount
10:1–11:1	The Missionary Sermon

Along the way, there are what Luz refers to as "signals," that is, passages that stand out because of a fuller significance they have when read in the larger context.[2] For example, the genealogy, with which the story begins (1:1–17), is marked by the names of four women, each of whom contributes to make it an unconventional genealogy: Tamar (Gen 38), Rahab (Josh 2), Ruth (Ruth 1–4), and Bathsheba (2 Sam 11–12). Gaventa contends that what the women have in common is that none of their stories fits the way things are "supposed" to be, that each is presented as threatening the status quo and that each is threatened by it.[3]

The fact that Bathsheba is depicted the way she is ("the wife of Uriah the Hittite") tends to underscore the fact that she was included because she was non-Jewish (otherwise her ethnic identity is unknown), and she may have become with the other three women trailblazers for other non-Jews in the church. The only problem with this explanation is that Mary is a Jew and not a Gentile. Minear responds that though not all were Gentiles, "however humble or despised, they had been significant instruments through whom God had kept covenant with the people, maintaining them in existence from the beginning."[4]

It is intriguing that with the birth narratives we encounter two critical names for Jesus. One comes in a dream to Joseph as he wrestles with what to do with this pregnant wife. An angel tells him to name the baby Jesus, "for he will save his people from their sins" (1:21).[5] This naming falls on the heels of the explanation given by the same angel, who quotes the LXX of Isaiah 7:14 which uses Emmanuel, which means "God is with us" (1:23). The former name symbolizes the work to be done in connection with Israel's sins. The latter expresses the conviction of God's presence, the final promise made to the church (28:20).

The Sermon on the Mount (5:1–7:29) follows a clear outline. First, the blessings of the kingdom are offered (5:3–16) in terms of the "Beatitudes" (5:3–12) and the calls to discipleship (5:13–16). Then attention is drawn to "the righteousness that exceeds that of the scribes and Pharisees" (5:17–7:12). Five of the seven occurrences of the word "righteousness" (all added by the evangelist) appear in the Sermon. Following the so-called Golden Rule, readers are confronted with alternatives, either entering through the narrow or the wide gate or building one's house on sand or on rock (7:13–27).

The Beatitudes raise an interesting problem. Have they been ethicized by the evangelist so that they are entrance requirements into the kingdom of God, or are they "eschatological promises announced to the unsuspecting or undeserving"? Guelich makes a strong case for the latter, contending that they are similar to an announcement of congratulations as in Isaiah 61:1. The promise is not only future but also present.

> They address those who already *are* what they are identified as being. The identity of the Beatitudes' subjects first comes into being in the encounter with God through Jesus' ministry in which God's redemptive initiative in history confronts the individual and calls for a decision of surrender, to yield one's all to God. To those who so respond out of desperation, the subjects of the Beatitudes, the various promises of the future are given. These promises are given as assurance rather than reward.[6]

When one turns to the antitheses and the rules for piety in 5:17–6:18, one is confronted with statements severe and concrete in the demands laid on the readers. Hardly can one encounter harsher commandments in the New Testament. Those who casually comment that the Christian life is only a matter of living the Sermon on the Mount obviously haven't read it lately. Jesus radicalizes the law, turning hatred into murder, lust into adultery, and forbidding the remarriage of divorced people.

Two features in the text need attention in light of these tough words. First, human beings are not abandoned in their struggle to keep the law. In the middle of the main section of the Sermon comes the Lord's Prayer (6:9–15), suggesting that it is for active, engaged followers and not merely a prayer for a few. Subsections flank it dealing with various issues relating humans to God. "Human beings are not left to their own devices in their striving for superior righteousness and perfection. They are sustained by God. They are permitted to pray."[7] The word "father" occurs no fewer than ten times throughout this central section of the book. While readers are told to strive first for the kingdom and God's righteousness, they are promised "all these things will be given to you as well" (6:33). Perhaps this is what Jesus had in mind later when he spoke of his burden being easy and his yoke being light (11:30).

Second, "mercy and obedience, promise and demand—all are interlocked in Matthew."[8]

> The Sermon is not simply a promise of salvation, nor does it merely impose demands. Instead, it represents a continuing relation, confronting those men and women with whom God is prepared to walk with the demands he imposes upon them. At the same time, precisely because of those demands, it leads them to a sense of promise from that very God who dwells with human beings before they dwell with him.[9]

The section that begins with 9:35 and continues through 10:42 functions as a manual of instruction for missionaries. They are not to go to the Gentiles or to the Samaritans, but only to "the lost sheep of the house of Israel" (10:6), to carry on the ministry of Jesus, not to replace Jesus but to follow him as he continues to minister in the world. This involves declaring the good news that the kingdom of heaven has come near (10:7), as well as curing the sick, raising the dead, and casting out demons. The missionaries are not to go loaded down with belongings, nor are they to charge anyone for their services; however, they are to accept the generosity of the people if it is offered them. The disciples, like their Master, are to anticipate persecution, because the intrusion of God's kingdom into this world inevitably arouses opposition (5:10–12; 6:1–18; 10:16–23; 12:1–14; 14:1–12).

As Son of God, Jesus is for Matthew the reliable teacher. He does not advocate the abrogation of the Mosaic law, but rather provides its definitive interpretation. The Sermon on the Mount, for example, does not replace the Torah, but radically restates its demands in the light of God's kingly rule. Six antitheses are stated in the Sermon with the repeated pattern: "You have heard that it was said . . . but I say to you" (5:21–26, 27–30, 31–32, 33–37, 38–42, 43–48). Each antithesis represents a radicalizing of the Torah. At one point later in his ministry the Pharisees send to him a lawyer, rooted in the traditions of Israel, to flatter him and to put to him a trick question: "Which commandment in the law is the greatest?" He replies, " 'You shall love the Lord your God with all your heart, and with all your soul, and with all your mind. . . .' [A] second is like it: 'You shall love your neighbor as yourself.' On these two commandments hang all the law and the prophets" (22:34–40). The key to the Torah is love, even love of the enemy (6:44–47), and Jesus represents the full expression of love. In this sense, Jesus does not come to replace Moses but to complete what God has begun with Moses.

While Jesus is characterized in Matthew as a teacher, he is also the healer of a variety of sicknesses and exorcizer of demons. Between the Sermon on the Mount and the address to the missionaries (chap. 10) are ten accounts of miracles of healing. Perhaps the most moving story is that of the healing of the woman who had been hemorrhaging for twelve years, who reached out and touched Jesus' garment (9:18–26), which is sandwiched between the story of the restoration of the daughter of the synagogue leader. Both figures, coming from different walks of life, demonstrate considerable faith and are commended for it.

Of all the disciples Peter appears more prominently in Matthew than in any other Gospel. Three occasions are unique to Matthew. First, when the disciples are together in the boat on a stormy sea, Jesus comes to them walking on the water and tells them not to fear, for he is present with them. Then Peter makes a request, "Command me to come to you on the water." And Jesus says, "Come." When Peter courageously steps out of the boat, he is enabled, like

Jesus, to walk on the rugged sea. But, alas, Peter cannot walk on the sea for long. The boisterous storm becomes more than he can handle, and he begins to sink under the waves. He feels the tug between the chaotic sea and the firm hand of Jesus, and Jesus rescues him (14:28–31).

Second, each of the Synoptic Gospels records for us Peter's powerful confession about Jesus, "You are the Messiah, the Son of the living God" (16:16), but it is Matthew alone who goes on to include the blessing pronounced,

> "Blessed are you, Simon son of Jonah! For flesh and blood has not revealed this to you, but my Father in heaven. And I tell you, you are Peter, and on this rock I will build my church, and the gates of Hades will not prevail against it. I will give you the keys of the kingdom of heaven, and whatever you bind on earth will be bound in heaven, and whatever you loose on earth will be loosed in heaven." (16:17–20)

With some delight, many Protestants take note that when Peter has a difficult time with the meaning of what he confessed, he is chastised by his Lord: "Get behind me, Satan! You are a stumbling block to me; for you are setting your mind not on divine things but on human things" (16:23). The rock has become a stone over which people stumble. Matthew, however, does not hesitate to warn all the disciples about the life they are living. Twice the haunting phrase "weeping and grinding of teeth" (24:51; 25:30) is used to depict the place of deep darkness where the hypocrites are consigned.

The third distinctive appearance of Peter in Matthew's Gospel comes when the collectors of the temple tax query him as to whether his teacher advocates paying the temple tax or not (17:24–27). Before the destruction of the temple, payment of the half-shekel tax for the upkeep of the temple was a critical sign of solidarity for all Jewish families. After the destruction of Jerusalem, however, the Romans continued to collect the tax and used it for the temple to Jupiter in Rome. Jesus responds by declaring that the children are free. However, "so that we do not give offense" to the authorities, he then sends Peter to the sea and directs him to take the first fish that he catches, which will have a coin in its mouth, and to give that coin "to them for you and me." Senior comments, "This story provides the Jewish Christians a rationale for paying the tax without separating themselves too radically from their Jewish neighbors (prior to CE 70) or creating problems with the Roman authorities (after CE 70)."[10]

Chapter 18 contains the fourth major discourse of Matthew's, one depicting life in the ("Matthean"?) community. Two issues emerge in this discourse. One is the term "little ones," which becomes a critical phrase in the instructions to the community. Matthew first mentions "children" as of the essence of the kingdom of heaven (18:1–5) and moves quickly into a warning against despising "the little ones" (18:6, 10). Those who are prominent in the community are not to look down on the "little ones." As Boring puts it, "The point is clear: Heaven does not give up on the marginal, the lapsed, or the strayed, and what heaven values so dearly cannot be distained by the 'big people' in the church on earth."[11]

Second is the stress on church discipline. Apart from the Pastoral Letters, nowhere does one find in the New Testament canon such precise instructions laid out for the discipline of members of the community who have gone astray (18:15–20). Those members who have the responsibility of correcting fellow members are provided careful guidelines for what to do and even how to turn the evidence over to the church. Interestingly, the instructions are set between the parable of the Lost Sheep, with its stress on the searching shepherd (18:12–14), and Peter's concern about how often he should forgive another member of the church who sins against him (18:21–22).

The story of the rich young man figures prominently in chapter 19 (19:16–26). He had kept the commandments from his youth and yet he is aware that he lacks something in order to "have eternal life." Jesus directs him to give what possessions he has to the poor, in order to be "perfect." In the history of the church, this Matthean concern for perfection (see 5:48) has fueled the monastic movement, particularly involving the giving up of one's possessions to become perfect and implying that there were two levels of Christians, one group that kept the commandments (the ordinary Christians) and another group that renounced possessions (the monastics). Matthew, however, means by becoming perfect, being undivided in one's obedience to Christ. Jesus previously warned about storing up treasures on earth (6:19) and spoke a parable about selling what one has to purchase the pearl of great price (13:46).

Lest one think that Matthew's Gospel is exclusively one of demand, in which people do good and thus receive divine blessing, nothing jolts the sentimentality more than the parable of the Laborers in the Vineyard (20:1–16). In a vivid and even abrasive story, the offensive character of grace is depicted, inevitably leaving the reader pondering whether the owner was really fair and whether the laborers who worked all day didn't have a legitimate beef. The context needs to be kept in mind. Previously Matthew records the account of the rich young man, who refuses to leave all and to follow Jesus (19:16–26). The audience is primarily the disciples (19:23, 27; 20:17). The parable is a part of their instruction as they move from Galilee to Jerusalem (19:1; 20:18). The parable is told not to the crowds or even the seekers, but to insiders who presumably know something of the measure of grace. Finally, the story is bracketed by two reversal sayings (19:30; 20:16), both of which are threats to those who consider themselves the privileged who enjoy a special relationship with Jesus. Matthew makes it plain that divine grace does not rest on the merit system. The owner's decision to pay those who worked only a single hour the same as those who labored in the heat of the day upsets the entire societal order. Divine grace is a great equalizer, which rips away presumed privilege and puts all recipients on a par.

In chapter 25, Matthew tells the powerful story of divine judgment that falls on "the least of these my brothers and sisters" when they have failed to minister in his name. A critical interpretive issue arises in determining exactly who are the actors in the parable. Luz has traced three possible solutions that have recurred throughout the history of the church.[12] One he labels "the universal interpretive model," which identifies the "brothers and sisters" as all of the suffering people of the earth, both non-Christians as well as Christians. The passage is then the basis for a practical, nondogmatic Christianity. Freed from the specter of particularism, it plays well in a modern, post-Christian culture.

Luz's second solution is "the classic interpretive model," in which "the least of my brothers and sisters" are baptized members of the church. The intent is primarily to motivate the church to do acts of compassion and deeds of kindness. In the final judgment the criterion for Christians is the concern concretely expressed toward their fellow Christians, who are persecuted or suffering. The third possibility Luz labels "the exclusive interpretive model," which takes "all the nations" to read "all the pagans" and "the least" to be Christians. Thus it is only non-Christians who stand before the judgment bench and are judged by how they have treated Christians. Rather than carrying parenetic intent, the passage would offer comfort to the oppressed, persecuted missionaries.

Luz, having carefully surveyed what others have thought and written concerning this passage, makes a strong case in favor of the second alternative ("the classic interpretive model"), contending that Matthew has in mind the church as it answers to its heavenly Judge. In the suffering "sisters and brothers," he has in mind not every suffering human, but basically suffering disciples (so 23:8; 28:10), who have been sent into the world as missionaries of the gospel. The passage serves as a reminder to the church members of the earlier judgment scene in 7:21–23. It is the deeds that matter, not a right confession.

For the most part, Matthew follows closely Mark's crucifixion narrative, though Matthew's story is replete with the apocalyptic details—the darkness (24:45), the raising of many of the deceased saints, and the shaking of the earth (27:51–53). Moreover, in the account of the resurrection, Matthew, unlike Mark, has the women who come to the tomb early in the morning faithfully reporting what they had seen and heard (28:8), in contrast with their silence in Mark's Gospel (16:7–8).

At a final scene Matthew 28:16–20 provides an apt conclusion to the Gospel. On the one hand, Jesus gives a commission to his followers to "make disciples" not merely of "the lost sheep of the house of Israel" (10:6), but of "all nations." On the other hand, Jesus, the one to whom all authority now has been given, promises to be with the disciples "always, to the end of the age" (28:20; cf. 1:23; 11:28–29; 18:20). Through the death and resurrection of Jesus the non-Jewish world, as well as the Jews, is opened up now to hear and respond to the gospel.

A final word concerning the Christology of Matthew. Though the primary titles for Jesus appear profusely in Matthew's Gospel—Christ (fourteen times), Lord (thirty times), Son of God (seventeen times), Son of Man (thirty-one times), and Son of David (eight times)—and though debate has raged for many years around the significance of the titles, it seems unlikely that titles are the clue to Matthew's Christology. Matthew tells a story in which the promises of a redemptive God are fulfilled. From the outset Jesus is a redemptive figure who does not annul the moral teaching of the law and the prophets (5:17–20), for he is the one to save the people from their sins (1:21). "Sins," which are the obstacle to full humanity for Matthew, are not to be taken (as with Paul) as a demonic force, but rather the deeds, thoughts, and words, understood in the light of the law authoritatively interpreted through the Christ. "God's redemptive purpose, in the Matthean perspective, is thus carried out and con-firmed through the authority of the risen Christ. . . . Redemption is not grounded in his death as an atoning event, but in the authority of the risen Christ who does and will do what, according to the angel prior to his birth, he is supposed to do—save his people from their sins—by way of forgiveness."[13]

17

The Gospel of Luke

The author of the Gospel of Luke, whose name occurs three times in the Pauline corpus (Phlm 24; Col 4:14; 2 Tim 4:11), is sometimes identified as the friend of Paul, the "beloved physician." The name "Luke," however, is never mentioned in connection with the third Gospel or with the book of Acts. Both volumes are anonymous; both are dedicated to "Theophilus," most likely the author's patron. A continuity of the stories, a similarity in literary style, and a shared perspective support the contention that the two volumes have the same writer, whether he be Luke or someone else.

Commentators tend to agree on the structure of the third Gospel:

1. The prologue to Luke and to Acts (1:1–4)
2. Jesus' birth and John's birth (1:5–2:52)
3. Jesus' preparation for his public ministry (3:1–4:13)
4. Jesus' ministry in Galilee (4:14–9:50)
5. Jesus' journey toward Jerusalem with his disciples (9:51–19:27)
6. Jesus' ministry in and around Jerusalem (19:28–21:38)
7. Jesus' passion and resurrection (22:1–24:53)

The prologue is interesting because it reveals that other accounts of the life and ministry of Jesus were in circulation in the church as early as the time of Luke. The aim of Luke is to produce for the reader an accurate account of Jesus' life and ministry that leads to *asphaleian* (1:4). Though the NRSV translates the Greek word *asphaleia* as "truth," it might better be rendered as "security" or "assurance." "Truth" might imply criticism of older texts as if they were inaccurate or untrue, which is not Luke's intention. Rather Luke wishes to provide an account that will bring to the readers the certainty of the gospel.

Four aspects of the infancy narratives in Luke (chaps. 1 and 2) elicit our attention. First, the author interweaves the announcement, conception, birth, naming, and circumcision of John with the announcement, conception, birth, naming, and circumcision of Jesus. Back and forth, the narrative oscillates, from one character to the other, each account with its own details. One cannot but anticipate that the two figures will significantly influence one another in the years ahead.

Second, we note the powerful hymns and prophecies sung or spoken by Mary (1:46–55), by Zechariah (1:68–79), and by Simeon (2:29–31). Mary's "magnificat" is patterned after Hannah's prayer prayed at Samuel's birth (1 Sam 2:1–10). Like Hannah, Mary rejoices over God's activity on behalf of the lowly and the hungry, borrowing heavily from the LXX language. In addition to these hymns, the angelic choirs sing at the birth of the Christ child (2:14), giving the prologue a joyously liturgical cast.

Third, only Luke, in telling the story of Jesus confounding the elders in the temple, relates information about Jesus' boyhood (2:41–51). It is a fascinating gap in the narrative of Jesus' life that later spurred writers of the noncanonical gospels to speculate as to Jesus' precocious behavior and extraordinary powers. Luke's story seems tame alongside the others, and yet he shares with them the recognition of Jesus' greatness even in his childhood. For example, the Infancy Gospel of Thomas, sometimes dated as early as 150 CE, relates the story of how Jesus as a boy of about five makes clay birds in a stream on the Sabbath. When a Jewish man comes by and chastises Jesus for violating the Sabbath, Jesus claps his hands and the sparrows fly away, thus removing any evidence of his having broken the law. How different the account of Jesus' being left behind in Jerusalem, of his amazing understanding of the law, and of his return with his family to Nazareth!

Fourth, the dialogue between Mary and the angel Gabriel sets the tone for the book. Gabriel appears to Mary and proclaims that she is pregnant because of the Holy Spirit, concluding with the affirmation: "For nothing will be impossible with God." Mary responds simply, "Here am I, the servant of the Lord; let it be with me according to your word" (Luke 1:37–38). A theological case can be made that both Luke and Acts explicate the theme of the plan of God to which Mary (and others) are obedient. " 'Plan of God' refers to God as the one whose intention and oversight govern the events that unfold, both the events of Jesus' own life and the way in which the witness moves throughout the cities of the Mediterranean world."[1] Jesus as a boy, though able to converse with the elders in the temple and attentive to his Father's business, nevertheless exhibits appropriate obedience to his parents.

Several events in Luke's narrative serve as preparation for Jesus in his ministry. First is the location of the time and place with reference to the calendar, the authority structures of the Roman Empire, the political leadership, and the high priests (3:1–2). Luke as historian provides a date and place for the narrative that will unfold. This is no fairy tale, "once upon a time" story, but a narrative that unfolds in real time, amid the power structures who control the empire and for whom Jesus is bound to be a threat.

Second, there is the proclamation of John the Baptist (3:2–20), who thunders away at the people, calling them to repentance and forgiveness. John is clear that he is not the Messiah, but in the words of Isaiah, he is "the voice of one crying in the wilderness," urging the people to prepare for the coming of the Lord. Tax collectors are to take no more from the people than the law allows, and soldiers are to extract heavy fees from their subjects no longer (3:3–14).

Third, Jesus is baptized and a voice comes from heaven, "You are my Son, the Beloved; with you I am well pleased" (3:22). This confirmation of Jesus by John and by the voice out of heaven underscores who Jesus is. In the descent of the Spirit on Jesus as a dove and in the later story of the reading of the scroll at Nazareth, with the words of Isaiah 61:1, "The Spirit of the Lord is upon me, because he has anointed me to bring good news to the poor" (Luke 4:18), Luke presents Jesus as the one who himself is anointed with the Spirit and who then dispenses it. It may be surprising that Luke, however, makes very little use of Jesus' possession of the Spirit throughout the remainder of his narrative.

Fourth, an abbreviated genealogy takes Jesus back to Adam (3:23–38). Interestingly, in distinction from Matthew's Gospel, there is no mention of Abraham nor of the four women who represent the distinctiveness of Matthew's line. Luke simply concludes the genealogy with "son of Adam, son of God" (3:38).

Fifth, Luke relates the temptation of Jesus in the wilderness (4:1–12). Quoting Deuteronomy three times, Jesus uses the Word of God to counter the wiles of the devil and to authenticate the reign of the new anointed Son of God.

Following his baptism and testing by Satan, Jesus returns to Nazareth, where he has been reared and where his ministry actually begins (4:14–30). He goes to the synagogue on the Sabbath, and is invited to join in reading the lesson of the morning, which includes portions of Isaiah 58 and 61.

> The Spirit of the Lord is upon me, because he has anointed me to bring good news to the poor. He has sent me to proclaim release to the captives and recovery of sight to the blind, to let the oppressed go free, to proclaim the year of the Lord's favor. (Luke 4:18–19)

When he finishes reading the lesson, he declares, "Today this scripture has been fulfilled in your hearing." Today in the presence of Jesus himself salvation has arrived. The newness of the messianic hope has taken on concrete form in the presence of this young man from Galilee. Jesus' word is fulfilled time and thus is not confined to past history, nor is it relegated to the future.

The local attendants at the synagogue are pleased with Jesus and speak well of him. They acknowledge that this is Joseph's son and that he reads the text effectively. He responds that they would no doubt expect him to do the same miracles in Nazareth that he has done in Capernaum, but that they need to know that he has come to serve a broader audience than simply the hometown group. He uses as illustrations Elijah's ministry to the widow of Zarephath and Elisha's healing of the Syrian Naaman. There were no doubt needy people within the bounds of the Jewish community at the time, but in both cases outsiders were healed. The reminder of that portion of their history infuriates the citizens of Nazareth, who then attempt to push him off a cliff.

The neighbors' wrath is aroused when they perceive that the good news includes the poor of all nations and not of the Jews alone. "It is this veiled intimation that the prophet would be for all and not just for them—and in the reader's understanding, that God's visitation and salvation were to be for the poor and oppressed of all nations and not just for Jews—that arouses the neighbors' wrath, impelling them to fulfill Jesus' statement: he is not acceptable in his own country because his mission extends beyond his own country."[2]

Chapters 5–9 of Luke's Gospel contain stories of Jesus' healing, his work of exorcism, his calling of the disciples, and the so-called Sermon on the Plain (6:17–49). Since the latter passage is paralleled by a section in Matthew (5:1–7:29), it is worth considering some of the differences. For example, the first of the Beatitudes states simply "Blessed are you who are poor" (6:20) and is accompanied later by a "woe" ("But woe to you who are rich, for you have received your consolation" [6:24]). Poverty and wealth stand out throughout the Gospel as prominent themes. Jesus declares that he has no place to lay his head (9:58), and he depends on the support of others (8:1–3). Luke understands wealth as a temptation to prestige and security apart from God and warns against "all kinds of greed" (12:13–21, 33–34). This stance toward wealth takes on added significance in that giving to someone, without expecting reciprocation, was the same as embracing that person as family. Thus, the rich young man in refusing to sell what he had and give to the poor was making not only an economic decision but also a social one (18:18–23). The same holds true for the rich man who distances himself from Lazarus, the beggar at his gate, and who finds himself in Hades after death (16:19–31).

A break in the narrative comes at 9:51 when Jesus "sets his face to go to Jerusalem" and as he instructs his followers along the way. The narrative now focuses on Jesus and his destiny. The journey to Jerusalem becomes the occasion for his teaching concerning what it means to be a true disciple.

Jesus takes heavy criticism for eating with sinners and in response tells several parables about the lost being found. The section is flooded with parables of grace as well as demands of discipleship. Included in these chapters are the parables of the Lost Sheep and the Lost Coin; the parable of the Prodigal Son; the parable of the Rich Man and Lazarus; the parable of the Widow and the Unjust Judge; and the parable of the Great Dinner. The familiar story of the prodigal son seems to be about the return of a lost son and the begrudging stance of his elder brother, and yet the remarkable character is the generous father, who meets both sons with openness and acceptance. These stories show God to be at work actively in changing history. For example, the parable of the Rich Man and Lazarus (Luke 16:19–31) demonstrates how the reversal takes place. "What seems to be beyond dispute is that the vision of a history reshaped by the power of God is Luke's contribution to the understanding of gospel."[3]

The section from 9:51–19:27 concludes with the parable of the Ten Pounds. Luke's version of the parable differs significantly from both Mark (13:34) and Matthew (25:14–30) and is no doubt set in a political context involving Archelaus, son of Herod and his effort to gain the kingship from Rome. Luke's parable also supplies a corrective to the notion that the kingdom of God is to appear soon (19:11). There is work to be done (i.e., trading the pounds), and opposition still lies ahead before the kingdom of God comes.

The parable of the pounds seems to contradict the preceding story of Jesus' encounter with Zacchaeus. Jesus declares to Zacchaeus, "Today salvation has come to this house. For the Son of Man came to seek out and to save the lost" (19:9–10). This is a part of the establishing of the will of God. As Tiede puts it, "Jesus is not merely acting on a whim. He is enacting the will and reign of God and is under some constraint from his mission to go to this house."[4]

The next section of Luke's Gospel (19:28–21:38) begins with the entry into Jerusalem (19:28) and concludes with the crowds coming to the temple in the early morning to listen to Jesus teach (21:37–38). As he had earlier attacked the Pharisees (11:37–44) and the lawyers (11:45–52), Jesus includes in this teaching an attack on the scribes (20:45–57). No scene in the Gospel is more poignant than Jesus' description of the scribes "who like to walk around in long robes, and love to be greeted with respect in the marketplaces, and to have the best seats in the synagogues and places of honor at banquets. They devour widows' houses and for the sake of appearance say long prayers. They will receive the greater condemnation" (20:46–47). Luke then sets this description over against the poor widow, who puts into the collection box two small copper coins. She out of her poverty gives away all she has to live on (21:4).

The passion narrative in Luke is dominated by the Passover meal that Jesus eats with his disciples (22:7–30). The meal is interpreted in light of his upcoming death (22:15, 20) and his eschatological anticipation ("I will not eat it until it is fulfilled in the kingdom of God. . . . [F]rom now on I will not drink of the fruit of the vine until the kingdom of God comes" [22:16, 18]). Whereas Mark's institution of the Lord's Supper is rather terse (14:22–25), Luke expands the institution to include two cup-words (22:17–18, 20), plus the postresurrection revelation to the men walking to Emmaus (24:30). Forgiveness lies at the heart of the story. Luke alone of the Gospel writers has the crucified Jesus ask pardon for those who crucified him (23:34) (though this verse is missing in many early and diverse manuscripts).

In addition to forgiveness, Luke is concerned about the witness of the church to the world. The character of that witness emerges in the unique stories of Jesus' appearances (1) to the women who had come early in the morning to the tomb (24:1–12), (2) to the two men with whom he walked to Emmaus (24:13–35), and (3) to the disciples with whom he shared a breakfast on the beach (24:36–49).

1. The women had stuck by Jesus through the time of his rejection and crucifixion, not fleeing as the disciples had fled. Coming to the tomb to embalm the body of Jesus, they are met by two men in dazzling white attire, who remind the women that Jesus had promised that he would be crucified and raised from the dead. The women remembered and went to spread the word to disbelieving and skeptical disciples. Only Peter is sufficiently convinced by the witness of the women to investigate further and find out for himself (24:1–12).

2. The two disciples headed toward Emmaus are fascinated enough with Jesus incognito to listen to his interpretation of the Scriptures and invite him to stay at their home. After Jesus broke bread, their eyes were opened, and they recognized him. Though Jesus departs, the two walk back to Jerusalem, find the disciples, and report convincingly what had happened to them (24:13–35).

3. Finally on Luke's postresurrection list are the disciples as a whole, who initially react to the risen Jesus with paralyzing fear, thinking him to be a ghost. But he shows them his hands and feet, and, though they still harbor doubts, they watch him eat and listen to his words, words that interpret the Scriptures for them. All three groups serve as models for mission, a prominent theme of Acts.

Perhaps the most difficult interpretive problem in Luke concerns the delay of the parousia. The time of Jesus' return is placed somewhat in doubt in chapters 12 and 19 in connection with the parables (especially 12:35–38, 39–40, 41–46) and in chapter 21 in connection with the coming end time (21:5–8, 9–19, 20–24, 25–36; cf. 17:22–37). The focus is on the dangers that must take place before the return of Jesus.

Furthermore, if Acts is a second volume to Luke, then why write a history of the church if one is daily expecting the end of the world? At least the writer does not expect the return of the Lord at an immediate moment. The world continues day by day and does not come to a drastic end. The church faces a crisis, and if it is to continue, it has to adapt itself to a new situation of continued life in this world.[5]

Hans Conzelmann responded to this issue by replacing the church's eschatological anticipation with "a history of salvation." Luke, he contended, divided history into three phases: the time until John the Baptist (Luke 16:16), the time of Jesus, and the time of the church. Luke "de-eschatologized" the gospel, according to Conzelmann—that is, by anchoring the life of Jesus in the past as a historical event, and then sharply delineating it from the continuing history of the church, Luke replaced the imminent parousia with a historical scheme that includes the duration of God's plan.[6]

The problem with Conzelmann's reading of Luke is his failure to take seriously the variegated way in which the parousia is presented. The end is surely to come; it is only with regard to its timing that Luke remains agnostic.[7] Furthermore, as Carroll points out, in the dramatic presence of the Spirit the eschatological era has already arrived (Luke 11:20). And yet there will be no escaping end-time events. "God's rule is already operative in Jesus' acts of mercy and power. Yet the agenda remains unfinished. . . . God's sovereign rule has not yet been established in its fullness; it remains a matter of hope."[8]

Rather than a preoccupation with the delay of the parousia, the writer of Luke-Acts accepts the God-given Spirit as an expression of the "already" of the kingdom and acknowledges the "not yet" fulfillment of God's promise in hope and confidence. An eschatological dialectic like this must have been at work in the life and thought of the early church since there is little effort to push the parousia into the distant future nor to drop its driving force.

18

The Historical Jesus

Each of the gospel writers paints a distinctive picture of Jesus and his ministry appropriate for the community for which the narrative is written. Mark tells of Jesus' announcing the coming kingdom of God as a new wine that holds the potential of bursting the old wineskins. Jesus' presence on the human scene is likened to the binding of a strong man, whose house then can be ransacked. The conflict implied between Jesus and those who oppose him leads to his rejection and crucifixion. Mark's story is clearly not a dispassionate chronicle of the remembered events of his life, but a proclamation of God's activity based on the historical event of Jesus' life, ministry, and death. It is a declaration of the good news of Jesus Christ, the Son of God.

Matthew, on the other hand, presents Jesus as an authoritative teacher of righteousness, who came not to abolish but to fulfill the law and the prophets. The five sermons that stand out in Matthew's narrative, perhaps paralleling the five books of Moses, suggest an intended reading audience of Jewish Christians for whom the Scriptures were sacred. Throughout the Gospel a final judgment is presupposed and a reward is given, though the reward is not something that humans can earn. The critical issue is: who is the judge of the world? "It is Jesus: the same who is now God's Immanuel and the traveling companion of the community, the same who is now proclaiming God's commandments to the community, and who is leading them in prayer to their Father in heaven."[1]

Luke tells a beautiful story, enriched by several parables not appearing in the other Gospels, such as the parables of the Good Samaritan, the Prodigal Son and his Elder Brother, and the Lost Sheep and Lost Coin. Luke's account of the two men, following the resurrection, who walk to Emmaus and who are joined by the risen Jesus, provides a wonderful conclusion to the narrative, particularly in contrast to the abrupt ending of Mark. John's Gospel, where from the beginning Jesus is the Word made flesh and who throughout declares the great "I am"s, relates a very different story of Jesus from that of the Synoptic Gospels.

Each of the Gospel narratives begins at a different place and provides a different conclusion to the story. The question that has haunted scholars of the Bible since the Enlightenment is which Gospel presents the more historically accurate picture of Jesus. What can one say about a Jesus who is rendered so differently in the four stories that the church has seen fit to canonize? Does one choose Mark's ending to the narrative, where the women go away in fear and trembling and keep silence about what they have seen (Mark 16:8)? Or does one find the Lukan conclusion to the story more reliable (Luke 24:44–53)? Can one harmonize the accounts by smoothing off the rough edges and letting them tell a common story?[2]

We begin by defining what is meant by the term "the historical Jesus." By employing the adjective "historical," a significant issue is raised. Reimarus, the eighteenth-century biographer of Jesus, was probably most instrumental in initiating the understanding of the phrase. He declared that it represents a Jesus as he really was before Christians began to interpret him in ways he did not intend. The phrase quickly took on an antitheological, even anti-Christian cast. Reimarus wanted to draw a clear distinction between what Jesus had said and done and what the evangelists had reported that he had said and done. There was for him a clear distinction between the Jesus of history (i.e., Jesus as he actually was) and the Christ of faith (i.e., what the Gospel writers picture him as being and doing).[3] He drew a sharp line between Jesus as a historical figure and Jesus who is the object of worship in a community of believers. He contended that the latter was highly biased.

When of course any figure of the past is turned over to the historians for investigation, several things occur. For one thing, historians must be skeptical toward their sources, probing them to prove their authenticity. Second, they must resist giving theological answers to historical questions. Did Jesus think himself to be the Messiah? One cannot argue that, because the texts say that he was the Messiah, he must have thought he was the Messiah. What do the historical sources say about who he "thought" he was? The term "the historical Jesus" thus designates not Jesus as he was, but Jesus as the historians can reconstruct him by applying their methods and sifting through their sources. Of necessity they must be skeptical, query their sources, and challenge widely held opinions. They have to deal with verifiable reality, with cause-and-effect relationships.

One inevitable outcome to the problem has been to separate faith from history and to turn the former over to the theologians and the latter to the historians. The problem is that the distinction between beliefs and facts is not so simple. Most historians acknowledge that ideology plays a role in their discipline, that what can be determined as facts is partially dictated by the criteria set forth to measure fact from faith. That historians evidence such biases does not of course invalidate their work; however, a failure to acknowledge one's presuppositions certainly colors the results one offers.

A brief survey of the church's struggle with the reality of the historical Jesus helps to clarify the issue.[4] During the late eighteenth, nineteenth, and early twentieth centuries a plethora of biographies emerged out of this new historical sensitivity. Liberal scholars were eager to liberate the Jesus of history from the scholastic prison house in which the dogmas of the theologians had confined him. They were anxious to let history have its say. David Friedrich Strauss and Ernest Renan, plus a host of lesser lights, produced biographies of Jesus, some of which had a wide influence on the church. (Renan's *Life of Jesus* in 1863 sold over sixty thousand copies in France and was quickly translated into German, Italian, Dutch, and English. The full text is still available on the Internet.) Strauss employed the term "myth" to indicate that many New Testament stories are fashioned along the lines of Old Testament parallels and did not take place as they purport to have been. The point of recording the stories by the evangelists, he contended, is not to provide a historical account of the life of Jesus, but to communicate significant religious ideas. It is the ideas that matter, he argued, and not the accounts themselves.

At the beginning of the twentieth century Albert Schweitzer wrote an influential book, surveying the biographies written up to the moment, and in doing so, exposed two of the failings of the historical biographers. First was their almost naïve tendency to reflect their own era or their own personal interests in their presentations of Jesus. As Schweitzer warns the reader early in his survey, "There is no historical task which so reveals a [person's] true self as the writing of a Life of Jesus."[5] About the Frenchman Renan's romantic portrait of Jesus, Schweitzer writes, "There is scarcely any other work on the subject which so abounds in lapses of taste. It is Christian art in the worst sense of the term—the art of the wax image. The Gentle Jesus, the beautiful Mary, the fair Galileans who formed the retinue of the 'amiable carpenter,' might have been taken over in a body from the shop-window of an ecclesiastical art emporium in Place St. Suplice."[6]

Second, Schweitzer called attention to the consistent failure of the biographers to come to grips with the apocalyptic character of Jesus' life and teaching. Jesus' frequent sayings about the end time always seemed an embarrassment to liberal scholars and were for the most part ignored by the life of Jesus movement. Previously only Reimarus had taken these apocalyptic sayings into account in his portrait of Jesus as an unsuccessful political leader. He had contended that the Gospels were rewritten in light of the hopes of the later church. The story of the resurrection of Jesus, for example, was a deliberate fraud so that the disciples could maintain their positions of power and privilege in the community. Schweitzer himself did not preclude the search for the historical Jesus. He simply felt that no one had written a biography that had taken into account the apocalyptic character of Jesus' ministry and teaching.

Almost contemporary with Schweitzer, Martin Kähler, a teacher of Paul Tillich and a figure highly influential for Rudolf Bultmann, offered an even more devastating critique of the biographers of Jesus. Kähler had no time at all for their historical treatments. He argued that the Gospels do not lend themselves as sources for composing such biographies. They simply do not provide tidbits of data that can be strung together to make a "life of Jesus." They yield no information that lets the reader into Jesus' inner life and development, nor do they offer any help to penetrate Jesus' self-consciousness. Rather, the Gospels are written from a post-Easter perspective by believing people who confess a crucified and risen Lord. The faith of the church rests not on a figure whom the historians can uncover behind the Gospels, but rather on the one whom the Gospels proclaim. To quote Kähler, "It is the task of the dogmatician, in defense of the plain Christian faith, to set limits on the learned pontificating of the historians."[7] The result was a complete divorce between the Jesus of history and the Christ of faith.

Though one could discern a few dissenting voices from time to time (mostly from Great Britain),[8] the arguments of Kähler, developed and refined by Bultmann and Karl Barth, controlled the theological landscape during the first half of the twentieth century. Schweitzer, who had repudiated the liberal lives of Jesus, insisted that Jesus could be recovered, but as an apocalyptic preacher, quite different from both orthodox and liberal expectations of him.

Then in 1953 Ernst Käsemann, in presenting a paper to a gathering of former pupils of Rudolf Bultmann, called for a reopening of the quest for the historical Jesus. Fully cognizant of the weaknesses of the old quest, Käsemann nevertheless argued that to separate the earthly Jesus from the risen Christ was to fall into docetism as well as to forfeit the possibility of drawing a line between the Easter faith of the community and pure folklore. The task was not to produce another biography of Jesus, but, having accepted the Gospels as kerygmatic documents, to trace connections between what the earthly Jesus said and did and what the early church affirmed about him. "My own concern is to show that, out of the obscurity of the life-story of Jesus, certain characteristic traits in his preaching stand out in relatively sharp relief, and that primitive Christianity united its own message with these."[9]

The "new quest," which followed Käsemann's lead, was not enormously productive in terms of books about Jesus. The most widely read volume was Günther Bornkamm's *Jesus of Nazareth*, written in 1956 and translated into English in 1960. Bornkamm makes no effort to write a biography. There is no attempt to deal with the historical or psychological development of Jesus as a human being; there is very little chronology. Neither does Bornkamm dismiss a story as "inauthentic" simply because it reflects the interests and language of the early Christian community. As he states the issue methodologically, "Our task, then, is to seek the history *in* the Kerygma of the Gospels, and in this history to seek the Kerygma. If we are asked to differentiate between the two, that is only for the purpose of revealing more clearly their inter-connection and interpenetration."[10] "Understood in this way, the primitive tradition of Jesus is brimful of history."[11]

Through the period of the 1960s, 1970s, and 1980s, before the days of the Jesus Seminar, liberation theologians became very concerned with what sort of person Jesus really was. Their concern for the concrete praxis of faith led them away from any Christology that tended toward a universal abstraction and in favor of understanding Jesus as anchored in history. Jon Sobrino offers two reasons why it makes sense to begin with the historical Jesus.[12] First, he discerns a noticeable resemblance between the situation in Latin America and the situation in which Jesus lived. It is not simply the poverty and exploitation that characterized first-century life in Palestinian villages and that parallels his situation, but that such poverty and exploitation are "acutely felt and understood to be a sinful situation." Second, the understandings of Jesus in the first-century communities, while diverse, are not fabricated, but generated by people who had been with Jesus from the baptism of John until his death (Acts 1:21–22). Thus, most of the Christology developed by liberation theologians is rooted in the historical Jesus.

A century after Schweitzer and Kähler, we are confronted with the third quest of the historical Jesus, including scholars associated with the Jesus Seminar[13] (led by Robert Funk, John Dominic Crossan, and Marcus Borg) and those unrelated to or even opposed to the Jesus Seminar (such as John Meier, E. P. Sanders, N. T. Wright, and Dale Allison). Opinions vary widely about which sources are most appropriate, what criteria are to be used in determining the authentic sayings of Jesus, how to relate Jesus' actions to his teaching, and to what extent faith is dependent on the results of the historians' conclusions.

For example, in *The Five Gospels*, which reports the results of the Jesus Seminar's efforts to answer the question, "What did Jesus really say?" the commonly accepted two-source theory is embraced. Mark is the earliest written Gospel, and Q is a sayings source employed by Luke and Matthew in the composition of their narratives. The only difficulty is that Mark is given a fairly late dating (approximately 70 CE), and some scholars (Crossan) divide it into two sources (the Secret Gospel of Mark and the Gospel of Mark), and Q is split into at least two sections (an early nonapocalyptic Q and late Q). Furthermore, the noncanonical Gospel of Thomas, customarily dated in the second century and normally thought of as heavily shaped by Gnostic ideas, is treated by the Jesus Seminar as earlier and more trustworthy than Mark. Crossan adds as a very early source for the passion the Cross Gospel, which is embedded in the apocryphal Gospel of Peter.[14] Clearly the canonical decisions of the early church carry no weight at all.

What sort of Jesus emerges from the Jesus Seminar? He is basically a traveling sage who dapples in the wisdom tradition. For most members of the Seminar he becomes a political threat to the Roman forces, who are eventually responsible for his death.[15] Horsley pictures Jesus as "a revolutionary, but not a violent revolutionary."[16] In no way is Jesus to be thought of as an eschatological or apocalyptic figure in the sense of anticipating or predicting the end of the world. The sayings referring to the "coming Son of Man" (e.g., Mark 8:38; 13:24–27; Matt 16:27; Luke 12:8–9; 17:24–30) are creations of the post-Easter church and in no way represent Jesus' own identity. As Borg has written, "The movement which Jesus began will be seen not as an end-of-the-world movement unconcerned with culture, but as a 'contrast-society' or 'alternative community,' a community seeking to live in history under the kingship of Christ."[17]

Many not engaged in the Jesus Seminar (or writing in opposition to it) have proposed that Jesus was an apocalyptic prophet.[18] The sayings of the coming Son of Man are too widely scattered throughout the sources to be ignored or discounted. It would have been unlikely that the early Christians invented these sayings since they assumed that Jesus was the Son of Man. Jesus thus predicted the coming judgment of God through the cosmic Son of Man and that this coming is imminent. This lesson is by no means all that Jesus taught, but the note that he would usher in a final judgment is sounded clearly and repeatedly in the earliest sources. Jesus' followers were to live in light of the coming reign of God.

There are various interpretations of Jesus as an apocalyptic figure, often depending on the background against which he is set. For example, E. P. Sanders argues that Jesus' life and ministry can best be understood in relation to the perspective of restoration eschatology, prevalent in first-century Judaism. He begins not with the sayings of Jesus, but with a list of the "almost indisputable facts about Jesus."[19] Two events are of paramount significance: his cleansing of the temple and his call of the twelve disciples. With each incident he anticipates that God will intervene and establish a new and glorious temple, with the disciples being the leading figures in the restored assembly. The divine restoration of Israel is imminent. On the one side, John the Baptist employs apocalyptic language to anticipate a divine intervention in history. On the other side, Paul expected the end to arrive soon (1 Thess 4:13–17). Between the two, Jesus thought of himself as having the full authoritative voice to speak for God, and his miracles were "signs of the beginning of God's final victory over evil."[20]

John Meier in a sense steers a middle course between Sanders's Jesus, who is a typical Jew, and Crossan's Jesus, who is hardly Jewish at all. Meier refers to Jesus as "a marginal Jew," which may mean that he was ignored by the Jewish historians of the day, or it may reflect his effort to see Jesus as within the Jewish environment, yet as remarkably distinct.[21] Moreover, Meier is willing to give attention to John's Gospel, otherwise ignored by most of the Jesus scholars of the day. For example, he feels that John is historically correct in stretching the public ministry of Jesus out for more than one year and in acknowledging that he paid several visits to Jerusalem, more than the single visit highlighted in Mark and Matthew.

What the Jesus Seminar and its opponents reveal is the decisiveness of the preconditions the historian brings to her or his work (as Schweitzer noted). How one dates sources, what criteria one chooses to determine an authentic or inauthentic saying of Jesus, and how Jesus' sayings are related to his actions influence the picture the historian paints of the individual or the movement.

One hotly debated criterion is that of "dissimilarity." If an event in Jesus' ministry seems hard to explain, then its likelihood of its having occurred is increased. Thus, Jesus' baptism by John in the Jordan River is plausible since such an event implies Jesus' subordination to John. As Perrin put it, "If we are to seek that which is most characteristic of Jesus, it will be found not in the things which he shares with his contemporaries, but in the things wherein he differs from them."[22]

The difficulty is that those who rely heavily on this criterion often end up with a Jesus cut off from his roots in Judaism or even an anti-Jewish figure. Some scholars want to eliminate Jesus' involvement with the rituals of the first century or with apocalyptic eschatology. They are embarrassed by the fact that Matthew (16:28) and Mark (9:1) attribute to him the notion that some of the people who were alive at that time would remain alive until the Son of Man came. In the effort to prevent Jesus from making an error, even one of timing, apocalyptic eschatology is thus eliminated from the historical Jesus. The result, of course, is to cut Jesus off from his religious and historical context. Furthermore, in stressing the criterion of dissimilarity and in disassociating Jesus from Judaism, some have removed from him "the scandal of particularity" and turned him into a modern man.[23]

And so what do we do with this Jesus of history? Is faith immune to the historian's investigations? Well, yes and no. It is certainly true that faith cannot look to the historian for vindication, to bolster an otherwise shaky foundation and make it more believable. If the historian could document that the events in the Gospels happened just as they are reported, it would not remove the scandal of the cross and make faith easier and the story more believable. In this regard, Kähler is right. Human faith depends on the faithfulness of God shown in the crucified and risen Jesus and not on what the historians can confirm about what Jesus said or didn't say, what he did or didn't do.

On the other hand, historical research does hold the potential for falsifying faith. Suppose the historians unanimously concluded that Jesus died in old age of natural causes. Then the whole meaning of his life and death is up for grabs, Paul's theology is emasculated, and we are left with an inoffensive message of trivial love. The church has always confessed that God's revelation came in a specific human being, Jesus, the Jew of Nazareth ("the scandal of particularity") and at a designated time in history ("he suffered under Pontius Pilate").

A faith that claims it is rooted in history must of necessity be open to the risk of historical investigation. Historians not only have the right but the responsibility to bring their best methods and resources to consider a person like Jesus of Nazareth.

All the while the church listens to the historians, it must always be sensitive to the possibility that under the historians' research may lie a hidden Christology that requires neither resurrection nor canon nor creed. When this happens, a reconstructed Jesus supplants the crucified and risen Christ as the object of faith, and the historian subtly replaces the canon.[24]

Mark Allen Powell fittingly concludes his study of this third quest by describing a group of young believers who sing and long for a Jesus to love:

> Their quest is for a Jesus of a story, a story of which history is but a part, sometimes but a shadow. Stories, unlike history, cannot always be divided neatly along a chronological axis. Good stories involve so many anachronies—foreshadowings, predictions, flashbacks, memories— that we lose track of what was post- and what was pre-, what was then and what was now, and finally we don't care. We just let the story take us where it is going.[25]

19

The Acts of the Apostles

There is little disagreement among scholars that Acts is the second of a two-volume work written by the same individual who wrote the Gospel of Luke. The introduction to Acts speaks of a "first book" that recorded all that Jesus had begun to do and to teach (Acts 1:1–2), and the second book takes up where the Gospel of Luke leaves off. The ascension of Jesus occurs in both, albeit in more detail in Acts than in Luke. Again, the theme of witness is critical in that the apostles are commissioned as "witnesses" in 1:8, and the book tells the story of the church's witness in characters such as Peter, John, Cornelius, Paul, and Barnabas.

Readers of Acts have often noted that the book is about the church and its leaders and particularly about the geographical expansion of the church "in Jerusalem, in all Judea and Samaria, and to the ends of the earth" (1:8). Starting with the day of Pentecost at Jerusalem, the narrative moves through Judea and Samaria, and finally to Rome. Sometimes this progressive movement is seen as the thematic role of the book. From Jerusalem to Rome indicates the movement from the main city of the Jews to the main city of the Roman Empire.

What is the point of tracking the mission of the early church from Jerusalem to Rome, if the church was anticipating an early return of Jesus? Why did Luke add this second volume? Various suggestions have been made. In the mid-nineteenth century, F. C. Baur suggested that Luke writes to forge a compromise between the strongly Jewish and anti-Jewish factions within the church.[1] The struggle between the Petrine and Pauline wings of the church is resolved in this second-century document called Acts, which papers over the cracks in the ecclesiastical walls of the first century, creating a picture of harmony and agreement. The purpose of Acts, according to Baur's perspective, was to present a mediated picture between the Jewish and Gentile wings of the first-century church. "Paul was not Judaised, nor Peter Paulinised, but both Paul and Peter were Lucanised, i.e., Catholicised."[2]

But one has to ask whether there existed such factions in the church strictly along Jewish and Gentile lines, and whether Acts in fact represents an early "catholizing" process. For example, the conflict evidenced in the Letter to the Galatians seems not to have been strictly a Jew-Gentile controversy, but a conflict between Paul's mission to the Gentiles and another Jewish mission to the Gentiles, which advocated law observance. It is difficult to conceive of Acts as a settling of the problem in the Galatian communities.

A second suggestion takes the political context seriously and argues that the church has spread throughout the Greco-Roman world and that it has a proper place as a legal religion within the empire. The empire has nothing to fear from the church. The church is in fact loyal to the empire. Acts is written to defend the church against charges that it exists or acts in violation of Roman law. To cite Henry J. Cadbury, writing about Acts, "If Judaism was a *religio licita* and Christianity was not, it was important to show that Christianity was only a legitimate form of Judaism and could shelter under the Jewish name."[3] Despite Paul's appeal to the Roman emperor, it is difficult to see the church in Acts as a tame and muted voice seeking to find acceptance as a legal religion like the Jews. From the very beginning, Peter's speech in Solomon's portico (3:11–26) is hardly an appeasement of the Jews. Nor is his comment after being arrested by the temple police, "We must obey God rather than any human authority" (5:29). Moreover, the conclusion of Acts, which leaves Paul in prison for two years (28:30), even though he remains a citizen of Rome, would indicate a failure to persuade the Romans that he as a spokesman for the Christian faith was politically harmless.

A third suggestion also takes the political situation into account and argues the case that the church need not fear the empire. Acts is an *apologia pro imperio* written for the church, in which Luke emphasizes the positive aspects of Roman involvement in the history of the Christian community and tones down the anti-Roman elements in his sources. His intent is to help the church live effectively amid the social and political realities of the present situation.[4] But Paul's imprisonment and his inability to get a hearing with Nero are hardly encouragements to the church to accept the Roman government as a friendly ally.

In a fourth suggestion, Gaventa, however, pushes beyond the social and political features of the writings and calls attention to the frequency of the phrases "word of God" and "plan of God." She argues that in the narratives of the two volumes readers encounter God's plan for human history. Beginning with Gabriel's word to Mary, "Nothing will be impossible with God" (Luke 1:37–38), the narrator repeatedly announces that he would relate "the things that have happened among us," meaning things impossible that God has enacted.

Frequently the Greek word *dei* ("must") appears, implying that whatever is happening is of "divine necessity." From Peter's sermon at Pentecost which begins "Friends, the scripture had to be (*edei*) fulfilled . . ." (Acts 1:16) to Paul's report of a visit by the angel of God amid the storm, telling him, "You must (*dei*) stand before the emperor" (27:24), God works the divine purpose for his people. " 'Plan of God' refers to God as the one whose intention and oversight governs the events that unfold, both the events of Jesus' own life and the way in which the witness moves throughout the cities of the Mediterranean world."[5]

This stress on the divine plan reveals that both Luke and Acts evidence a strong theological character.[6] Rather than being concerned with a superficial unity of Jewish and Gentile believers or with its political setting amid the Roman Empire, the angle of these books have more to do with God and God's action in history. The formation of the church at Pentecost and the witness of the people of God throughout the Mediterranean world happen under the direction of God's plan. At times the Spirit does not allow the proclamation in certain areas (16:6–7), in order to open other territories to the witness of the community (16:9–10).

Acts relates several stories critical to the life and mission of the early church, beginning with the arrival of the Spirit at Pentecost (2:1–13). This diverse gathering of people was composed of "devout Jews," members of the Diaspora, each of whom heard others speaking in their own language about "God's deeds of power" (2:11). This element of communication distinguishes this incident of "speaking in tongues" from other such incidents in Acts or in the Pauline letters. Not in a common language, but each person in his or her own language hears the message of divine power. Though bystanders thought the believers were drunk, it was too early in the day for drunkenness. Peter's sermon (2:14–36) clarified what God was up to in fulfilling the promise made to the prophet Joel (see Joel 2:28–32). The crucified Jesus was handed over to his murderers "according to the definite plan and foreknowledge of God" (2:23). Now God's gift of newness is actualized both through human failure and divine intention (2:23; 4:28). Christians become beneficiaries of the Spirit. They are empowered in new and marvelous ways to proclaim the gospel.

What about Peter's speech at Pentecost? Ancient historians often freely composed speeches and placed them on the lips of characters in their histories. Several of the sermons given by Peter and Paul in particular carry the same theme, which make them more likely to have been creations of Luke. Many years ago C. H. Dodd wrote *The Apostolic Preaching and Its Developments*, in which he isolated the basic message of the early church, derived not only from Peter's sermon in Acts 2, but also from passages like 1 Cor 15:3–5.[7] Dodd made the case that the early Christian preachers had a common message (called the *kerygma*):

> Prophecies are fulfilled; the new age is inaugurated by the coming of Christ. Born of the seed of David;
>
> He died according to the Scriptures, to deliver us from the present evil age; He was buried;
>
> He arose on the third day, according to the Scriptures;
>
> He is exalted at the right hand of God, as Son of God and the Lord of the living and the dead;
>
> He will come again as Judge and Savior of all people.

There are other portions of Dodd's argument that are stretched and have proved inaccurate (e.g., his sharp division between *kerygma* and *didachē*), but his identification of the fundamental preaching of the early church has been helpful. Thus, the speeches in Acts are, to be sure, in Luke's words, yet they represent the common preaching of the church (with possibly the exception of Paul's speech on Mars Hill in 17:22–34). Each speech is tailored to suit the context, as with Peter's answering the questions raised at Pentecost (2:14–36) or his explanation of the healing of a crippled beggar (3:11–26) or with Paul's sermon at Pisidian Antioch (13:16–41). In each instance the sermon is not just padding to the narrative, but rather introduces hearers to the grand scheme that God has for his people.

A second critical narrative in Acts recounts the elaborate stories of Peter and Cornelius (10:1–11:18), a portion of which is listed as the lectionary reading for Easter Sunday (10:34–43). Scene one tells of Cornelius, who was a centurion but a God-fearer, who lived at Caesarea and who had given generously to care for the needs of the poor. His dream was that he should send envoys to Peter, who was staying at Joppa (10:1–8). Scene two relates Peter's dream in which he learned that "what God had made clean, he was not to call unclean" (10:9–16). Scenes three and four tell of Cornelius's envoys, which had been sent from Cornelius to Joppa, of Peter's welcome of them, and of the journey from Joppa to Caesarea (10:17–29). Cornelius and Peter each make "speeches" explaining what had transpired (10:30–43).

The narrative closes with two confirmation scenes, one in which the Spirit comes on the Gentiles (10:44–48) and another in which the church at Jerusalem hears Peter's report and acknowledges the receipt of Gentiles into the community of faith (11:1–18). The confirmation scenes are important in the overall history of the early church, in that apart from Paul a breakthrough has occurred for the Gentiles to be received into the church on the same terms as the Jews, and this has occurred as the Gentiles have received the Spirit of God.

A third critical story in Acts recounts the so-called Jerusalem council (Acts 15:1–35). Paul and Barnabas were commissioned by the church at Antioch to deal with a complaint against their reception of non-Jews into the community of faith. Though welcomed by the apostles and elders at Jerusalem, some of the Pharisees argue that the Gentiles must receive circumcision and that the Law of Moses be kept. Peter speaks up and claims that the Spirit has been given to the Gentiles and to ignore this would be putting God to the test. James seems then to have made the most decisive speech at the council, quoting Amos 9:11–12 to show that the inclusion of the Gentiles has always been a part of God's plan (Acts 15:12–21).

Finally the council decides to welcome the Gentiles, only requiring that they abstain from things polluted by idols, from fornication, from whatever has been strangled, and from blood. This addendum was evidently important to some participants at the council since it was put in a letter to be sent to all the churches.

A fourth critical story from Acts is Paul's defense before King Agrippa (Acts 26:1–23). Because he had claimed his rights as a Roman citizen, Paul eventually was able to plead his case before Festus and King Agrippa. He began his defense by acknowledging his status as a faithful Pharisee, who had harassed "the saints" and sided with those who put them to death. But on his way to Damascus he was struck by a blinding light and heard a voice, saying, "Saul, Saul, why are your persecuting me?" What Saul discovers is that the Lord has identified with these people he has been persecuting and that he has been riding the train in the wrong direction. He is then commissioned to preach to the Gentiles "so that they may turn from darkness to light and from the power of Satan to God, so that they may receive forgiveness of sins and a place among those who are sanctified by faith" in Christ (26:18).

Though Festus and King Agrippa both see no reason for not giving Paul his freedom, once Paul has appealed to the emperor, to the emperor he must go. Acts then closes with the voyage to Rome, the shipwreck, and the fifth critical scene: Paul's arrival and stay at Rome (28:16–31). There he calls together the local leaders of the Jews to explain his situation. They declare that they have heard no negative reports concerning him and set a time for him to speak to them about the gospel and "this sect we know that everywhere it is spoken against" (28:22).

Paul's preaching to them about Jesus "from the law of Moses and the prophets" is accepted by some and rejected by others, leading to a quarrel among them. Then somewhat mysteriously Paul cites to them Isaiah 6:9–10, concluding with the comment "Let it be known to you then that this salvation of God has been sent to the Gentiles; they will listen" (28:28). The comment does not imply that God has given up on the promises made to Israel any more than at the original time Isaiah wrote the citation. It may imply that the Gentiles will listen, because they have no hope outside of these promises. Since some Jews do respond to Paul's preaching (28:24), then by no means is the door closed to them. They may have been among the group ("all who came to him," 28:30), who listened for two years to his preaching and teaching about the Lord Jesus Christ.

In any case, this narrative of Acts ends where it began—with the proclamation of Jesus as Lord and the kingdom of God. For "two whole years" Paul lived in Rome, under a kind of house arrest, but free to speak "with all boldness and without hindrance." We learn nothing more from Acts about Paul's fate.

Historically, one would have to say that the ending to Acts is a bit disappointing. Paul gets to Rome, but never has the opportunity to present the gospel to the emperor. Nor do we know what happened in the two years he remained under house arrest. Was Luke planning a third volume? Or did he stop here because this is all that had occurred? One tradition has it that Paul was martyred shortly after the conclusion of the two years, likely by Nero, a factor perhaps hinted at in his speech to the Ephesian elders at Miletus (Acts 20:22–25, 38). For those who contend for Pauline authorship of the Pastoral Letters, the most plausible construction is to argue for a release from imprisonment and a journey to the west, followed by a second Roman imprisonment and perhaps then martyrdom. In any case, what we have is Acts concluding with the unfettered preaching of the gospel by the apostle to "all who came to him" (28:30).

20

The Gospel and Letters of John

Of all the narratives of the life and ministry of Jesus, the Gospel of John is probably the most popular with church people. The various "I am" statements ("I am the bread of life"; "I am the light of the world"; "I am the way, the truth, and the life") carry universal appeal. The narratives are longer than those in the Synoptics, and so characters develop and plots emerge with more depth. A story like the feeding of the five thousand becomes the framework for extensive teaching.

Along with its popularity, however, comes also a tendency toward exclusivism. The statement that Jesus is the only way, truth, and life (14:6) has led many to think that the world is divided between "us" and "them" and that "we" as believers in Jesus are the true people of God. Although at times it fosters a harmless sectarianism, this way of thinking also leads to an arrogance that rejects many in the name of Christ.

In our post-Holocaust context, some narratives also smack of anti-Judaism. Repeatedly "the Jews" are singled out as the primary opposition to Jesus. Although some prefer the translation "the Judeans" or "the religious authorities," one would be hard-pressed to discount completely the Jewish hostility toward Jesus and his followers.

J. Louis Martyn has helped this issue with his study of chapter 9, in which he uncovers a two-level plot taking place. On one level, the narrative witnesses to an event during Jesus' earthly lifetime. On another level, it witnesses to Jesus' presence in events experienced in the Johannine church. At the time of the latter, there are apparently groups of Jews who have confessed Jesus as Messiah. They continue to live happily within the confines of the synagogue, keeping the law and observing the festivals and rites of Judaism. But the spirit of nationalism begins to darken in the fifties and erupts in revolt against Rome in 66. As a result of the fatal struggle, the Jews are banished from Jerusalem and grow increasingly hostile toward those of their number who openly confess Jesus as Messiah.

The Jews, who reconstitute themselves at Jamnia, institute a curse (*minim*) in a Benediction against Jewish deviants or heretics who are believers in Jesus. As a result, many Jewish Christians are exiled from the synagogues, which creates an enormous social dislocation, involving the breakup of families and the disruption of close relationships. Those excommunicated establish a congregation based on faith in Jesus as Messiah, a congregation we call the "Johannine community."

This community is predominantly made up of a group of believing Jews who confess Jesus as Messiah, who have been exiled from the synagogue, who have established their own "church down the street," and who live in considerable tension with their kinfolk. Martyn describes how the text captures these communal antagonisms.

> In the two-level drama of John 9 the man born blind plays not only the part of a Jew in Jerusalem healed by Jesus of Nazareth, but also the part of Jews known to John who have become members of the separated church because of their messianic faith and because of the awesome Benediction.[1]

Several factors further complicate the situation. First, the Gospel seems to indicate that the new Christians evidently associate with Samaritans and Gentiles. For them Jesus is not only the Jewish Messiah but also Savior of the world (4:42), a stance that further alienates the Johannine community from their kinfolk in the synagogues, who were establishing strict communal borders in a strongly nationalistic environment.

Second, this association with "outsiders" led to a persecution of the Christians (15:18–25). "They will put you out of the synagogues. . . . And they will do this because they have not known the Father or me" (16:2–3).

Third, some Christians remained within the synagogue as "secret believers." These closet Christians were fearful of the Jews and unwilling to make a public profession of faith, as imaged in the story of the blind man whose parents kept their distance from their healed son "because they were afraid of the Jews; for the Jews had already agreed that anyone who confessed Jesus to be the Messiah would be put out of the synagogue" (9:22–23). The Gospel describes other secret believers, such as Joseph of Arimathea who is identified as a "secret disciple." Nicodemus, who is associated with Joseph (19:38–39), also seems to be a secret disciple because he came to Jesus "by night" (3:2; 19:39).

As such, these "secret believers" are challenged by the open communities to embrace Jesus and be born anew. The clarification in the Nicodemus story that being born "from above" means "being born of water and Spirit" (3:5) might well entail baptism, which would have been a public event and would have necessitated full identification with the Christian group. David Rensberger writes:

> Baptism is thus viewed in John in the same light as public confession, as an acknowledgment of adherence both to Jesus as divine Son of God and to the community whose testimony to him is thereby accepted. It forms a boundary between those in the believing community and those outside it, and to be baptized is to cross that boundary in an open recognizable way. To be "born from above" is to undergo a change of communal affiliation and is therefore a social as well as a spiritual event.[2]

In the context of this ancient hostility, "the Jews" (or as it is often colloquially put "the synagogue down the street") refers to a particular group and not to the Jewish people as a whole. When gentile readers of John's Gospel today use and interpret the expression "the Jews," care has to be exercised that it does not degenerate into anti-Semitism, as it often has in the church's history. It is fundamentally different for first-century Jews to speak harshly to one another than for Gentiles to accuse Jews.

The structure of the Fourth Gospel is clear:

1:1–51	Introduction
2:1–12:50	Public ministry (often called "the book of signs")
13:1–17:26	Farewell discourses
18:1–20:31	Passion, death, and resurrection of Jesus
21:1–25	Epilogue

While the other Gospels begin with the adult Jesus or with the birth of the Messiah, the Fourth Gospel begins with creation. It is an appropriate beginning and provides a distinct witness to the reality of the Word made flesh. First of all, the Gospel's introduction speaks about the Word's presence in creation. It draws from the creation-story in Genesis 1 ("In the beginning") and continues the role of personified Wisdom in the Jewish tradition, which can be traced through Job 28 and Proverbs 8.[3] There is no negation of creation in the Word-made-flesh, but rather its fulfillment.

Second, the Word became flesh and "tented" (NRSV: "lived") among us (1:14), an allusion to the presence of Yahweh with the Israelites at the "tent of meeting" (Exod 25:8; 29:43–46). The Word is, however, rejected by the very world he has created. And so, third, he moves to change the situation. The Word's becoming "flesh" is not just a way of saying that God became human, but of God's assuming the nature of Adam after the fall. As Barth comments, "The Logos put himself at the side of his opponents,"[4] and as John the Baptist is soon to testify, "Here is the Lamb of God who takes away the sin of the world" (1:29). The Word in John's Gospel is not only a creative and incarnate Word, but also a redemptive Word.

John the Baptist (1:6–8; 3:27–30) is a remarkable character in the Fourth Gospel. He does not appear as the thundering preacher of social righteousness as in the Synoptics, but as a self-effacing witness to Jesus. He is content to be the best man and not the groom. He makes no pretense to be the light but embraces a modest task: to bear witness to the light (1:19–23). His words denying that he is the Messiah are memorable: "He must increase, but I must decrease" (3:30).

The second chapter contains two incidents pointing to the radical newness of the gospel, a theme highlighted in the Fourth Gospel. The first is the exchange of water to wine at the wedding feast at Cana (2:1–11). The stone pots are explicitly there for the purpose of the purification rites of the Jews. At Jesus' touch, the water they contain is transformed, however, into wine, no doubt symbolizing the dynamic of the reign of God.

The other incident recorded in chapter 2 is Jesus' cleansing of the temple, which appears in the other Gospels immediately following the triumphal entry into Jerusalem. John's cleansing story is expanded to include Jesus' comment, "Destroy this temple, and I will build it back in three days," and the narrator's comment that he was speaking of "the temple of his body" and that after he was raised from the dead his disciples remembered and believed.

These two incidents, coming where they do in the overall story at the outset of Jesus' ministry, set the direction for the remaining narrative. As Moody Smith comments, "It is highly significant that both narratives portray Jesus as bringing or embodying what is new, displacing the old."[5] Nicodemus, who comes "by night," is told that he must be born "from above" (3:3). He takes the expression (in Greek *anōthen*) to imply a second birth from his mother, whereas it is clear from the narrative that Jesus is calling for a more radical birth by the Spirit. The Samaritan woman is introduced to the new worship in the Spirit (4:24). The man, helpless at the Sheep Gate for thirty-eight years (5:1–18), is healed by the authority of this one who walks on the water (6:16–21). The newness of the gospel is demonstrated time and again as Jesus moves in and among the people.

Chapter 2 also introduces the reader to the word "signs" (2:18, 23), which becomes a critical term for what in the Synoptic Gospels is called "mighty works" or "wonders" and which we commonly refer to as "miracles." In John 2, "signs" refers to Jesus' transformation of water to wine, but the Fourth Gospel also designates other astounding acts as "signs," such as acts of healing (4:54). Unlike the Synoptic Gospels where Jesus persistently refuses to perform a deed that would validate his divine origin (Mark 8:11–12; Luke 23:8), in the Fourth Gospel "signs" are meant to lead to insight and faith (2:11; 4:53–54; 20:30–31). Some people see and believe; others, however, fail to get beyond the deed to the One to whom the sign pointed (2:23–25; 4:48). The final query of the risen Jesus to Thomas was "Have you believed because you have seen me? Blessed are those who have not seen and yet have come to believe" (20:29).

A climax is reached in chapter 11. Jesus, delaying to come to Bethany on hearing of Lazarus' illness and death, announces to Mary, "I am the resurrection and the life" (11:25) and then proceeds to raise her dead brother. The "nowness" of the future resurrection is transparent. Unfortunately the public ministry of Jesus ends with the lament that people have rejected the light in favor of the darkness (12:44–50). Jesus' demonstration of his power over death provides such a threat that his enemies plot to kill Lazarus as well as Jesus (12:9–11).

At the end of his public ministry Jesus does what strikes many contemporary readers as a strange thing. He takes a towel and a basin of water and washes the feet of the disciples (13:1–17). When Peter objects to having his feet washed, Jesus insists that he *must* allow his feet to be washed. Only after Jesus' death and resurrection does it become clear that to be washed is to participate in the death and resurrection of Jesus. Allowing Jesus to wash his feet is a gift of grace that draws the participant into the ministry of Jesus. "So if I, your Lord and Teacher, have washed your feet, you also ought to wash one another's feet" (13:14).

The Farewell Discourses, which provide the primary teaching element for the Fourth Gospel, are intriguing in that they contain no parables, no Sermon on the Mount, no exorcisms, no institution of the Lord's Supper, and no agony in the garden.

Four themes are prominent in these chapters. First, Jesus commands his disciples to love one another. In fact, the washing of the disciples' feet is prefaced by the statement that Jesus "having loved [those] who were in the world, he loved them to the end" (or to the uttermost [13:1]). The foot washing becomes a picture of what love entails. "No one has greater love than this, to lay down one's life for one's friends" (15:13). Following the foot washing, we are told of the "new commandment, that [we] love one another." Just as Jesus has loved us, we are to love one another (13:34–35; cf. Lev. 19:18).

The commandment to love one another is placed in the context of his betrayal by Judas and his denial by Peter, which means that the newness in the community of Jesus' disciples is to be characterized by love, even in the face of opposition.

A second theme is the warning about the hatred that the church is to receive from the world (15:18–16:4). No doubt this hatred was occurring in the life of the Johannine community at the time of writing. Those who were excommunicating Jewish Christians from the synagogues thought they were doing God a favor (16:2), but John teaches that the world had hated Jesus before it hated the believers, and they should not be surprised at the hostility toward them.

The third theme prominent in the final discourses is the Spirit, called the "Paraklete" and "the Spirit of truth." The term *parakletos* depicts one who comes along side to counsel or to comfort and to be the advocate for another. Five times the term occurs in the Fourth Gospel (14:15–17, 26; 15:26–27; 16:5–11, 12–15). As far as Jesus is concerned, the coming of the Spirit is predicated on his departure from them. Thus the "I will not leave you orphaned" (14:18) is an appropriate word for the disciples. Jesus will not abandon them, even in his physical absence from them. Moreover, John writes that the Spirit comes on Easter evening, when Jesus appears to the disciples, "breathe[s] on them," and says, "Receive the Holy Spirit" (20:22). The Spirit represents the presence of Jesus as the teacher of truth, who enables the disciples and their followers to remember what Jesus said and did and to let it guide their lives.

The fourth theme is that of the glorification of Jesus, which includes the glorification of the Father (13:31–32; 14:13; 15:8; 16:14; 17:1–5, 10) and is evident in Jesus' death. The term "glorification" in the Fourth Gospel means revelation and involves the complex relations of the Trinity. It is not something Jesus has earned or achieved, but who he is, as defined by his crucifixion. His glory is his own only in that it is given to him by the Father. His "hour" is a unique time, anticipated throughout the Gospel and which finally arrives at the beginning of his passion. The moment of death strangely is also the moment of Jesus' glorification. "Glorification entails death: exaltation implies the cross."[6] Yet how different John is from Mark and Paul, who find it difficult to refer to Jesus' crucifixion as a time of "glorification."[7]

Jesus' Farewell Discourses clarify the eschatological situation of the present and prepare the reader for Jesus' death (11:1–17:26). Gail O'Day declares that 16:33 is probably "a summary of the Johannine Gospel" ("I have said this to you, so that in me you may have peace. In the world you face persecution. But take courage: I have conquered the world!") It promises that one can move from the present sorrow to future joy.

> The measure of what is to be hoped for is the promises of Christ (16:23, 26–28). Both the present and the future are redefined by Jesus' death and resurrection and are held in a delicate balance. When one lives in hope, the present moves toward the promises and possibilities of the future, and the future transforms the sorrows and seeming impossibilities of the present. *The Fourth Gospel's distinctive contribution*

*to the church's conversation about hope and the future is the value that it
places on the present moment as the arena in which God's future is already
under way.* For the Fourth Evangelist, the decisive Easter proclamation is "In the world you face persecution. But take courage; I have
overcome the world!"[8]

Jesus' final word from the cross becomes significant in light of the whole
Gospel. "It is finished" (19:30). No cry of dereliction, only the word that he
completed what his Father has given him to do (cf. 4:34; 5:36; 17:4). Jesus dies
with dignity. Then we read, "He bowed his head and gave up his spirit." His
giving up his spirit no doubt carries a typically Johannine double meaning:
Jesus dies, gives up his breath (*pneuma*). But at the same time, he gives (actually in the Greek "gives over") his Spirit (*pneuma*) to the disciples.

John 21 seems to be an epilogue, added to the Gospel by a later editor, since
the Gospel projects its purpose so effectively in 20:30–31. Though there is no significant manuscript that does not include chapter 21, the language, style, and contents of chapter 21 differ from chapter 20. For instance, John 21 is distinct in that
it is the only Gospel to record appearances of the risen Christ both in Jerusalem
and in Galilee. Chapter 21 alone contains the threefold questioning of Peter and
his responses. Furthermore, only in 21:20–23 do we find an implied death for
Peter and the role of the Beloved Disciple spelled out as the authentic witness.

The epilogue was likely added in order to scotch rumors about Peter's death
and to honor the Beloved Disciple as the faithful witness of the community.
Peter is commissioned not only as a leader, but also as a follower of Jesus
(21:19). Chapter 21 teaches that leadership in the Christian community is destined to misuse its prerogatives and fail unless at the same time it is embraced
as discipleship.

The purpose of the Fourth Gospel is given at the end of chapter 20. The
"signs" are written "that you may continue to believe" that Jesus is the Messiah (20:31 NRSV margin). Other manuscript traditions take the verb
"believe" as an aorist tense rather than a present tense, with the translation
then being "that you may come to believe that Jesus is the Messiah" (NRSV).
The manuscript evidence is fairly evenly divided between the present and
aorist tenses. The intent of the Gospel, however, seems more to be the
strengthening of a community of faith (present tense) rather than as an evangelistic appeal (aorist tense).

THE LETTERS OF JOHN

Each of the three letters of John has certain common characteristics, and yet
each has distinctive qualities. The language, style, and ideas of the first letter

are definitely similar to the Gospel, and some scholars make the case that the two documents came from the same hand or at least emanate from the same community (or "school").[9] The second and third letters come from "the elder" but have different addressees: the second letter "to the elect lady," and the third to "the beloved Gaius."

First John has few characteristics of a letter; in fact, it reads much more like a homily or an essay. It stresses the nature of God and reflects the life of a community. An exhortation follows each theme. For example, God is light, and in him there is no darkness. Thus the community is exhorted to walk in the light just as Jesus is in the light, which means following Jesus honestly and sincerely, not being deceived by self-congratulatory ways that lead away from the light. If readers deny their need for forgiveness and persist in their self-deceptive lives, they negate the atoning sacrifice made for them by Jesus (2:2).

A second example is that God is love, and the readers are exhorted to love one another (2:3–11). This is the "new commandment," but of course is not really new in that it is found in Leviticus 19:18. Its newness lies in the reality that it has come in a unique way into the life of the community. It is "true in him and in you, because the darkness is passing away and the true light is already shining" (2:8). This comports well with the "new commandment" in the Gospel: "a new commandment, that you love one another. Just as I have loved you, you also should love one another" (John 13:34).

Third, the love that believers are to demonstrate to one another is not a mawkish sentimentality. God is righteous, and "everyone who does right has been born of him" (2:29); even the Cains of this world are to love the Abels (and vice versa), and we are to share our goods with one another and with the poor. The change of address to "brothers and sisters" in 3:13 confirms that the writer is not simply addressing his comments to the general public but to the members of the Johannine community and in a sharp way. Jesus laid down his life for us, and we should lay down our lives for others (3:16).

Some members have apparently left the community because they are unable to affirm that Christ has really come in the flesh. The writer seeks to weed out his opponents by insisting on a public confession of Jesus' humanity (1 John 4:2; 2 John 7). Have those who left the community done so in reaction to the otherwise high Christology of the Fourth Gospel (e.g., John 10:30), or is there some other reason for their failure to embrace Jesus' humanity? Whatever their reason, they are identified with "false prophets" (1 John 4:1–2), with "deceivers" and even "the anti-Christ" (2 John 7).

That God is love dominates the letter and determines the quality of life that Jesus' followers are to manifest to the world. The love that they share is their distinguishing mark. "And this is his commandment, that we should believe in the name of his Son Jesus Christ and love one another, just as he has commanded us" (3:23).

Second John possesses many more characteristics of the letter-form than 1 John. It is written from "the elder" to "the elect lady and her children," which may refer to an individual and her family or to a congregation and its members.

Two features characterize the letter. One is the commandment to love one another, a common command in the Johannine tradition. Again the writer says that it is not a new commandment, but one that they are to walk in and obey. Second John emphasizes the importance of hospitality for obedience to this commandment.

Second the brevity of the letter hides the point, made in 2 John 7, that some have departed from the community because they no longer confess that the risen Christ has come in the flesh. These "deceivers" apparently deny that the human Jesus can be identified with the divine Christ.

Third John, like 2 John, has many characteristics of a letter. Gaius, its addressee, is not known outside of this letter, but is highly commended for his hospitality. To practice hospitality as Gaius has done is to demonstrate love and thus to fulfill the new commandment. In a sense he is to be contrasted with Diotrephes, who is self-centered and has been busy spreading false charges against the elder and Demetrius (3 John 9–10a). He refuses to practice hospitality and is engaged in expelling people from the church rather than welcoming them (3 John 10b).

PART FOUR

The General Epistles

21

Introduction to the General Epistles

The term "General Epistles" (or "Catholic Epistles") was employed for the remaining eight letters in the New Testament canon at least in the early portion of the fourth century, in the time of Eusebius of Caesarea. The list usually included Hebrews; James; 1 and 2 Peter; 1, 2, and 3 John; and Jude. In earlier lists only seven were included, since Hebrews, though written anonymously, was often counted as a Pauline letter, and in the third century papyrus, P[46], it even follows Romans in the canonical order.

The adjective "general" or "catholic" seems to have derived from the fact that the authors and audience are not so specific as are the Pauline letters. Cyril of Jerusalem (c. 348 CE) used the term to designate the universal church in distinction from the local congregation (Catechetical Letters 18:23). As Paul's letters were written to specific communities of Christians, it was thought that these letters were intended for the church at large, and likely encyclical in nature.

In the canonical order of the early manuscripts, they appear in different places. Sometimes, with Acts, they follow Paul's letters; sometimes they follow Acts but precede the Pauline letters.

Since the three Johannine letters have been treated already in connection with the Gospel of John, we shall operate with only five "general letters": Hebrews, James, 1 and 2 Peter, and Jude.

22

Hebrews

When compared with the Pauline letters, Hebrews hardly seems like a letter at all. It closes with the standard conventions of the letter (13:20–25), but at the beginning it lacks the name of a sender, recipients, an initial greeting, and a prayer of thanksgiving. The writer identifies the writing as "a word of exhortation" (13:22), a term used elsewhere for a sermon (Acts 13:15) and a fitting description of the contents of Hebrews. The writer, who was obviously at home in the Septuagint, writes in a highly sophisticated style throughout and has constructed some rhetorically impressive sentences (such as 1:1–4).

The initial audience, though likely including people of Jewish background (since so many Old Testament texts from the Septuagint are cited) was no doubt a Christian group. In fact, the purpose of the document is to encourage such people not to lose heart, not to fall away from their initial profession of faith. The community is one facing a crisis. Some have ceased to attend church (10:25); others suffer from "drooping hands" and "weak knees" (12:12). Many seem to be second-generation Christians (2:3), who have endured persecution (10:32–34). Still others may have been disillusioned by the delay of the return of Christ (10:25, 35–39). The letter attempts to renew the commitment of the readers, who are growing lax. The methods are a series of exhortations (hortatory subjunctives abound throughout the letter), and the readers are severely warned regarding apostasy (6:4–8; 12:14–17). At the same time, the letter contains a strong statement of the significance of Jesus. The Christology drives the exhortations, not vice versa.

In response to this situation, the writer seeks to expose the superiority of the revelation in Jesus Christ over all other realities and in doing so to urge the hearers and readers not to forsake their initial confession. We see this in the way in which the writer depicts (1) Jesus, (2) his sacrifice, and (3) the resulting salvation. These are not clean, discrete categories, and one would expect to find overlapping.

1. At the very beginning of the letter, Jesus is declared to be God's Son, who is God's ultimate word to humankind. "God spoke to our ancestors in many and various ways by the prophets, but in these last days he has spoken to us by a Son" (1:1–2a). Probably Jesus' preexistence is affirmed in the way the Son is set alongside God "through whom he also created the worlds" (1:2b). Using the words of wisdom (see Wis 7:26), Jesus is "the reflection of God's glory and the exact imprint of God's very being." Then, citing texts from the Septuagint, the writer goes on to establish the fact that the Son is superior to the angels (1:5–9).

The text becomes a bit clearer in 2:5–8 where Psalm 8:4–6 is cited. The psalm praises the creation of human beings in the context of God's larger creation. George Caird has pointed out that this citation from Psalm 8 (taken from the Septuagint) helps to clear up the confusion of how the beginning to this letter is related to the rest of the story.[1] The author affirms that humanity was for a period created lower than the angels, but a time will come when God will crown humans with glory and honor and will put all things under their feet. It is as if history is divided into two periods: the present age under the authority of the angels and an age to come when the whole universe is put under God's subjection. The psalmist lays out God's intention for humankind: to bring many sons and daughters to glory (2:10).

Now we do not yet see that age which is to come, nor are we crowned with glory and honor. But we do see our representative figure, Jesus, who for "a little while" was made lower than the angels. Jesus' crowning then comes as a result of his suffering of death that was a representative death for all people (2:9).

But why angels? Two reasons. First, Hebrews 2:2 reflects the widespread belief in Second Temple Judaism that angels mediated the law at Sinai and were in some sense the law's guardians (cf. Gal 3:19–22; Acts 7:53). The author makes the point that Jesus, as mediator of the new covenant, is far superior to the mediators of the old covenant. Second, the angels to whom Jesus and humankind are superior in Hebrews 1 are the same angels that were previously "for a little while" in control of humans. It is only in light of the fact that Jesus embraced suffering and death that he and we are exalted and "crowned with glory and honor" (2:9). Throughout the letter the reader then is told in various ways that the speech of God is illumined in the new age by the presence of the Son. Jesus is "our confession" (3:1; 4:14; 10:23), to whom the readers are to hold fast.

Probably as strongly as anywhere else in the New Testament, Jesus is presented as a human being. He was one of us (2:11); he was tempted just as we are (4:15); he was totally obedient to God but amid "loud cries and tears"

(5:7–8); and he shared "flesh and blood" with us, including death (2:14–15). This depiction, of course, enables the writer to establish that Jesus was a high priest who knows and has experienced the human situation and is able to sympathize fully with our weaknesses (4:14–5:3).

2. Jesus' sonship is readily connected to his role as high priest, no doubt through the juxtaposition of Psalm 2:7 and Psalm 110:4. (cf. Heb 5:8–10). As high priest the image of Jesus moves in two directions: (a) as one who sympathizes with human beings in their weaknesses, who has been tested in every way as they are tested (4:14–16), and still deals gently with the ignorant and wayward (4:14–5:4). The motif of intercession always follows a statement about the high priest's exaltation (2:17–18; 4:14–16; 7:20–25). As a full human being, he "learned obedience through what he suffered" (5:8). (b) And yet this priest stands in a unique line of priesthood, namely that of Melchizedek, who has neither beginning of days nor end of life (7:3). Melchizedek is mentioned in the Bible only two times outside of Hebrews (in Ps 110:4 and Gen 14:17–20). His authority stems not from the law but from an indestructible life (7:16), and his office is eternal (7:24). The writer thus wants clearly to display for the readers a figure both like us and unlike us, both human and divine.

As high priest Jesus himself then becomes the perfect sacrifice. It was the function of the priest to enter the Holy of Holies once annually to atone for his own sins and the sins of the people. "But as it is, he (i.e., Christ, the high priest) has appeared once for all at the end of the age to remove sin by the sacrifice of himself" (9:26). Referring to the crucifixion as the sacrifice, he mediates not with the blood of bulls and goats, but with his own blood, and thereby he gains "eternal redemption" (9:12). It should be added that this act does not abolish the principle of sacrifice, but its own consummate provision is that it abolishes the guilt of sin.[2]

3. The salvation resulting from Christ's sacrifice is also spoken of in the dialect of the end time. He became "the source of eternal salvation" (5:9), so decisive that those who share it and fall away cannot be "restored" (6:4).[3] To experience this salvation is to receive the heavenly gift, to become a partaker of the Holy Spirit, to encounter God's word, and to taste "the powers of the age to come" (6:5).

At the end of the letter and in the midst of exhorting the readers to do good and to share what they have, the author reminds them that the priest burned the sacrifices "outside the city gate" and that "Jesus also suffered outside the city gate" (13:10–16). Thus, the word of exhortation to the readers is that they "go to him outside the camp and bear the abuse he endured." The timid, fearful, reluctant followers are called to embrace Christ's destiny outside the gate, where the stakes are high and the risks are real. Such an exhortation also depicts life in terms of a pilgrimage. "For here we have no lasting city, but we are looking for the city that is to come" (13:14).

The eschatology is deeply interwoven with the Christology and the salvation given in Christ. In the process of highlighting this way of salvation, new in Christ, the writer underlines the fact that the old sacrificial system is obsolete, that the old way is no longer adequate ("He abolishes the first in order to establish the second" [10:9]), which includes the methods of atonement. "In speaking of 'a new covenant,' he has made the first one obsolete. And what is obsolete and growing old will soon disappear" (8:13).

Not always, however, is the presentation of the past so negative. In fact, in probably the most familiar passage in the book (11:1–12:2), the author calls on the experience of a number of figures in Israel's history as attested examples of a faith that perseveres amid various forms of opposition (so Abel, Enoch, Noah, Abraham and Sarah, Jacob, Joseph, Moses, et al.). They did not receive the promise offered them, "since God had provided something better so that they would not, apart from us, be made perfect" (11:40). Often the circumstances belied the promise, and thus the emphasis falls on the endurance of faith. Jesus "the pioneer and perfecter of our faith" is depicted as the climatic example of this list of heroes, who learned through discipline how to endure (12:2).

A fundamental tension thus exists between continuity and discontinuity in Hebrews, as the author relates the past to the present and the present to the future. Such a tension tones down the otherwise supersessionist tendency of the letter. Not all that *has* happened is to be rejected, nor is what has immediately occurred or about to occur necessarily to be embraced. As Pfitzner puts it, "Past revelation was not defective; it was the penultimate, not the ultimate word from God."[4]

Notice how all three of our concerns—Christology, Jesus' sacrifice, and the resulting salvation—are stated in the eschatological tension so characteristic of the other New Testament writers. The "already" but "not yet" dimension comes through in connection with Jesus, who though he is the word spoken in these last days, is nevertheless "appointed heir of all things" (1:2), the single descendant of Melchizedek. His sacrifice transcends the sacrifice of bulls and goats, "so Christ, having been offered once to bear the sins of many, will appear a second time, not to deal with sin, but to save those who are eagerly waiting for him" (9:28). Furthermore, believers at the time of the writing join the heroes of the Old Testament community in looking for the city prepared for them (11:13–16).

It is critical to note that though the writer uses exhortations as the means by which to call this struggling community back to faith in Christ and to service in the world, he does so by laying a strong christological base. Unlike the book of James, Hebrews underscores *why* they should return to the faith they have abandoned.

23

James
———

At first blush the Letter of James seems terribly disjointed, heavy on exhortations, and impossible to outline. It reads more like a miscellaneous collection of moral sayings, with no solid theological base. "Jesus" is named only twice in the letter (1:1; 2:1), although some of the occasions of the use of "Lord" may refer to Jesus rather than God. There is no acknowledgment of the human slavery to sin, no mention of Jesus' death and resurrection, and no interest in Christology or in the Spirit. Luther labeled this letter "a right strawy epistle," primarily because he heard nothing of the gospel in it. He remarked on one occasion that he would give his doctor's beret to anyone who could reconcile Paul and James.[1]

We do not know for sure who wrote the letter, though some think it was James, the brother of Jesus. It is addressed "to the twelve tribes in the Dispersion," which could be a congregation of Jewish Christians (though the expression is not used anywhere else for Christians). A case can be made that it wasn't really a letter at all, but more of a speech in which the orator is drawing heavily on a number of sources such as the wisdom literature of Hellenistic Judaism, the Greek moralists of the day, and even the sayings of Jesus.

The author of the letter writes very good Greek, bordering on being eloquent. His vocabulary is broad, and he uses vivid analogies (e.g., the patient farmer, the ship driven by a rudder, the bridled horse). He calls on figures from the Old Testament to drive his points home: Abraham, Rahab, and Job.

We examine here a number of the themes that emerge in the letter. First, most obviously to anyone familiar with Paul's letters is the conflict concerning the interpretation of Genesis 15:6 ("[Abraham] believed the LORD, and the LORD reckoned it to him as righteousness.") Twice Paul cites this same Old

Testament passage, only to arrive at the conclusion that Abraham was justified by faith and not by works (Rom 4:1–5; Gal 3:6–10a). James comes to exactly the opposite conclusion: "You see that a person is justified by works and not by faith alone" (Jas 2:22–24).

What do we do with the apparent contradiction posed by James's reading and Paul's reading of the same text? Is James seeking deliberately to counter Paul or vice versa? The contexts are critical. On one hand, James paints a picture of a homeless person, needing food and clothes, being told by the believing person to hit the road, without providing food and shelter (2:14–16). On the other hand, Paul confronts Jewish Christian leaders in Rome and Galatia, who say to the Gentiles that they cannot be a part of the people of God unless they assume the marks of being Jewish—that is, unless they agree to be circumcised.

In the James context, the contrast is not really between faith and the law, but between the empty profession of religion and its lively expression. James mentions "law" at least ten times, calling it "the perfect law," "the royal law," "the law of liberty" (1:25; 2:8, 12). James is clearly concerned about the same law that concerned Jesus and Paul, namely the love of neighbor (2:8).

A second theme appearing in James has to do with impartiality. The command to love one's neighbor as oneself simply does not allow for playing favorites, especially when the favorites turn out to be friends in the same social bracket as ourselves. Twice he pictures the situation of a poor, homeless person whose needs are ignored by the individual with resources to help (2:1–5, 15–16). In showing such partiality, "you commit sin and are convicted by the law as transgressors" (2:9).

The motif of impartiality leads to the issue of wealth. In 5:1–6 rich people are roundly condemned. It is difficult to determine whether this represents a blanket judgment on all who are affluent, or whether James has a particular group in mind, those who have defrauded their workers (5:3–6), have lived a luxurious existence, and have flaunted their wealth. A special group seems to be the target of James's prophetic word, since the second-person pronoun is used so prominently in 5:1–6 and since the readers themselves have been the victims of the rich (2:6).[2]

A fourth theme emerges in 3:1–12, when for a whole chapter the author examines the problems dealing with speech. For every person, but especially for teachers, this essay is extremely relevant. The tongue has enormous potential for either good or evil. Like a rudder guiding a ship or a bridle on a horse, our speech can yield enormous results. With our speaking we can praise and bless God or with it we can engage in all sorts of destructive gossip. We are created by speech (1:18), and we are redeemed by it (1:21).

At this point, one is inclined to ask: are these random sermonettes that the author has set in contrasting patterns, or is there a fundamental theological structure to the mini-sermons? L. T. Johnson has helped by isolating in 3:13–4:5 the dynamic of friendship with the world over against friendship with God.[3] Particularly, 4:4 asks, "Do you not know that friendship with the world is enmity with God? Therefore whoever wishes to be a friend of the world becomes an enemy of God." At the heart of each of these exhortations lies this basic dichotomy of God over against the world. "World" here is understood not as a term for the universe, but as a category of value.

Friendship with the world means accepting the world's system of values as one's own, buying into the closed system of the world. I can be "more" only if I have more. Another who has more then becomes a threat to me. Envy moves toward hostility and even murder. I can be more only if I eliminate the other. If I accept the world's closed system, I forget that everything comes from God (1:17). God's generosity is unbounded and endless.[4]

This sharp differentiation smokes out those who like to have it both ways, whom James names early in the letter as "double-minded" (1:8). Such individuals are vulnerable to whatever fad comes along. They are not just believers who have doubts. They are tossed to and fro by every wave in the sea and driven by whatever wind that blows. Their stable counterparts are ones who not only hear the word of God when it is taught, but also do it. As Johnson concludes, James

> not only challenges Christians to an integrity in thought, speech, and actions, but also by sketching a vision of the world opposite to the one offered by the logic of envy, it offers the possibility for Christians to enter into conversation with others who view the world as defined by a gift-giving God, a conversation in which the insights and clarity of James can contribute toward a genuine social ethic based on solidarity and peace rather than competition and violence.[5]

24

1 Peter

The context in which this letter was written is critical, even though one cannot be sure as to who the author was and exactly when the letter was written. It seems best located sometime after the failed uprising against the Romans (when "Babylon" begins to be used for Rome, cf. 5:13) and the end of the century (when Christians officially become targeted as enemies of Rome). This would put the letter between 70 and 90 CE. It seems improbable that the apostle Peter was the author since the Greek is highly sophisticated and unlike that of a rugged fisherman whose native tongue was Aramaic.

First Peter reads like a real letter, with a salutation (1:1–2), a blessing (1:3–9), a body (1:10–5:11), and a conclusion (5:12–14). Though some have interpreted it to be a baptismal liturgy because of the extensive baptismal imagery, it smacks of being genuine correspondence.

The book is addressed to "exiles of the Dispersion" in several provinces in Asia Minor. Since they "were ransomed from the futile ways inherited from [their] ancestors" (1:18; cf. also 1:14), they were predominately Gentiles who found themselves under considerable social and political pressure because of their faith in Christ. It was not that the Christian religion was illegal; it is rather that the Christian converts, when they ceased their participation in the worship of local deities, were seen as the scorn of the population.

How then is one to explain a book like 1 Peter, where the letter is clearly written to give encouragement and hope to *suffering* Christians? Obviously persecution was taking place. Two things can be said. First, because of their unwillingness to participate in the worship of the local deities and in the Roman cults, Christians in many settings were subject to severe harassment and persecution. It was not official and government-sponsored, but was spasmodic and local.

The crime was not in confessing Christ, but in the unwillingness to acknowledge the state gods as *deus et dominus*. Behind all of the local deities was a reverence for the emperor and for Rome. "The cult flourished as a way to maintain cultural stability and control in a situation of political subjugation."[1] To worship only one God made a person politically suspect.

Pliny the Younger, governor of Bythnia in Asia Minor (c. 112 CE) asked the emperor Trajan (98–117) for advice in handling the Christians. Christianity had spread fairly widely in his area, not only in the towns but also in the countryside. Pliny's report to Trajan indicated his alarm that so many Christians were being persecuted for their faith and not for having done anything illegal. Trajan's response was that Christians were not to be hunted down, but "if met with were to be punished." The intense pressure was relieved somewhat, but there were many pretexts left for those who wanted to injure the Christians. As Eusebius wrote, "Sometimes it was the common people, sometimes the local authorities, who devised plots against us, so that even without open persecution sporadic attacks blazed up in one province or another, and many of the faithful endured the ordeal of martyrdom in various forms."[2]

Second, due to their antisocial situation in the community, Christians tended to be blamed by the general populace for whatever went wrong, whether it be economic or criminal. They refused to take part in the local clubs, an action that was taken to be treasonous, because the clubs were government-sponsored. Locally, the Christians were seen as disturbers of the peace and became easy targets for those seeking scapegoats for their own misdemeanors. So Nero blamed the Christians for the burning of Rome.

When one looks at the passages that constitute the letter of 1 Peter and that seek to comfort the persecuted, one is inclined to think more in terms of the second category of harassment rather than the first. It is not that the two categories are all that separated since both have the union of religion and politics as a major dimension.

The beginning of the letter follows the general pattern of the Pauline letter-form. Though the three powerful verbs in the NRSV translation of 1:2 ("chosen," "destined," "sanctified") are actually not verbs in Greek, there is nevertheless an interesting movement in the text from the providential purpose of God the Father, through the holiness given by the Spirit, to obedience to Jesus Christ and the sprinkling of his blood. It is too early to be thinking of the Trinity and the role of each member in it, but from passages like this the Trinity later develops.

In the blessing that follows (1:3–12), the readers begin to sense the direction of the text in terms of three important gifts God has given them. First, God through the divine mercy has given the readers a living hope on the basis of a new birth through Jesus' resurrection of the dead. The Greek word behind "new birth" occurs in the New Testament only here and in 1:23, serving to reiterate the radical newness behind the living hope that is to sustain the believers amid suffering and trial.

The second of the important gifts given by God through Jesus' resurrection is an inheritance, impervious to the testing brought by the fiery ordeals, protected and sheltered. Having access to that inheritance, the readers can rejoice, even in the time of testing. The third gift is the eschatological salvation, which also endures any trial and suffering. The prophets dug deep into the Scriptures, making "careful search and inquiry" (1:10), seeking this salvation, but could only testify in advance to the gift of grace, which is the gospel (1:12).

What follows is a string of exhortations (though in Greek they are mostly participles), which conclude with a declaration that the readers are by divine election the church, chosen and precious in God's sight (2:4). The image of the stone, drawn from Isaiah 19:6 and 28:16, and Psalm 118:22, enables the writer to acknowledge both those who accept Christ and thereby constitute the church and those who reject Christ. Finally, however, the Isaiah passage concludes the section with a firm declaration: "But you are a chosen race, a royal priesthood, a holy nation, God's own people" (1 Pet 2:9) to the end of announcing God's mighty acts.

What the writer has been doing is to reinforce the church's identity as the one household of God. Connected to the rejected stone, members are drawn together into a spiritual household. The not-people have become God's people (3:10; Hos 1:9; 2:23) in order that they may proclaim the mighty acts of God.

One is struck with the profuse use of the Old Testament quotations and images that appear in the letter. Unlike the Pauline letters, where a care is expressed about the relationship of Christians and Jews as possible heirs of Israel, 1 Peter "simply takes over the images and phrases that the Old Testament applies to Israel and applies them to the church. Christians are now the people who were once no people; the church is the community of those who were without mercy but now have received mercy (2:10, quoting Hos 2:23)."[3] Perhaps the reason for this is the strong christological basis of the letter. "For 1 Peter, the Old Testament was not written to point to Israel but to point to Christ and through Christ to point ahead to the life of the church."[4]

Beyond this declaration comes another string of exhortations (2:11–3:12), especially for the context of the audience, including citizens yielding to the political authorities (2:13–17); slaves being obedient to their masters (3:18–25); wives accepting the authority of their husbands (3:1–6); husbands showing honor to their wives (3:7). But why these examples of submissiveness? Why introduce the household codes of Colossians and Ephesians here? First, there is the matter of a clear conscience. It is better to suffer for having done something good rather than from having done evil (3:13–17). To a people constantly under scrutiny and blamed for every disaster that occurred, with no appeal to a higher political power, this counsel may not be bad at all.

Second, Christ is a model for this submissiveness. "For Christ also suffered for sins once for all, the righteous for the unrighteous, in order to bring you to God" (3:18a), and on the basis of the resurrection now is at the right hand of God (3:22). When Christians suffer, they share in the suffering of Christ. Third, submissiveness is prefigured in baptism, which has to do with more than the removal of dirt from the body. It is a sign of one's ingrafting into Christ, the victorious Christ, who now rules by his own authority.[5]

The remainder of the letter deals with what it means to live amidst suffering, particularly with the end not so far off (4:7, 12). Believers still have to exist in a world where they must live as nonconformists and must be subject to various types of opposition. They are to love one another (4:8); to show hospitality (4:8); to manifest the grace of God in every way they can (4:10); to speak God's word whenever they have the opportunity (4:11). They are not to be surprised at all when suffering comes, but are to entrust themselves to a faithful God (4:19). Elders are singled out, to be examples to others (5:1–5). Resist evil, for like a roaring lion it stalks about looking for a chance to wreak havoc (5:7). Bartlett puts it as follows:

> Christians are exhorted to be exemplary aliens in the land that does not welcome them. This means that they are to be as upright as the most upright of their neighbors. More than that, they are to forge for themselves an identity that sets them apart without necessarily setting them in conflict with the pagans around them. They are to return good for evil, blessing for slander—hoping perhaps against hope, that in the judgment their fidelity may shame their slanderers into believing.[6]

25

2 Peter

To think in terms of "false teaching" or heresy in the first or second centuries is a bit of an anomaly. Yet many of the books in the New Testament are directed at false teachers, who have twisted the gospel in one way or another and have taught their brand of the Christian faith to others. In the region of Galatia, Paul encountered a Jewish Christian group of teachers who advocated circumcision as necessary for membership in the people of God. Paul put up a vigorous argument in light of the freedom and grace of the gospel. The letter to the Colossians was directed to a similar distortion of the gospel, which was a dispute over Christology. At heart was the nature of the gospel and who Jesus was and is.

Second Peter is written to address such a situation, except that here the opponents scoff at the Christians and seek to remove elements of the faith that seem embarrassing in a pagan culture. The anticipation that Christ would return as judge of heaven and earth had not happened, and this called into question the moral life they were seeking to live. They were exploited with "deceptive words" (2:3). The result is this document, partially a letter (1:1–2) and partially a farewell speech (1:3–15).

Two passages are commended in the lectionary as epistolary readings for specific Sundays. Second Peter 1:16–21 is the recommended reading for the last Sunday in the Epiphany season, and the passage carries both christological and eschatological significance. It reflects the story of the transfiguration of Jesus on the mountain, when the voice is heard, "This is my Son, my Beloved, with whom I am well pleased" (1:17). The readers apparently were familiar with some form of the synoptic story (Mark 9:2–9). Set over against "cleverly devised myths" (1:16) is this eyewitness account of Jesus' moment of

173

glorification and the voice that declares Jesus to be God's beloved Son. The christological impact is heightened not only by the voice, but also by Jesus' reception of honor and glory from the Father.

But not only does the passage carry christological significance, it also reflects eschatological significance and the fulfillment of past promises. Whereas the synoptic writers refer to the fulfillment by means of the presence of Moses and Elijah on the mountain with Jesus, 2 Peter points forward to the second advent (*parousia*, 1:16). Jesus' coming again is not a myth. The witness to the transfiguration becomes a sure testimony that the readers can rely on God's faithfulness. They can live in hope.

Finally, this passage bears witness to the validity of Scripture and to the necessity of the Spirit in the interpretation of the text. Though the apostolic tradition results from eyewitnesses and not from "cleverly devised myths," true "interpretation" only happens when men and women are moved by the Spirit and thus speak in accord with God's intention.

The other text recommended by the lectionary (2 Pet 3:8–15a) develops as a response to the words of the scoffers, who challenge the prospect of Jesus' second advent. They are not well-meaning doubters, but brazen and cynical, who see themselves above moral constraint. Nothing has changed, they contend, since the creation of the world. Why should they await another coming? "Where is the promise of his coming? For ever since our ancestors died, all things continue as they were from the beginning of creation!" (3:4).

Two responses are given by the text. The first declares that the continuance of the world is not to be taken for granted (3:5–7). The judgment of God came through the flood. Only if one ignores the reality of the creation and the judgment by water can one say that nothing has occurred.

The second response reaffirms the advent of Christ (using Ps 90:4), but not by limiting the event to the current generation. The writer admits the delay of the time of the parousia, but affirms nevertheless from God's perspective that the promise of God is sure. Human life is ephemeral; God's perspective is everlasting. "But, in accordance with his promise, we wait for new heavens and a new earth, where righteousness is at home" (3:13; Rev 21:1). Meanwhile, we can take the present as a time of the Lord's patience and salvation (3:15).

26

Jude

I am indebted to R. S. Dietrich, a former colleague, a pastor, and a poet, for this rendition of Jude. Dr. Dietrich has pointed to the rich but fierce metaphors in the letter. As he comments, "The letter is strange, especially in the sense of wonderful, because of its imagery: rain clouds empty of rain, lunatic waves capped with shame instead of foam, misguided stars confusing the night sky. It begs for a poetic translation. Though everything in the letter is not immediately relevant to a modern audience, it still raises enduring questions: What is the nature of human evil? How much is it related to what we think and how much to what we do? How dangerous is it to others? And, how do we best resist it? Or, must we, at times, simply flee?"

Jude, to those God loves

I, Jude, a servant of Jesus, the Christ,
And James's brother, write: to those God calls,
to those God loves, to those Christ keeps. To you
be mercy, peace, abundant love.
                                    My hope
had been to write to you about salvation,
the joy we share. Instead, I find, I write
about the faith, the trust that we've been given:
Hold on to it. Hold hard. For certain men
(I wrote about before, God-hating men,
already damned—long since!)—are secretly
stealing in again among you to deny
that Jesus Christ is our one, only Lord
and Master. Would he bind us so, they ask,
whose grace is free? Grace sets you free: believe,

then, what you will do . . . what you will. You're free;
it doesn't matter.
                    But, all this you know.
Remember though that the same Lord who saved
his people out of Egypt, not long later
destroyed those who did not believe. I say:
Even the angels who abandoned him—
where are they? Kept in darkness, still, in chains,
from then to now to Judgment Day, in chains.
Of Sodom and Gomorrah, it's much the same.
They turned away; they turned the towns around them
to loveless sex, perversion; and they burned.
And burn, continuously.
                        Now, these fellows,
lured by their dreams—nightmares! They lie in filth,
they lie to you, they curse the angels. Michael,
remember, wouldn't even curse the devil,
when they were arguing about the body
of Moses, only said, "The Lord rebuke you."
But these men curse whatever they don't get.
The little they do doesn't come to them
by any sort of normal, human thinking
but by instinct, the way dogs run to garbage—
with the same wretched, retching result.
The Lord rebuke them, walking beside Cain,
palms out like Balaam, joining Korah's troop
of fools. And still you let them eat with you?—
as if you didn't know how they corrupt
your meals for their own fat and hollow pleasures:
for they are like rain clouds bringing no rain;
or, like fruit trees empty of fruit (dead even,
rooted in rot). Or they're like lunatic
waves capped with shame instead of foam. Lost stars,
confusing the night sky.
                        They are, as Enoch,
in Adam's seventh generation, said
(that long ago) "godless." "See here," he said,
"the Lord is coming with his thousand thousands
to judge us all, and to convict the godless—
their godless acts, their godless ways, the harsh
and godless words that godless sinners speak
against him." Like these men, grumbling, fault-finding,
following their own ill desires then boasting
of it and flattering you to go along.
Remember what the Lord's apostles said,
my friends—to you: "There will be scoffers, then,
though stuffed with lust, completely void of sense,"
desiring only, as I said before,
what instinct tells them to. What else could they?
There is no Spirit in them.[1]

PART FIVE

Revelation

27

The Revelation of John

The last book in the New Testament canon is called "apocalypse" of John. Somewhat surprisingly, this is the only time the word "apocalypse" occurs in the book. The term usually refers to a revelation, given by God to a seer, which has to do with events soon to take place. John Collins proposes the following definition: " 'Apocalypse' is a genre of revelatory literature with a narrative framework, in which a revelation is mediated by an otherworldly being to a human recipient, disclosing a transcendent reality which is both temporal, insofar as it envisages eschatological salvation, and spatial, insofar as it involves another, supernatural world."[1] Readers of the Bible often avoid the genre. It appears too confusing and difficult to understand. Others are repulsed by its violence and its cries of vengeance. Martin Luther, for example, is one who found the book objectionable. Still others, however, are fascinated by its symbols and move quickly to identify them with historical figures. Readers can produce all manner of strange interpretations that turn out to be an embarrassment to the church and occasionally precipitate events of tragic consequences.

Perhaps the majority of Bible readers are among those who simply ignore the book of Revelation. It makes no sense. The visions do not provide a satisfying key to unlock the door to an obvious meaning for today. It is not simply a matter of breaking a code and then being able to discover the answers to life's serious questions.

Revelation is unusual in three particular ways. First, though clearly an apocalypse, it nevertheless functions as a prophetic apocalypse in that it communicates to a concrete historical situation and brings to the implied readers "a prophetic word of God, enabling them to discern the divine purpose in their situation and to respond to their situation in a way appropriate to this purpose."[2]

Second, Revelation is a circular letter addressed to seven churches in Asia Minor. Each message written in 2:1–3:22 is aimed at specific congregations, and yet the seven messages are introductory to the rest of the book as can be seen from the promise to "conquer," which concludes each message. Moral exhortations, normally absent from apocalypses, are prominent here.

Third, usually apocalyptic writings were penned in a time of persecution, when people were disenfranchised from their bases of power. The writings not only provided comfort and reassurance that God was ultimately in control of history despite the current appearances, but also served as protest literature. They encouraged their readers not to accept the worldview and value system embraced by the dominant culture.

If, however, one takes seriously the settings of the seven churches of Asia Minor, specifically addressed in 2:1–3:22, one is impressed with the variety of conditions to which this document is written. Ephesus, a church with patience, has endured great suffering, but also has abandoned their initial love. They are called to repent. Smyrna is a poor church that despite its poverty is spiritually rich. Sardis is also a community vulnerable to divine judgment, though distinguished by a few people who "walk with me, dressed in white, for they are worthy" (3:4). Laodicea is a wealthy community, which has prospered and seems to lack nothing, except that blinded by its wealth it is in need of the gospel and of repentance.

What these churches have in common is the need for endurance, for habits of resistance to keep them from the hour of trial that is coming on the whole world. Whether wealthy or poor, each community is called to withstand whatever suffering that may come. "Apocalypse offers a converted sense of history, so that one might see in every event not only the reality of death but also the Word of God; not only the demonic and the dehumanizing, but also the power of the resurrection; not only the portents of doom, but also hope for oneself and one's society."[3]

The structure of the book is fairly clear:

1:1–20	The Prologue
2:1–3:22	The message to the seven churches
4:1–11:19	The opening of the seven seals
12:1–14:20	The conflict with the two beasts
15:1–16:21	The seven bowl plagues
17:1–19:10	The fall of Babylon
19:11–20:15	The final victory
21:1–22:5	The new Jerusalem
22:6–21	The conclusion

Several narratives within the book serve to give it coherence. Perhaps the most prominent is the story that begins at 12:1, where a dragon chases a pregnant woman. The dragon had been a part of an unsuccessful rebellion against God and had been booted out of heaven, but was worshiped by people from all over the world. The pregnant woman successfully gives birth to a baby boy, which angers the dragon even more. He launches an attack on the offspring of the woman, and is joined in the struggle by two beasts, one from the sea and the other from the land. War is waged particularly against "those who keep the commandments of God and hold the testimony of Jesus" (12:17). Of the people, 144,000 individuals are rescued, the same number that in the vision of the seer were "sealed" from the twelve tribes of Israel (7:4–8). The conclusion to the narrative comes when the hostile force, known as the great whore, Babylon, envisioned in terms of Rome (17:1–18), is finally defeated. "They will make war on the Lamb, and the Lamb will conquer them, for he is Lord of lords and King of kings, and those with him are called and chosen and faithful" (17:14).

Three further features of Revelation help to undergird the critique of Roman power and to prepare for the coming of the new heaven and the new earth. The first is the highly theocentric perspective that runs throughout the book. The prologue ends with a divine self-revelation. " 'I am the Alpha and the Omega,' says the Lord God, who is and who was and who is to come, the Almighty" (1:8). When added to these designations "the one who is seated on the throne" (4:9; 5:1, 7, 13; 6:16; 7:15; 21:5), we are concerned "with the indispensable expressions of Jewish monotheism in Revelation."[4] This language is not at all anthropomorphic. It relies on the Old Testament for its force and effectiveness. Unlike human gods and idols, God is "the utterly incomparable One, to whom all nations are subject, whose purpose none can frustrate (cf. Isa 40:12–26)."[5] From this theocentric base, the criticism of all human powers that challenge God's purposes and plans emerges.

This theocentric perspective, given the failure of the myth of progress and the decline of secular hope, is the only credible eschatology that can provide the world with a satisfying conclusion. It is a transcendent one that looks for a resolution of history that exceeds any possible immanent outcome of history.[6]

The second feature that runs through the book of Revelation is the predominant emphasis on worship. In the critical fifth chapter, when no one is worthy to open the scroll and break its seal, one of the elders declares that the Lion of the tribe of Judah, the Root of David has conquered and can open the scroll and its seven seals. The image of Jesus as the Lamb who has been slaughtered then takes the scroll, and "they sing a new song. And the angels heartily join in

> "Worthy is the Lamb that was slaughtered
> to receive power and wealth and wisdom and might
> and honor and glory and blessing!"

Then I heard every creature in heaven and on earth and under the earth and in the sea, and all that is in them, singing,

> "To the one seated on the throne and to the Lamb
> be blessing and honor and glory and might
> forever and ever!" (Rev 5:11–13)

Throughout the book the new song is sung, until the vision of a new heaven and a new earth is apparent and "the one who was seated on the throne [says], 'See, I am making all things new'" (21:5).

The purpose of such worship is set in opposition to pagan idolatry, which Rome propagated in the name of peace and economic prosperity. One of the beast's heads receives a mortal wound, but the beast is surprisingly healed, making him a much-revered figure (13:3–4). The allusion is likely to Nero and to the chaotic events immediately following his death. There was fear in the empire that it might disintegrate. But the Flavian dynasty restored the imperial power. So "the mortal wound" was healed. Thus to worship God was to resist the Roman pretensions to power and to leave oneself vulnerable to persecution and to death. Twice John prostrates himself before the angel who mediates the divine revelation to him, only to be told by the angel that he is but a fellow servant and directs John to worship God alone (19:10; 22:8–9).

The third feature of Revelation is the importance of Jesus and his relationship to God. The prologue ends with the statement, "'I am the Alpha and the Omega,' says the Lord God, who is and who was and who is to come, the Almighty" (1:8). The affirmation is repeated in 21:6. And yet Jesus is also designated as "the first and the last" (1:17) and in the conclusion he identifies himself, "I am the Alpha and the Omega, the first and the last, the beginning and the end" (22:13). This is remarkable. As Bauckham notes, "As a way of stating that Jesus Christ belongs to the fullness of the eternal being of God, this surpasses anything in the New Testament."[7] It is in Christ's coming again that God who is the beginning of all things will also become the end of all things. Though as decisive as the resurrection is for Jesus, these titles he shares with God point to the fact that he shared them with God before the creation of the world.

Conclusion
Studying the New Testament

It was Karl Barth who first coined the phrase "the strange new world within the Bible."[1] He perhaps more than any other theologian of the twentieth century understood and articulated the oddness of the Bible and acknowledged that he was reaching beyond himself even to discuss it. Initially entrance into this new world baffles the reader and yet despite all our human limitations "the holy scriptures will interpret themselves to us." For example, there is plenty of history in the Bible, and the learned historians will seek to discover how it all happened, to ask how it is that one event follows another, why the people responded the way they did. It is just at the crucial point that "the Bible meets the lover of history with silences quite unparalleled." The moralist goes to the Bible to find models of good behavior, but comes up empty-handed. The Bible constantly amazes us with its remarkable indifference to our conceptions of good and evil. Even the individual that seeks the right religion finds himself stymied. "It is not the right human thoughts about God which form the content of the Bible, but the right divine thoughts about [humans]." Instead of history and morality, the Bible offers us the knowledge of God. The strange new world of the Bible is a place where one sees and understands that the Spirit creates a new heaven and a new earth, where there are new people, new families, new relationships, and new politics; where the voice of the one sitting on the throne resounds, "See, I am making all things new" (Rev 21:5).

If Barth is correct, then our Enlightenment notions of objectivity and autonomous reason go out the window, and we who read must be open to new thoughts and ideas, even new ways to read the text. Our heritage from Descartes that the individual can think and interpret the text on one's own is left in shambles. What the eighteenth and nineteenth centuries had freed us

183

from, namely the domination of ecclesiastical control of interpretation, has left interpreters confused in trying to move from the original context to what the text might mean for today. Surely the Bible is not to be read like a pottery shard, interesting in its own time and place, but hardly as a living word for readers.

Thus, as we read and study the text we are guided by the Spirit. Anyone who reads very far in the Scriptures discovers that the study of the Bible is not a purely academic matter. If one starts with Genesis, it is not long before one encounters a serpent that can speak. Or if one begins with Matthew, immediately one reads of a baby conceived and born not by natural processes, but by the Spirit. The Bible is full of miracles. They trouble the Enlightenment person who must find a way to explain how and if it "really happened." If one, however, trusts the guidance of the Spirit in interpreting the text, one is led beyond the issue of historicity. The Spirit did not cease acting when the books were canonized. Rather, the promise of Scripture itself is that the Spirit will be present at the reading of the text to illumine and enlighten us as we struggle to grasp its meaning for today. Thus the initial principle in our study of the Scriptures is our need for openness to the Spirit, who promises to lead us into this "strange new world."

Now in a time of the growth of fundamentalism around the world, it should be noted that the Spirit's presence in our reading of the text does not imply an inerrancy or that the Spirit comes as a part of the book itself and protects it as God's Word. Calvin claimed that the Spirit came alongside the text and was not limited to the text. Rather, the Spirit takes what we bring to the text—our experiences, our social location, who we are—to lead to an understanding, often nudging us forward to new places we have never been before.

Does this work of the Spirit mean that books of scholars who have worked on the biblical narrative in the past should be jettisoned? A second principle of interpretation advocated in the Reformed tradition is "the rule of faith," which says that the Bible is always to be read in light of past and present readings of the text (not only in commentaries but in the creeds and confessions of the church). We don't start de novo at the task of studying Scripture. We are not the first people who have come across the issues in a given passage, and we need to be guided by the wisdom of those who have plowed these fields before us, as well as those who are plowing them now. At the same time it has to be said that we are never locked into the interpretations of the past. One can think of the many ways African Americans and women have taught us to read the text in recent days.

A third principle guideline for the study of the Scripture is one that John Calvin particularly stressed: Scripture interprets Scripture. At least two things need to be said about this guideline. One is obvious—namely, that the reader should interpret the opaque parts of the text by those parts that are clear, the complex by the simple, the peripheral by the central, and the parts by the whole. Another thing is that the Old Testament needs to be read in terms of the New Testament. The movement is from back to front. As Lou Martyn puts it, "There are no through-trains from the scriptural, patriarchal traditions and their perceptive criteria to the gospel of God's Son."[2] Paul, for example, did not come to the Christian faith from his study of the Old Testament writings, but rather from his encounter with the risen Christ. After his transformation, however, he became an acute reader of Old Testament texts and quite a different reader from before the advent of the gospel. Equally, one cannot understand the New Testament apart from the Old. The Old gives the reader the categories, the movement, and the promise, which lead to the coming of the Christ.[3] For example, Christ is interpreted by and himself reinterprets the categories of "prophet, priest, and king." This is a way of saying that the Bible has to be read intertextually.

A fourth principle in interpretation is the conviction that Jesus Christ is the center of Scripture. Nowhere does this become more obvious (and relevant) than at the time of the Barmen Declaration, written against the Nazi forces in 1934. "Jesus Christ, as he is attested to us in Holy Scripture, is the one Word of God which we have to hear and which we have to trust and obey in life and death," so the Declaration states. For a long time this christological focus was interpreted in the categories of the Old Testament as promise and the New Testament as fulfillment. To be sure, a lot of New Testament texts claim that the Old Testament texts have been fulfilled in Jesus. The canonical approach, heralded by Brevard Childs, however, has broadened the perspective so that all Scripture is read in the church according to the confession that Jesus is Lord (see Childs's work on Ps 8:4–5).[4] The Old Testament is read not merely as a prologue to the New. It is interesting to note that the great thinkers of the past, such as Augustine, Aquinas, Luther, and Calvin did not consider themselves specialists in only one part of Scripture, but saw their own readings in light of the whole Bible and as an activity integrated into the life of the community.

The key here is the imagination the reader exercises in coming to the text, in contrast to the Enlightenment's search for objectivity. Imagination is the capacity to envision the existence of something that does not yet exist. It demands resourcefulness and hard work. Reading a text is an art that grows out of engagement, in contrast to the detached objectivity championed by the Enlightenment.[5]

The Bible is the church's book, and thus a fifth principle of interpretation is that the Bible needs to be read in community with others. It should be read "personally" but not "privately." This is especially true when the community is composed of those of diverse ethnic, racial, and economic backgrounds.

Each person in bringing his or her own gifts and limitations to the table can enrich and be enriched by the readings of those from whom he or she may differ. In this sense the text is "contextualized." It is read from a particular location that needs to be acknowledged.

In the Reformed tradition, one might add "the rule of love" as a sixth principle of interpretation. Jesus himself, quoting interestingly the Old Testament, said that the law and the prophets are summed up in two commandments: to love God with all our heart, soul, mind, and strength, and to love our neighbors as ourselves. An interpretation that degrades people or leads to contempt for God is, by definition, a false reading of the text. This should be thought of in a cultural as well as a personal way. The Bible has been used to justify holy wars and inquisitions, segregation and apartheid, the abuse of power, and the subjugation of people under tyrannical governments. Then what do we do, for example, with those texts that demean women? We have tried to speak to such texts as they have occurred in the course of the study of the New Testament. Each passage is fraught with a different set of problems and grows out of a different context, and yet "the rule of love" pushes us always to get beyond the situation in the ancient world to a point where all people are to be accepted and acknowledged as God's creatures.

This leads to a seventh principle. The Scriptures are always to be read in light of the literary form and the social and historical context in which they are written. To take the eleven chapters of Genesis as literal history can lead to all sorts of distortions. On the other hand, we immediately recognize the parable of the Good Samaritan as a made-up story and don't go searching for the Jericho police records to see if there was an account of a mugging of a Jewish traveler. Sometimes the failure to detect the literary form in which a text appears and the attempt to literalize everything reminds one of Data, the android character in the Star Trek series, who cannot recognize jokes. He literalizes everything and is puzzled when one speaks humorously.

An eighth principle states that because we are sinful people and interpret Scripture before a living God, every particular reading is provisional. The interpreter must be open to change (as the church has done in its treatment of women). The recognition of our limitations and the work of the Spirit can lead in directions we have never gone before.

Finally, to return to what is said in the Introduction to this book, we read the text for all it is worth. As Ricoeur put it, the text has "a surplus of meaning." It demands more than our historical-critical methods, but neither can it ignore them. It pushes beyond the "distantiation" of the biblical text to speak to the church a timely message of hope and anticipation. It brings the reader face-to-face with the judging, redeeming, and living God.

Notes

Introduction

1. Paul Feine and Johannes Behm, *Introduction to the New Testament*, ed. W. G. Kümmel, 14th rev. ed. (Nashville: Abingdon Press, 1966), 25.
2. Adolf Hilgenfeld, *Historisch-kritische Einleitung in das Neue Testament* (Leipzig: L. F. Fues, 1875).
3. William Baird, *History of New Testament Research*, vol. 1, *From Deism to Tübingen* (Minneapolis: Fortress Press, 1992), 274.
4. Paul Ricoeur, *Essays on Biblical Interpretation* (Philadelphia: Fortress Press, 1980), 54.
5. Paul Ricoeur, *Interpretation Theory: Discourse and the Surplus of Meaning* (Fort Worth: Texas Christian University Press, 1976), 92.
6. Paul Ricoeur, "The Model of the Text: Meaningful Action Considered as a Text," in *Hermeneutics and the Human Sciences*, ed. John B. Thompson (Cambridge: Cambridge University Press, 1981), 201; cited by Dan R. Stiver, *Theology after Ricoeur: New Directions in Hermeneutical Theology* (Louisville, KY: Westminster John Knox Press, 2001), 91.
7. Paul Ricoeur, *The Symbolism of Evil* (Boston: Beacon Press, 1967), 349.
8. Hans-Georg Gadamer, *Truth and Method*, rev. ed. (New York: Crossroad, 1991), 306.
9. Ricoeur, *Interpretation Theory*, 45–69.
10. See Brevard S. Childs, *The New Testament as Canon: An Introduction* (Philadelphia: Fortress Press, 1984), 144–48.
11. See David Rhodes, *The Challenge of Diversity: The Witness of Paul and the Gospels* (Minneapolis: Fortress Press, 1996).
12. For example, the tomb of Joseph of Arimathea is twice called "a new tomb" (Matt 27:60; John 19:41).
13. Charles B. Cousar, "The Concept of Newness in the New Testament: An Exegetical Inquiry into the Shape and Life of the New Order" (PhD diss., University of Aberdeen, 1960), 1–17.
14. Walter Brueggemann, *An Introduction to the Old Testament: The Canon and Christian Imagination* (Louisville, KY: Westminster John Knox Press, 2003), 2.

Chapter 1: Introduction to the Pauline Letters

1. Harry Y. Gamble, *Books and Readers in the Early Church: A History of Early Christian Texts* (New Haven, CT: Yale University Press, 1995), 98.
2. Ibid., 99.
3. A. M. Hunter, *Paul and His Predecessors* (London: SCM Press, 1961), 10.
4. The period from the death of Jesus until the earliest writing that we have (probably 1 Thessalonians) is occasionally referred to as the twilight period, because our understanding of it is reflected from a later period. For two radically different interpretations of the decades of the thirties and forties of the first century of the Common Era, see John Dominic Crossan, *The Birth of Christianity* (San Francisco: Harper, 1998), and Paul Barnett, *The Birth of Christianity: The First Twenty Years* (Grand Rapids: Wm. B. Eerdmans, 2005).
5. Harry Y. Gamble, *The New Testament Canon: Its Making and Meaning* (Philadelphia: Fortress Press, 1985), 45–46.
6. So surmises Bruce Metzger, *The Canon of the New Testament: Its Origin, Development, and Significance* (Oxford: Clarendon Press, 1987), 42.
7. See, most recently, Stanley Porter, "When and How Was the Pauline Canon Compiled? An Assessment of Theories," in *The Pauline Canon*, ed. Stanley Porter (Leiden: Brill, 2004), 95–127.
8. Francis Watson, *Paul, Judaism, and the Gentiles: A Sociological Approach*, SNTS 56 (Cambridge: Cambridge University Press, 1986), 28–38.
9. Daniel Boyarin, *A Radical Jew: Paul and the Politics of Identity* (Berkeley: University of California Press, 1994), 39, 58–59.
10. Ibid., 106.
11. Terence L. Donaldson, *Paul and the Gentiles: Remapping Paul's Convictional World* (Minneapolis: Fortress Press, 1997), 293–307.
12. Robin Scroggs, *Pauline Theology I*, ed. Jouette Bassler (Minneapolis: Fortress Press, 1992), 214.
13. See Keck's comment, "'Apocalyptic' is an adjective which characterizes a type of theology, not merely a type of eschatology," in "Paul and Apocalyptic Theology," *Interpretation* 38 (1984): 233.
14. See John J. Collins, *The Apocalyptic Imagination: An Introduction to the Jewish Matrix of Christianity* (New York: Crossroad, 1987).
15. Keck points to those ways in which Paul, though interpreting the Christ event as thoroughly apocalyptic, significantly differed from Jewish apocalyptic in "Paul and Apocalyptic Theology," 235–41.
16. See J. Louis Martyn, *Theological Issues in the Letters of Paul* (Nashville: Abingdon Press, 1997), 89–110.

Chapter 2: Romans

1. I am assuming that chapter 16 is an integral part of the letter and not a later addition to an abbreviated letter. See the discussion in Karl P. Donfried and Thomas Walter Manson, eds., *The Romans Debate*, rev. and enl. ed. (Minneapolis: Augsburg Press, 1991).
2. J. Louis Martyn, *Theological Issues in the Letters of Paul* (Nashville: Abingdon Press, 1997), 37–45.
3. Karl Barth, *A Shorter Commentary on Romans* (Richmond: John Knox Press, 1959), 20.
4. C. H. Dodd, *The Epistle of Paul to the Romans* (New York: Harper & Row, 1932), 50–55.

5. John A. T. Robinson, *Wrestling with Romans* (Philadelphia: Westminster Press, 1979), 18–19.
6. Paul W. Meyer, "Romans," in *The HarperCollins Bible Commentary*, rev. ed., ed. James L. Mays et al. (New York: HarperCollins Publishers, 1988), 1043–44.
7. Several exegetical decisions are evident in this translation, the most controversial of which is likely the treatment of the Greek phrase *pisteos Insou Christou* in 3:22 as "the faithfulness of Jesus Christ" rather than "faith in Jesus Christ." Cf. Richard B. Hays, *The Faith of Jesus Christ: An Introduction of the Narrative Substructure of Galatians 3:1–4:11* (Chico, CA: Scholars Press, 1983).
8. Richard B. Hays, *Pauline Theology IV*, ed. E. Elizabeth Johnson (Atlanta: Scholars Press, 1997), 45. The rendering "faithfulness of Christ" also removes an otherwise redundant phrasing from the text.
9. Ernst Käsemann, *Commentary on Romans*, trans. William Bromiley (Grand Rapids: Wm. B. Eerdmans, 1980), 108.
10. Ibid., 137.
11. Paul J. Achtemeier, *Romans* (Atlanta: John Knox Press, 1985), 97.
12. Käsemann, *Commentary on Romans*, 141.
13. So, Ernst Käsemann speaks of "a remarkable caveat in the shape of an eschatological reservation," in *New Testament Questions of Today* (Philadelphia: Fortress Press, 1969), 132.
14. Martyn, *Theological Issues in the Letters of Paul*, 107–9.
15. For a careful treatment, see Paul W. Meyer, *The Word in This World: Essays in New Testament Exegesis and Theology* (Louisville, KY: Westminster John Knox Press, 2004), 57–77.
16. James D. G. Dunn, *Romans 1–8*, Word Biblical Commentary 38A (Dallas: Word Books, 1988), 399.
17. The Greek noun for "spirit" appears in Romans only four times prior to chap. 8, and it occurs twenty-one times in chap. 8.
18. The Jews are included through use of the language of the "remnant." Isa 10:22–23 is cited to make the case. See David M. Hay and E. Elizabeth Johnson, eds., *Pauline Theology III* (Minneapolis: Fortress Press, 1995), 211–39.
19. Meyer, "Romans," 1063.
20. Hay and Johnson, *Pauline Theology III*, 227–28.
21. These and other linkages are developed by Michael B. Thompson, *Clothed with Christ: The Example and Teaching of Jesus in Romans 12:1–15:13*, Journal for the Study of the New Testament: Supplement Series 59 (Sheffield: JSOT Press, 1991), 78–86.
22. Meyer, "Romans," 1162.
23. John Calvin, *The Epistle of Paul the Apostle to the Romans and the Thessalonians*, eds. David W. Torrance and Thomas F. Torrance; trans. Ross Mackenzie (Grand Rapids: Wm. B. Eerdmans, 1995), 271.
24. A strong verb, meaning to "receive into one's home or circle of acquaintants," W. Bauer, W. F. Arndt, F. W. Gingrich, and F. W. Darker, *Greek-English Lexicon of the New Testament and Other Early Christian Literature*, 2nd ed. (Chicago: University of Chicago Press, 1979), 883.

Chapter 3: 1 Corinthians

1. See Walter Bauer's comment: 1 Corinthians is "that unit among the major Pauline letters which yields the very least for our understanding of the Pauline

faith," in Walter Bauer et al., *Orthodoxy and Heresy in Earliest Christianity* (Philadelphia: Fortress Press, 1971), 219.

2. See the convincing argument of Margaret M. Mitchell, *Paul and the Rhetoric of Reconciliation: An Exegetical Investigation of the Language and Composition of 1 Corinthians* (Louisville, KY: Westminster/John Knox Press, 1991).

3. George Alexander Kennedy, *New Testament Interpretation through Rhetorical Criticism* (Chapel Hill: University of North Carolina Press, 1984), 5–6.

4. Richard B. Hays, *First Corinthians*, Interpretation (Louisville, KY: John Knox Press, 1997), 83.

5. Cf. John Calvin, *Institutes of the Christian Religion*, ed. John T. McNeill, trans. Ford Lewis Battles, Library of Christian Classics 20 (Philadelphia: Westminster Press, 1960), 689–90.

6. Ernst Käsemann, *Essays on NT Themes*, Studies in Biblical Theology (London: SCM Press, 1964), 110.

7. Martin Luther, *Works*, vol. 31, ed. J. J. Pelikan et al. (St. Louis: Concordia Publishing House, 1955), 51–52.

8. In his treatment of 1 Cor 15, Martinus C. de Boer concludes, "Paul's argument against the deniers and for the resurrection of the dead with his cosmological-apocalyptic understanding of death is thus an extension of his theology of the cross," in *The Defeat of Death: Apocalyptic Eschatology in I Corinthians 15 and Romans 5*, Journal for the Society of the New Testament: Supplement Series 22 (Sheffield: JSOT Press, 1988), 140.

9. Much of this material on 1 Cor I developed more fully in "The Theological Task of 1 Corinthians: A Conversation with Gordon D. Fee and Victor Paul Furnish," in *Pauline Theology II*, ed. David M. Hay (Minneapolis: Fortress Press, 1993), 90–102.

Chapter 4: 2 Corinthians

1. My own position is that 2 Corinthians likely contains two letters, and that probably chaps. 1–9 were written before chaps. 10–13. See Victor Paul Furnish, *II Corinthians*, Anchor Bible 32A (New York: Doubleday, 1984), 35–55.

2. Frances M. Young and David Ford, *Meaning and Truth in 2 Corinthians* (Grand Rapids: Wm. B. Eerdmans, 1987), 54.

3. John Howard Schütz, *Paul and the Anatomy of Apostolic Authority*, Society for New Testament Studies Monograph Series (London: Cambridge University Press, 1975), 232.

4. See the treatment of 3:1–4:6 in Richard B. Hays, *Echoes of Scripture in the Letters of Paul* (New Haven, CT: Yale University Press, 1989), 122–53.

5. Bruce Malina, *The New Testament World: Insights from Cultural Anthropology* (Louisville, KY: Westminster John Knox Press, 2001), 75.

6. For the Old Testament development of this notion, see Walter Brueggemann, *Deep Memory, Exuberant Hope: Contested Truth in a Post-Christian World*, ed. Patrick D. Miller (Minneapolis: Fortress Press, 2000), 69–75. See also the treatment of this theme in 2 Cor by Young and Ford, *Meaning and Truth in 2 Corinthians*, 172–80.

7. Brueggemann, *Deep Memory, Exuberant Hope*, 75.

Chapter 5: Galatians

1. J. Louis Martyn, *Galatians: A New Translation with Introduction and Commentary*, Anchor Bible 33A (New York: Doubleday, 1997), 90–91.

2. Ibid., 99.

3. Ibid., 136.
4. Bernard C. Lategan, "The Inter- and Intra-Jewish Political Context of Paul's Letter to the Galatians," in *The Galatians Debate: Contemporary Issues in Rhetorical and Historical Interpretation*, ed. Mark D. Nanos (Peabody, MA: Hendrickson, 2002), 420.
5. See the discussion of Paul's call by Krister Stendahl (*Paul among Jews and Gentiles* [Philadelphia: Fortress Press, 1976], 7–23), who eschews both the term "conversion" for Paul's experience and the critique by Gaventa, who prefers the word "transformation," which demands not a rejection of the past but a changed way of understanding, "a new perception, a re-cognition of the past." See Beverly Roberts Gaventa, *From Darkness to Light: Aspects of Conversion in the New Testament* (Philadelphia; Fortress Press, 1986), 10–11.
6. George Howard, *Paul: Crisis in Galatia: A Study in Early Christian Theology* (Cambridge: Cambridge University Press, 1990), 58.
7. J. Louis Martyn, *Theological Issues in the Letters of Paul* (Nashville: Abingdon Press, 1997), 199.
8. Richard B. Hays, "Galatians," in *The New Interpreter's Bible* (Nashville: Abingdon Press, 1994), 323.
9. Ibid., 334–45.

Chapter 6: Philippians

1. A number of scholars have identified Philippians as a letter of friendship, each building on the research of his predecessors. See Peter Marshall, *Enmity in Corinth: Social Conventions in Paul's Relations with the Corinthians* (Tübingen: Mohr Siebeck, 1987); L. M. White, "Morality between Two Worlds: A Paradigm of Friendship in Philippians," in *Greeks, Romans, and Christians: Essays in Honor of Abraham Malherbe*, ed. D. L. Balch, E. Ferguson, W. Meeks (Minneapolis: Fortress Press, 1990), 201–21; Stanley Stowers, "Friends and Enemies in the Politics of Heaven: Reading Theology in Philippians," in *Pauline Theology*, vol. 1, ed. Jouette Bassler (Minneapolis: Fortress Press, 1991), 105–21.
2. Gordon D. Fee, *Paul's Letter to the Philippians*, New International Community on the New Testament (Grand Rapids: Wm. B. Eerdmans, 1995).
3. Paul Schubert, *Form and Function of the Pauline Thanksgivings* (Berlin: A. Töpelmann, 1939), 71–82.
4. Loveday Alexander, "Hellenistic Letter-Form and the Structure of Philippians," *Journal for the Study of the New Testament* 37 (1989): 87–101.
5. Ernst Käsemann, "The Saving Significance of the Death of Jesus in Paul," in *Perspectives on Paul*, trans. Margaret Kohl (Philadelphia: Fortress Press, 1971), 37.
6. See Walter Grundmann, *Theological Dictionary of the New Testament*, ed. G. Kittel and G. Friedrich, trans. G. W. Bromiley (Grand Rapids: Wm. B. Eerdmans, 1972), 1–26.
7. Karl Barth, *The Epistle to the Philippians* (Richmond: John Knox Press, 1962), 59.
8. See Ralph P. Martin, *A Hymn of Christ: Philippians 2:5–11 in Recent Interpretation & The Setting of Early Christian Worship* (Downers Grove, IL: InterVarsity Press, 1997); Richard J. Bauckham, "The Worship of Jesus in Philippians 2:9–11," in *Where Christology Began: Essays on Philippians 2*, ed. R. P. Martin and B. J. Dodd (Louisville, KY: Westminster John Knox Press, 1998).
9. Ernst Käsemann, "A Critical Analysis of Phil 2:5–11," *JTC* 5 (New York: Harper and Row, 1968), 72.

10. See William S. Kurz, "Kenotic Imitation of Paul and of Christ," in *Discipleship in the New Testament*, ed. Fernando Segovia (Philadelphia: Fortress Press, 1985), 113.
11. Marshall, *Enmity in Corinth*, 163–64; cf. 1–18.
12. Seneca, *Ad Lucilium Epistulae Morales* 9:13.

Chapter 7: Philemon

1. Allen Dwight Callahan, *Embassy of Onesimus: The Letter of Paul to Philemon* (Valley Forge, PA: Trinity Press International, 1997), 69–70.
2. See Norman R. Petersen, *Rediscovering Paul: Philemon and the Sociology of Paul's Narrative World* (Philadelphia: Fortress Press, 1985), 65–78.
3. Peter Lampe, "Keine 'Slavenflucht' des Onesimus," *Zeitschrift für die neutestamentliche Wissenschoft und die Kunde der älteren Kirche* 76: 135–37.
4. Petersen, *Rediscovering Paul*, 92.
5. N. T. Wright, *The Epistles of Paul to the Colossians and to Philemon*, Tyndale New Testament Commentary (Grand Rapids: Wm. B. Eerdmans, 1986), 169.
6. John M. G. Barclay, *Colossians and Philemon*, New Testament Guides, (Sheffield: Sheffield Academic Press, 1997), 119–26.

Chapter 8: 1 Thessalonians

1. Douglas Harink, *Paul among the Postliberals: Pauline Theology beyond Christendom and Modernity* (Grand Rapids: Brazos Press, 2003), 35.
2. Abraham Smith, "The First Letter to the Thessalonians," in *The New Interpreter's Bible* (Nashville: Abingdon Press, 1994), 9:720.
3. Beverly R. Gaventa, *First and Second Thessalonians*, Interpretation: A Bible Commentary for Teaching and Preaching (Louisville, KY: Westminster John Knox Press, 1998), 27.
4. Ibid., 42.
5. Smith, "The First Letter," 9:702.
6. Gaventa, *First and Second Thessalonians*, 87.

Chapter 9: Introduction to the Pauline Tradition

1. Paul Feine, Johannes Behm, and W. G. Kümmel, *Introduction to the New Testament*, 14th rev. ed. (Nashville: Abingdon Press, 1966), 185–90, 237–72; Bart D. Ehrman, *The New Testament: A Historical Introduction to the Early Christian Writings*, 3rd ed. (New York: Oxford University Press, 2004), 372–94.
2. See David G. Meade, *Pseudonymity and Canon* (Tübingen: Mohr, 1986); J. D. G. Dunn, "The Problem of Pseudonymity," in *The Living Word* (Philadelphia: Fortress, 1987), 65–85; Raymond F. Collins, *Letters That Paul Did Not Write: The Epistle to the Hebrews and the Pauline Pseudepigrapha* (Wilmington, DE: Glazier, 1988), 57–87.

Chaper 10: Ephesians

1. Karl Barth, *Wolfgang Amadeus Mozart* (Grand Rapids: Wm. B. Eerdmans, 1986, Eng. trans.), 23.
2. Andrew T. Lincoln, *Ephesians*, Word Biblical Commentary (Waco, TX: Word, 1990), lxxv.
3. Andrew T. Lincoln and A. J. M. Wedderburn, *The Theology of the Later Pauline Letters* (Cambridge: Cambridge University Press, 1993), 82.
4. Eduard Norden, *Agnostos Theos* (Berlin: Teubner, 1913), 253 (cited by Lincoln, *Ephesians*, 11).
5. Lincoln and Wedderburn, *Theology of the Later Pauline Letters*, 97.

6. Lincoln, *Ephesians*, 133.
7. Lincoln and Wedderburn, *Theology of the Later Pauline Letters*, 137.

Chapter 11: Colossians

1. Morna D. Hooker, "Were There False Teachers in Colossae?" in *Christ and Spirit in the New Testament*, eds. B. Lindars and B. B. Smalley (Cambridge: Cambridge University Press, 1973), 313–31.
2. Margaret Y. MacDonald, *Colossians and Ephesians*, Sacra pagina (Collegeville, MN: Liturgical Press, 2000), 56.
3. Christopher Tuckett, *Christology and the New Testament: Jesus and His Earliest Followers* (Louisville, KY: Westminster John Knox Press, 2001), 75.
4. Some scholars have taken the phrases "the church" in 1:18 and "through the blood of the cross" in 1:20 as additions to the original hymn. See Ernst Käsemann, *Essays on New Testament Themes* (London: SCM Press, 1964), 149–68.
5. Andrew T. Lincoln and A. J. M. Wedderburn, *The Theology of the Later Pauline Letters* (Cambridge: Cambridge University Press, 1993) 48–53.

Chapter 13: The Pastoral Letters

1. Margaret Y. MacDonald, *The Pauline Churches: A Socio-Historical Study of Institutionalization in the Pauline and Deutero-Pauline Writings* (Cambridge: Cambridge University Press, 1988).
2. Frances Young, *The Theology of the Pastoral Letters* (Cambridge: Cambridge University Press, 1994), 97–121.
3. Ibid., 121.
4. Dennis R. MacDonald, *The Legend and the Apostle: The Battle for Paul in Story and in Canon* (Philadelphia: Westminster Press, 1983), 334–53.
5. Raymond F. Collins, *I & II Timothy and Titus: A Commentary*, New Testament Library (Louisville, KY: Westminster John Knox Press, 2002), 58.
6. Jouette M. Bassler, *1 Timothy, 2 Timothy, Titus*, Abingdon New Testament Commentaries (Nashville: Abingdon Press, 1996), 119.

Chapter 14: Introduction to the Synoptic Gospels

1. It was traditionally thought that Matthew was the earliest Gospel and that Mark used Matthew in constructing his Gospel. Almost universally that view has been abandoned in favor of Markan priority. See Christopher Tuckett, *The Revival of the Griesbach Hypothesis* (Cambridge: Cambridge University Press, 1983). Though some scholars date the Gospel of Thomas as early as Mark, e.g., Helmut Koester, *Ancient Christian Gospels: Their History and Development* (Philadelphia: Trinity Press, 1990), it reads more clearly as a second-century document. See Christopher Tuckett, "Thomas and the Synoptics," *Novum Testamentum* 30 (1988): 132–57; and J. P. Meier, *A Marginal Jew: Rethinking the Historical Jesus*, vol. 1 (New York: Doubleday, 1991), 112–66.
2. Origen, *Contra Celsus* 1.34, 1.40, 1.58, 1.68, 2.24, 2.55, etc. See Harry Y. Gamble, *Books and Readers in the Early Church: A History of Early Christian Texts* (New Haven, CT: Yale University Press, 1995), 103.
3. *Dialogue with Trypho* 10.2.

Chapter 15: The Gospel of Mark

1. Graham N. Stanton, *Jesus and Gospel* (Cambridge: Cambridge University Press, 2004), 3.
2. Donald Juel, *A Master of Surprise: Mark Interpreted* (Minneapolis: Fortress Press, 1994), 35.

3. Joel Marcus, *Mark 1–8*, Anchor Bible (New York: Doubleday, 2000), 176.
4. Ibid., 238.
5. See Ched Myers, *Binding the Strong Man: A Political Reading of Mark's Story of Jesus* (Maryknoll, NY: Orbis, 1988).
6. Joachim Jeremias, *The Parables of Jesus* (New York: Scribners, 1963), 150n.
7. See John R. Donahue, *The Gospel in Parable* (Philadelphia: Fortress Press, 1988), 39–46; Marcus, *Mark 1–8*, 298–308; Arland J. Hultgren, *The Parables of Jesus: A Commentary* (Grand Rapids: Wm. B. Eerdmans, 2000), 453–67; Juel, *Master of Surprise*, 45–63.
8. Robert C. Tannehill, "The Gospel of Mark as Narrative Christology," *Semeia* 16 (1979): 75–76.
9. Ibid., 76.
10. Martin Kähler, *The So-Called Historical Jesus and the Historic Biblical Christ* (Philadelphia: Fortress Press, 1964), 80.
11. David Bartlett, *What's Good about This News? Preaching from the Gospels and Galatians* (Louisville, KY: Westminster John Knox Press, 2003), 42.
12. John R. Donahue, "Mark," in *The HarperCollins Bible Commentary*, rev. ed., ed. J. L. Mays (New York: HarperCollins, 2000), 917.
13. Ibid.
14. Jeremias, *The Parables of Jesus*, 152. cf. Cousar, "Eschatology & Mark's *Theologia Crucis*," *Interpretation* 24 (1970): 321–35.
15. William Manson, "Eschatology in the NT," in *Eschatology: Papers Read at the Society for the Study of Theology*, ed. T. F. Torrance and J. K. S. Reid (Edinburgh: Oliver & Boyd, 1957), 8.
16. The noun "prolepsis" is a rhetorical term that denotes the anticipation of possible objections and the answering of them in advance.
17. James Barr, "*Abba* isn't 'Daddy,'" *Journal of Theological Studies* 39 (1988): 28–47.
18. See the survey by Raymond E. Brown, *The Death of the Messiah* (New York: Doubleday, 1998) 2:900–909, 1043–58.
19. Ibid., 2:1044.
20. Ibid., 2:1046.
21. Martin Hengel, *Crucifixion in the Ancient World* (Philadelphia: Fortress Press, 1977).
22. Eduard Schweizer, *The Good News according to Mark* (Richmond, VA: John Knox Press, 1970), 355.
23. Christopher Tuckett, *Christology and the New Testament* (Louisville, KY: Westminster John Knox Press, 2001), 116.
24. Andrew T. Lincoln, "The Promise and the Failure," *Journal of Biblical Literature* 108 (1989): 290.
25. Juel, *Master of Surprise*, 120.

Chapter 16: The Gospel of Matthew

1. Graham Stanton, *A Gospel for a New People: Studies in Matthew* (Louisville, KY: Westminster/John Knox Press, 1993), 160.
2. Ulrich Luz, *The Theology of the Gospel of Matthew*, New Testament Theology (Cambridge: Cambridge University Press, 1995), 2–3.
3. Beverly Roberts Gaventa, *Mary: Glimpses of the Mother of Jesus* (Columbia: University of South Carolina Press, 1995), 38.
4. Paul S. Minear, *Matthew: The Teacher's Gospel* (New York: Pilgrim Press, 1982), 30.
5. Linguistically, this explanation is not quite right. Jehoshua means, "God is help." See Luz, *Theology of the Gospel of Matthew*, 30.

6. Robert A. Guelich, *The Sermon on the Mount* (Waco, TX: Word, 1982), 111.
7. Luz, *Theology of the Gospel of Matthew*, 50.
8. Ibid.
9. Ibid., 49.
10. Donald Senior, *The Gospel of Matthew*, Interpreting Biblical Texts (Nashville: Abingdon Press, 1997), 143. On Jesus and taxation, see Richard Bauckham, *The Bible in Politics* (Louisville, KY: Westminster John Knox Press, 1989), 73–84.
11. M. Eugene Boring, "The Gospel of Matthew: Introduction, Commentary, and Reflections," in *The New Interpreter's Bible* (Nashville: Abingdon Press, 1994), 8:375.
12. Ulrich Luz, "The Final Judgment (Matt 25:31–46): An Exercise in 'History of Influence' Exegesis," in *Treasures New and Old: Recent Contributions to Matthean Studies*, ed. D. R. Bauer & M. A. Powell (Atlanta: Scholars Press, 1996), 271–310. I find Luz's argument convincing and have thus changed my own position from a previous writing. See Charles Cousar, "The Sacrament of the Poor: Some Reflections on Matthew 25:31–46," *Columbia Theological Seminary Bulletin* 60 (1967): 14–19.
13. Arland J. Hultgren, *Christ and His Benefits: Christology and Redemption in the New Testament* (Philadelphia: Fortress Press, 1987), 76.

Chapter 17: The Gospel of Luke

1. Beverly Roberts Gaventa, *The Acts of the Apostles*, Abingdon New Testament Commentaries (Nashville: Abingdon Press, 2003), 39.
2. Luke Timothy Johnson, *The Gospel of Luke*, Sacra pagina (Collegeville, MN: Liturgical Press, 1991), 82.
3. David L. Bartlett, *What's Good about This News? Preaching from the Gospels and Galatians* (Louisville, KY: Westminster John Knox Press, 2003), 82.
4. David L. Tiede, *Luke*, Augsburg Commentaries on the New Testament, (Minneapolis: Augsburg Press, 1988), 323.
5. W. C. van Unnik, "Luke-Acts: A Storm Center in Contemporary Scholarship," in *Studies in Luke-Acts*, ed. Leander Keck et al. (Nashville: Abingdon Press, 1966), 26–27.
6. Hans Conzelmann, *The Theology of St. Luke* (New York: Harper and Brothers, 1960), 95–136, 207–34.
7. Joel B. Green, *The Theology of the Gospel of Luke* (Cambridge: Cambridge University Press, 1995), 97–100.
8. John T. Carroll, *The Return of Jesus in Early Christianity* (Peabody, MA: Hendrickson, 2000), 50. See a more detailed treatment in Carroll's dissertation, *Response to the End of History: Eschatology and Situation in Luke-Acts*, Society of Biblical Literature Dissertation Series (Atlanta: Scholars Press, 1988).

Chapter 18: The Historical Jesus

1. Ulrich Luz, *The Theology of the Gospel of Matthew*, New Testament Theology (Cambridge: Cambridge University Press, 1995), 61.
2. The *Diatessaron*, compiled by Tatian, who studied under Justin Martyr, consisted of a harmonization of the four Gospels, plus some use of noncanonical documents, in Syriac. It held an authoritative position in the Syrian church until the fifth century. There is a long history of efforts to harmonize the four Gospels. See John Calvin, *A Harmony of the Gospels: Matthew, Mark, and Luke*, trans. A. W. Morrison (Grand Rapids: Wm. B. Eerdmans, 1994).

3. See Leander Keck, *A Future for the Historical Jesus: The Place of Jesus in Preaching and Theology* (Nashville: Abingdon Press, 1971), 17–25.

4. This historical survey is mostly adapted from C. B. Cousar, "The Historical Jesus: So What?" *Journal for Preachers* 23 (2000): 10–15.

5. Albert Schweitzer, *The Quest of the Historical Jesus: A Critical Study of Its Progress from Reimarus to Wrede* (New York: Macmillan, 1961), 4.

6. Ibid., 182.

7. Martin Kähler, *The So-Called Historical Jesus and the Historic Biblical Christ* (Philadelphia: Fortress Press, 1964; translated from the 1896 German edition), 73.

8. For example, one thinks of Donald M. Baillie, *God Was in Christ: Essays on Incarnation and Atonement* (London: Faber & Faber, 1948), and the New Testament work of C. H. Dodd.

9. Ernst Käsemann, "The Problem of the Historical Jesus," in *Essays on New Testament Themes*, Studies in Biblical Theology (London: SCM, 1964; translated from the 1960 German edition), 46.

10. Günther Bornkamm, *Jesus of Nazareth* (London: Hodder & Stoughton, 1960), 21.

11. Ibid., 26.

12. Jon Sobrino, *Christology at the Crossroads: A Latin American Approach* (Maryknoll, NY: Orbis, 1978), 10–14.

13. Robert Funk and John Dominic Crossan initiated the Jesus Seminar in the 1980s to challenge fundamentalists. It was composed of a group of scholars who initially set out to answer the question, "What did Jesus really say?" The Seminar actively courted public attention by voting on each proposed saying of Jesus and by publishing a new red-letter edition of the New Testament, *The Five Gospels: The Search for the Authentic Words of Jesus* (New York: Macmillan, 1994). See the review of the volume and the work of the Seminar by Richard B. Hays, in *First Things* 43 (1994): 43–48.

14. John Dominic Crossan, *The Historical Jesus: The Life of a Mediterranean Jewish Peasant* (New York: HarperCollins, 1992), 427–50.

15. So John Dominic Crossan, Robert Funk, Marcus J. Borg.

16. Richard Horsley, *Jesus and the Spiral of Violence: Popular Jewish Resistance in Roman Palestine* (San Francisco: Harper & Row, 1973), 326.

17. Marcus J. Borg, *Jesus in Contemporary Scholarship* (Valley Forge, PA: Trinity Press International, 1994), 61.

18. So E. P. Sanders, Dale Allison, Bart D. Ehrman.

19. Cited by Mark Allen Powell, *Jesus as a Figure in History: How Modern Historians View the Man from Galilee* (Louisville, KY: Westminster John Knox Press, 1998), 114–29. Powell provides a careful survey of the contemporary seekers after the historical Jesus.

20. E. P. Sanders, *The Historical Figure of Jesus* (London: Penguin Press, 1993), 168.

21. See the discussion of Meier by Powell, *Jesus as a Figure in History*, 135–47.

22. Norman Perrin, *Rediscovering the Teaching of Jesus* (New York: Harper, 1967), 39.

23. E. P. Sanders, "Jesus, Ancient Judaism, and Modern Christianity," in *Jesus, Judaism, and Christian Anti-Judaism: Reading the New Testament after the Holocaust*, ed. P. Fredriksen and A. Reinhartz (Louisville, KY: Westminster John Knox Press, 2002), 44.

24. See the insightful analysis of "the third questers" by M. Eugene Boring, "The 'Third Quest' and the Apostolic Faith," *Interpretation* 50 (1996): 341–54.

25. Powell, *Jesus as a Figure in History*, 184.

Chapter 19: The Acts of the Apostles

1. Ferdinand Christian Baur, *Paul, the Apostle of Jesus Christ*, 2 vols. (London: Wiliams & Norgate), 1873–1876.
2. W. G. Kümmel, *The New Testament: The History of the Investigation of Its Problems* (Nashville: Abingdon Press, 1972), 176.
3. Henry J. Cadbury, *The Making of Luke-Acts* (London: SPCK, 1927), 308.
4. Paul Walaskay, *"And So We Came to Rome": The Political Perspective of St. Luke*, Society for New Testament Studies Monograph Series (Cambridge: Cambridge University Press, 1983).
5. Beverly Roberts Gaventa, *The Acts of the Apostles*, Abingdon New Testament Commentary (Nashville: Abingdon Press, 2003), 31.
6. Ibid., 162–75.
7. C. H. Dodd, *The Apostolic Preaching and Its Developments* (New York: Harper & Row, 1934).

Chapter 20: The Gospel and Letters of John

1. J. L. Martyn, *History and Theology in the Fourth Gospel*, 2nd ed., New Testament Library (Louisville, KY: Westminster John Knox Press, 2003), 41.
2. David Rensberger, *Johannine Faith and Liberating Community* (Philadelphia: Westminster Press, 1988), 69.
3. See Sir 24:1–34; Bar 3:9–4:4; Wis 7:7–11:1; Col 1:15–20.
4. Karl Barth, *Witness to the Word: A Commentary on John 1* (Grand Rapids: Wm. B. Eerdmans, 1986), 89.
5. D. Moody Smith, *John*, Abingdon New Testament Commentaries (Nashville: Abingdon, 1999), 91.
6. Marianne Meye Thompson, *The Humanity of Jesus in the Fourth Gospel* (Philadelphia: Fortress Press, 1988), 96.
7. A Johannine hymn is "In the Cross of Christ I glory, towering o'er the wrecks of time. All the light of sacred glory, gather round his head sublime," whereas a Markan or Pauline hymn is "O Sacred Head now wounded, with grief and shame weighed down . . ."
8. Gail O'Day, "The Gospel of John," *The New Interpreter's Bible* (Nashville: Abingdon Press, 1994), IX:785 (italics mine).
9. R. Alan Culpepper, *The Johannine School*, Society of Biblical Literature Dissertation Series (Missoula, MT: Scholars Press, 1975).

Chapter 22: Hebrews

1. George B. Caird, "The Exegetical Method of the Epistle to the Hebrews, *Canadian Journal of Theology* 5 (1959): 47.
2. William Manson, *The Epistle to the Hebrews* (London: Hodder & Stoughton, 1957), 145.
3. This verse is very difficult to interpret in that it seems to make apostasy the unforgivable sin. Historically, it supplied timber for the Montanists and Novatians to stoke the fire against any who fell away from the church, during, say, a time of persecution. James Moffatt (*A Critical and Exegetical Commentary on the Epistle to the Hebrews* [New York: Scribner's, 1924], 77–80) has attacked various attempts to water down the difficulties of the verse. The most likely explanation is that the verse served as a warning in the form of a hyperbole and thus is followed by a word of encouragement and a declaration that "God is not unjust" (6:9–10).
4. Victor C. Pfitzner, *Hebrews*, Abingdon New Testament Commentaries (Nashville: Abingdon Press, 1997), 49.

Chapter 23: James

1. See Roland Bainton, *Here I Stand: A Life of Martin Luther* (Nashville: Abingdon Press, 1955), 259–61.
2. Interestingly, 5:1–6 does not appear as a lectionary reading.
3. "Friendship with the World/Friendship with God: Discipleship in James," *Discipleship in the New Testament*, ed. Fernando Segovia (Philadelphia: Fortress Press, 1995), 166–83.
4. Ibid., 174–75.
5. L. T. Johnson, "The Letter of James," *The New Interpreter's Bible* (Nashville: Abingdon Press, 1994), XII:224.

Chapter 24: 1 Peter

1. Paul Achtemeier, *First Peter*, Hermeneia (Minneapolis: Fortress Press, 1996), 28n.
2. Eusebius, *The History of the Church* (Baltimore: Penguin Books, 1965), 33.1.
3. David L. Bartlett, "The First Letter of Peter," *The New Interpreter's Bible* (Nashville: Abingdon Press, 1994), XII:236.
4. Ibid., 237.
5. Some contend, as mentioned at the outset, that the letter is a baptismal paschal liturgy, but baptism is not a major theme in the letter. See F. L. Cross, *First Peter: A Paschal Liturgy* (London: Mowbray, 1955).
6. Bartlett, "First Letter of Peter," XII:241.

Chapter 26: Jude

1. R. S. Dietrich, "Jude, to Those God Loves" (verse translation with introduction), *Presbyterian Voice* 13, no. 5 (October 2002): 5.

Chapter 27: The Revelation of John

1. John J. Collins, "Introduction to *Apocalypse*," *Semeia* 14 (1979): 9.
2. Richard Bauckham, *The Theology of the Book of Revelation* (Cambridge: Cambridge University Press, 1993), 7.
3. Christopher Rowland, "The Book of Revelation," *The New Interpreter's Bible*, XII, (Nashville: Abingdon Press, 1994), 589.
4. Bauckham, *Theology of the Book of Revelation*, 32.
5. Ibid., 27.
6. Richard Bauckham and Trevor Hart, *Hope Against Hope: Christian Eschatology at the Turn of the Millennium* (Grand Rapids: Wm. B. Eerdmans, 1999), 35.
7. Bauckham, *Theology of the Book of Revelation*, 54–58.

Conclusion

1. This was the title of an essay appearing in *The Word of God and Word of Man* (New York: Harper & Bros., 1957), 28–50.
2. J. Louis Martyn, *Theological Issues in the Letters of Paul* (Nashville: Abingdon Press, 1997), 221.
3. This provides the occasion to note that the Jewish community reads the Old Testament and does not arrive at Jesus as the Messiah. In Brueggemann's terms, the Old Testament is powerfully polyphonic, leading some in one direction and others in a different direction. The church certainly has no interpretive monopoly on the Old Testament. See Walter Brueggemann, *Theology of the Old Testament* (Minneapolis: Fortress Press, 1997), 729–35.
4. Brevard Childs, *Biblical Theology in Crisis* (Philadelphia: Westminster Press, 1970)
5. See the article by Ellen F. Davis and Richard B. Hays, "Beyond Criticism," *Christian Century* (April 20, 2004), 23–27.

Select Bibliography

Matthew

Kingsbury, Jack Dean. *Matthew as Story.* 2nd edition. Philadelphia: Fortress Press, 1988.

Luz, Ulrich. *The Theology of the Gospel of Matthew.* Cambridge: Cambridge University Press, 1995.

Mark

Juel, Donald. *The Gospel of Mark.* Interpreting Biblical Texts. Nashville: Abingdon Press, 1999.

Marcus, Joel. *Mark 1–8.* Anchor Bible. New York: Doubleday, 1999.

Myers, Ched. *Binding the Strong Man: A Political Reading of Mark's Story of Jesus.* Maryknoll, NY: Orbis Books, 1988.

Luke

Culpepper, R. Alan. "Luke." *The New Interpreter's Bible.* IX:1–490. Nashville: Abingdon Press, 1994.

Green, Joel. *The Theology of the Gospel of Luke.* Cambridge: Cambridge University Press, 1995.

Johnson, Luke Timothy. *The Gospel of Luke.* Sacra pagina. Collegeville, MN: Liturgical Press, 1991.

Tiede, David. *Luke.* Augsburg Commentaries on the New Testatament. Minneapolis: Augsburg Press, 1988.

John

O'Day, Gail R. "John." *The New Interpreter's Bible*, IX:492–867. Nashville: Abingdon Press, 1995.

Rensberger, David. *Johannine Faith and Liberating Community.* Philadelphia: Westminster Press, 1988.

Smith, D. Moody, Jr. *John.* Abingdon New Testament Commentaries. Nashville: Abingdon Press, 1999.

Acts of the Apostles

Gaventa, Beverly Roberts. *Acts*. Abingdon New Testament Commentaries. Nashville:
   Abingdon Press, 2003.
Spencer, F. Scott. *Acts*. Sheffield: Sheffield Academic Press, 1997.

Romans

Barth, Karl. *A Shorter Commentary on Romans*. Richmond, VA: John Knox Press, 1950.
Grieb, A. Katherine. *The Story of Romans: A Narrative Defense of God's Righteousness*.
   Louisville, KY: Westminster John Knox Press, 2002.
Käsemann, Ernst. *Commentary on Romans*. Grand Rapids: Wm. B. Eerdmans, 1980.
Keck, Leander E. *Romans*. Abingdon New Testament Commentaries. Nashville;
   Abingdon Press, 2005.
Meyer, Paul. *The Word in This World: Essays in New Testament Exegesis and Theology*.
   Edited by John T. Carroll. New Testament Library. Louisville, KY: Westmin-
   ster John Knox Press, 2004.

First Corinthians

Hays, Richard B. *First Corinthians*. Interpretation: A Bible Commentary for Teaching
   and Preaching. Louisville, KY: Westminster John Knox Press, 1997.
Horsley, Richard A. *1 Corinthians*. Abingdon New Testament Commentaries.
   Nashville: Abingdon Press, 1998.

Second Corinthians

Furnish, Victor Paul. *II Corinthians*. Anchor Bible. New York: Doubleday, 1984.
Matera, Frank. *II Corinthians*. New Testament Library. Louisville, KY: Westminster
   John Knox Press, 2003.
Young, Frances, and David F. Ford. *Meaning and Truth in 2 Corinthians*. Grand Rapids:
   Wm. B. Eerdmans, 1987.

Galatians

Cousar, Charles B. *Galatians*. Interpretation: A Bible Commentary for Teaching and
   Preaching. Atlanta: John Knox Press, 1982.
Hays, Richard B. "The Letter to the Galatians." *The New Interpreter's Bible*.
   XI:181–348. Nashville: Abingdon Press, 2002.
Martyn, J. Louis. *Galatians*. Anchor Bible. New York: Doubleday, 1997.

Ephesians

Lincoln, Andrew T. *Ephesians*. Word Biblical Commentary. Waco, TX: Word, 1990.
Perkins, Pheme. *Ephesians*. Abingdon New Testament Commentaries. Nashville:
   Abingdon Press, 1997.

Philippians

Bockmuehl, Markus. *The Epistle to the Philippians*. Black's New Testament Commen-
   taries. London: A. & C. Black, 1998.
Hooker, Morna D. "The Letter to the Philippians." *The New Interpreter's Bible*.
   XI:467–550. Nashville: Abingdon Press, 2000.

Colossians

Lincoln, Andrew T. "The Letter to the Colossians." *The New Interpreter's Bible*.
   XI:551–670. Nashville: Abingdon Press, 2000.
Schweizer, Eduard. *The Letter to the Colossians*. Minneapolis: Augsburg Press, 1982.

First and Second Thessalonians

Gaventa, Beverly Roberts. *First and Second Thessalonians.* Interpretation: A Bible Commentary for Teaching and Preaching. Louisville, KY: Westminster John Knox Press, 1998.

Smith, Abraham. "The First and Second Letter to the Thessalonians." *The New Interpreter's Bible.* XI:673–772. Nashville: Abingdon Press, 2000.

The Pastoral Letters

Bassler, Jouette. *1 Timothy, 2 Timothy, Titus.* Abingdon New Testament Commentaries. Nashville: Abingdon Press, 1996.

Collins, Raymond. *I & II Timothy and Titus.* New Testament Library. Louisville, KY: Westminster John Knox Press, 2002.

Philemon

Barclay, John M. G. *Colossians and Philemon.* New Testament Guides. Sheffield: Sheffield Academic Press, 1997.

Hebrews

Lindars, Barnabas. *The Theology of the Letter to the Hebrews.* Cambridge: Cambridge University Press, 1991.

Pfitzner, V. C. *Hebrews.* Abingdon New Testament Commentaries. Nashville: Abingdon Press, 1997.

James

Johnson, Luke Timothy. *The Letter of James.* Anchor Bible. New York: Doubleday, 1995.

First Peter

Bartlett, David. "The First Letter of Peter." *The New Interpreter's Bible.* XII:227–319. Nashville: Abingdon Press, 1994.

Second Peter & Jude

Bauckham, Richard J. *Jude, 2 Peter.* World Biblical Commentary. Waco, TX: Word, 1983.

1, 2, and 3 John

Brown, Raymond. *The Epistles of John.* Anchor Bible. New York: Doubleday, 1982.

Lieu, Judith. *The Theology of the Johannine Epistles.* Cambridge: Cambridge University Press, 1991.

Black, C. Clifton. "1, 2, and 3 John." *The New Interpreter's Bible.* XII:363–470. Nashville: Abingdon Press, 1994.

Revelation

Bauckham, Richard J. *The Theology of the Book of Revelation.* Cambridge: Cambridge University Press, 1993.

Schüssler Fiorenza, Elisabeth. *Revelation: Vision of a Just World.* Edinburgh: T & T Clark, 1993.

Index of Scripture

Index of Commentators
and Modern Authors